To Have
but not
To Hold

A Novel By
Fay D. Hayton

© Fay Hayton Australia 2015

The right of Fay Hayton to be identified as the author of this work has been asserted by her.

Set up and design by
Gondor Writers' Centre

To Have
but not
To Hold

© Fay Hayton Australia 2015

ISBN:978-0-9942463-8-7

All rights reserved.
This book is sold subject to the conditions that it shall not, by way of trade or otherwise, be lent, hired out or otherwise circulated in any form of binding or cover other than that in which it is published. No part of this publication may be reproduced, stored in a retrieval system, or transmitted in any form or by any means (electronic, mechanical, photocopying, recording or otherwise) without the prior written permissions of Fay Hayton.

This is a work of fiction. Names, characters, places, incidents, and dialogue are products of the author's imagination or are used fictionally. Any resemblance to actual people, living or dead, events, or locales is entirely coincidental.

Published November 2015.

Dedication

I would like to dedicate this book to my treasured husband Graham and all our wonderful children.

Also to a brave young boy 'Elijah', the inspiration for the character 'Harry' in my book.

Acknowledgements

I would like to thank those who helped me complete this book.

My husband, Graham, who always encouraged me and made sure I had plenty of time to write.

My resourceful, tender-hearted daughter Heather. (My other precious children live in N.Z.) Heather was always at the end of the phone ready to assist with problems as they arose. (And there has been quite a few.)

Also, the Gold Coast Writer's 'All Genre' writer's group that I have attended for the last four years. I learned so much at our meetings, the critiquing was always supportive and constructive. A great group of fellow writers.

To my editor, Elaine Ouston, from the 'Gondor Writer's Centre'. What a find she was. She helped my book come to life and offered me a great deal of support from her wealth of knowledge to do with the business of writing and publishing a book.

To my 'early-readers' Kym and Karen. Thank you for believing in me and inspiring me to keep writing.

Finally, our beautiful cavaliers, who kept me company as I wrote and reminded me when it was meal-time.

Wonglepong, Queensland.

Wonglepong is a rural community in the Scenic Rim Region of Queensland, Australia.

At the 2011 Australian Census, Wonglepong recorded a population of 367.

Wonglepong straddles a valley upstream from where Canungra Creek joins the Albert River. Development is centred along Beaudesert Nerang Road, which passes through the lowest elevations. In the east, the slopes of the valley rise sharply towards the Tamborine Mountain plateau.

Wonglepong is believed to be an Aboriginal name possibly meaning either 'forgotten sound' or referring to some feature of Mount Tamborine.

There was a railway station at Wonglepong along the Canungra railway line, which operated from 1915 to 1955.

Details gathered from Wikipedia. 12/11/2015.

Wonglepong May 2010

Chapter One

Vivid flashes of lightning streaked through the bus windows. Twenty-eight-year-old Kellie Lund nervously clutched her handbag as she sat staring through the rain-splattered glass. She had just seen 'Wonglepong 2km' on a signpost. *I'm nearly there*, she thought anxiously.

She made her way to the front of the bus and asked the driver if he could let her off at house number 26, further along the main road.

Happy to oblige, he answered, 'I'll do my best, love.'

'Thank y-you,' she replied politely.

This sad-faced young woman had first caught the bus-driver's eye when she boarded the bus in Southport. He'd kept an eye on her in his rear-vision mirror and several times noticed her dabbing her eyes.

In the distance, he made out a large '26' painted on a silver mailbox. Pulling up near the driveway, he gave Kellie a hand with her heavy suitcase as she stepped down from the bus.

'Take care, love. Get out of this blessed rain.'

'Thank you, I will.' She smiled through wobbly lips.

'Oh!' she squealed with fright as a deafening clap of thunder crashed right overhead. Nightfall had set in early because of the bad weather and the gloom added to her misery. Her heart thumped like a hammer and she breathed deeply trying to quell her rising panic. With frozen hands, she opened her umbrella and jerked out the handle on her travel bag.

The bus pulled away with a squelch of wet tyres and Kellie began the short haul up the gravel driveway. The skies opened and an almighty flash of lightning lit up the sky, outlining a house up ahead. Lights were on inside and she heard a dog bark. Crash! More lightning zigzagged through the sky striking a tree across the road with a huge bang! Terrified, she screamed and tried to move faster.

Finally, she reached the covered front entrance of the house, grateful to be out of the cold stinging rain. She stood her sodden umbrella against a brick-wall, gulped, and took a deep breath. Pulling herself together, she pushed a button lit up on the wall. A dog growled within.

'Oh!' She jumped with fright as another thunderclap exploded overhead. The door opened.

'Good evening,' said the tall, unsmiling man. Dr James Harvey looked down his nose at her saturated coat and filthy wet shoes.

'G... Good evening. I'm sorry to arrive this late, but only one bus comes out this w-way and it was late l-leaving,' babbled Kellie as she stood there shivering. Her head spun and she knew she wasn't making a good impression.

Dear God, what on earth made me think this was the answer. She'd come all the way out to a place she hadn't even known existed, to work for someone she knew virtually nothing about. Her heart raced and her lips trembled. There was no turning back. She was three and a half months pregnant and had nowhere else to go.

'Wait there,' he ordered and turned away. He promptly returned with two large towels. 'Here, take your coat and shoes off then dry yourself as much as you can.' Kellie felt like a stray dog as she obeyed his commands. She removed her jacket and hung it over a nearby wrought iron chair then propped her waterlogged shoes against the nearest wall.

As he lifted her suitcase, he glanced with distaste at the filthy wheels. 'Pass me the towel.' The doctor scowled as he carefully wiped them clean. 'Now, I'll show you to your room, where you can get out of those wet clothes.'

Carefully, she stepped inside, trying not to make too much mess on the carpet. The dog checked her out as she followed Dr Harvey down a wide hallway. Kellie glanced at the rooms they hurried past. They looked like something from a 'House and Garden' magazine, but the place smelt stale and needed a good clean.

He stopped near the end of the hallway and pushed open a door. 'This is your room and you have your own bathroom. The laundry's next door so please put your wet things in the tub.' He carried her suitcase through to an ensuite and deposited it on the tiled floor. 'When you're ready, join me in the kitchen. It's across the hallway.'

'Okay. Thanks.' He left and Kellie closed and locked the bedroom door.

In the gleaming white bathroom, she stripped off her wet clothes and had a lovely hot shower. Then, wrapped in a bath towel, she took a moment to look around her bedroom. 'Wow,' she whispered, 'I have never slept in such an amazing room.' The curtains were a soft green, patterned with burgundy and cream magnolias. They matched the puffy doona covering the queen-size bed. Gold lamps with burgundy glass shades sat on small, highly polished tables either side of the bed. A room-freshener gave off a sickly sweet perfume, which Kellie wasn't fussed on. It irritated her nose. 'I'll get rid of that,' she mumbled to herself.

The walls and carpets were a light biscuit colour and a large television set stood in one corner. There were two louvered doors opposite the bed – one into her ensuite and the other into a walk-in wardrobe.

'Well,' she whispered, 'I certainly can't complain about the accommodation!'

She partly dried her hair, then put on a tracksuit and made her way to the kitchen, trying to ignore the rumbling thunder over-head.

***

'Come in,' the doctor called. 'Can I get you a glass of water?'

She nodded. 'Yes please.'

He poured her a drink and pulled out a chair. 'Have a seat.'

Kellie sat down at a large wooden table and looked around. The big kitchen had a nice, cosy feel. A dark polished buffet with junk spread across the top stood to one side. Above that, a television sat on an adjustable wall bracket. A huge bay-window, with what looked like a super-comfy window seat beneath it, was at the far end. Multi-coloured cushions and old newspapers covered it. Lightning flashed in the distance, but the storm seemed to be moving away. Kellie sipped her water and wrinkled her nose as she spotted the dog's dirty food-bowl near the table. It stank of fish. *Yuk,* she thought.

Dr Harvey sat opposite her and cleared his throat. 'Since I spoke to you at our interview, the situation has somewhat changed.'

'What do you mean?' Butterflies started up in her tummy.

He hesitated. 'Originally you applied for a housekeeping position. The work will now include looking after a small boy.'

He briefly explained. He'd been married and had a young son, Harry. Two years ago, when the child was twelve months old, his wife left, taking the toddler with her. He had searched for them ever since even hiring a private investigator, but without success. Three days ago, the

Sydney Police contacted him to report that Harry had been found. The doctor went quiet.

Kellie studied her fingernails, feeling uncomfortable in the tense silence.

He coughed then carried on. 'I can't tell you what a relief it was to hear those words. They discovered him living in a squalid apartment block in Redfern, a suburb of Sydney. The area is well-known to the police. Drug addicts and criminals frequent that part of town. I was told Harry and his mother shared an apartment with such people. Apparently, most of the time, he was left by himself or with people he hardly knew. The officer thought Harry's mother may have worked on the streets.' At this point, he stopped speaking. Somewhere, a clock chimed the half-hour and then it was deadly quiet.

He raised a shaking hand to cover his mouth, waited a moment, and then continued. 'A neighbour heard continuous crying. She knew a young child lived there and felt uneasy at the distressing sound. She rang the police and told them of her concern. They came out, broke into the apartment, and found Harry in an appalling state. The child didn't utter a word. He just sobbed. The place was filthy. There was no edible food, the fridge didn't even work.' The doctor went on to explain how the police found paperwork with his name on. After a computer check, Harry's name and description came up on their missing person's file. 'They contacted me with this information.'

'Harry has an unusual crescent shaped birthmark on his right shoulder. I knew straight away this boy was my son.' He stood up and walked over to the bay-window where he gazed silently into the inky darkness. Kellie felt dreadful. She didn't know what to say or do.

A few minutes later, he turned. 'To cut a long story short, Harry's in the care of Child Services at the moment and tomorrow morning I'm flying to Sydney to be interviewed. All going well, Harry will come home with me tomorrow night.'

As the doctor had been talking, the small dog smooched up to Kellie. She thought he was gorgeous. His deep brown eyes were soft and full of love, but he badly needed a bath. She tickled him under the chin and his beautiful tail wagged excitedly.

'Meet Charlie. He's a Cavalier King Charles Spaniel. I found him injured on the side of the road a couple of years ago.' The dog rolled over to let Kellie rub his tummy, while his master walked over to a cabinet, returning with a bottle of red wine and two glasses.

'Would you care to join me?'

Kellie had never felt more like getting stuck into a bottle of wine in all her life, but knowing her condition she politely refused.

'Well, what do you think?' he asked anxiously. 'Are you prepared to mind Harry and look after the house? Your salary will be increased accordingly.' He waited.

Kellie could see he was afraid she'd refuse the job. 'Yes,' she replied, 'that's fine. I once applied for a job in a childcare centre. But they turned me down. I didn't have the necessary qualifications. I'd like to look after your little boy. I'd enjoy his company.'

The frown on the doctor's face lifted and he got to his feet. 'Thank you for that. I'm extremely grateful for your decision. He looked at the time. 'I'll quickly show you around the house. Please help yourself to a meal when you're ready. There's cold meat and salad in the fridge. It's fresh. I bought it earlier today from the supermarket. I'm sorry this is so rushed.'

Kellie glanced at him. She could see his thoughts were far away.

***

First, he showed her the laundry. It smelt musty from the unwashed clothes stuffed in a tall cane basket. He stepped over the wet things she had dumped on the floor, reached into a high cupboard, and handed Kellie a set of keys.

'I know you have a current driver's licence and,' he opened a side door, 'in through here there's a small car for your use. I drive the station wagon next to it.' He turned to her. 'I'll be leaving for the airport fairly early and I don't know what time we'll be home.'

He finished showing her the house then led Kellie back to the kitchen. 'Could you make up the bedroom next to yours ready for Harry?'

She nodded. 'Sure, Dr Harvey. Where do I find the sheets?'

'Please call me James. The linen cupboard is in the hallway next to your bedroom. If you have any queries, my mobile number is by the telephone. Oh, I almost forgot Charlie. He has a small cup of dry dog biscuits morning and night. They are kept in the cupboard under the laundry tub.'

Then he stood quietly for a moment and she could tell his mind was elsewhere. 'I think that's all. Once more, I apologize for leaving you to look after yourself when you've just arrived.' With a nod, he left the room.

Kellie returned to her bedroom, her head reeling from all his instructions. She locked her door and started to unpack. 'He seems all right, just a bit stressed,' she muttered to herself, 'and I don't think he looks like a rapist or an axe murderer, so maybe this job will be okay.'

The next morning, a rooster crowing his heart out woke her. *What a racket he makes,* she thought.

She opened one eye and peered at her bedside clock. *Five-thirty. The doctor has probably left for the airport by now.*

Outside, dawn was breaking and birds called and whistled to welcome in the new day. Kellie thought she might as well get up and make a cup of tea. She opened her bedroom door and found Charlie sitting there waiting patiently to be fed. She gave him a couple of pats and told him he was a lovely dog, even though he smelt whiffy, then made her way to the kitchen to fill the kettle. While she waited for it to boil, she walked over and opened the back door for a quick peek outside.

A covered veranda with white pillars went across the back of the house and tall potted palms stood like soldiers, one at each veranda post. A large wooden table and chairs were set to one side of the deck. Further down the backyard, a swimming pool enclosed by a high glass fence shimmered in the early morning light.

Tall trees surrounded the back garden. Gardenia bushes, growing in clumps near the rotary clothesline, gave off a fragrant perfume. Colourful lorikeets squabbled nosily in a nearby flowering eucalypt and a blue-tongue lizard snoozed lazily on the concrete, trying to catch some warmth from the early morning sun. It was a beautiful but badly neglected garden.

Back inside, Kellie made her tea, carried it over to the table, and sat down. She had just taken a few sips when, to her horror, she felt it coming back up!

She covered her mouth with both hands as she ran for the bathroom, terrified she would vomit over the floor before she made it to the loo. 'Oh no,' she whimpered. 'Why didn't I tell the doctor I'm three months pregnant? Maybe he wouldn't have minded.' She knew that wasn't true and felt guilt-ridden as she cleaned herself up.

Chapter Two

Kellie

With her mug of tea in one hand, Kellie went back outside and let her mind wander over the past few years and what had brought her to this place. She reflected on her idyllic lifestyle as an only child, born and raised in Te Puke, the capital of New Zealand's huge kiwifruit industry. Her eyes watered thinking about her much loved parents. She had never gotten over their loss in a horrific boating accident when she was twenty-three. It almost destroyed her. She remembered the pain and the misery, and the deep, dark depression that took hold of her for months on end.

Tears overflowed as she recalled that time. *I lived like a zombie, shutting out everyone and everything.* She wiped her eyes. *I felt so lost.*

Her best friend Samantha Stewart, who lived on the Gold Coast, came over for the funeral and stayed in touch. She was the reason Kellie came to Australia.

After a while, she had lost patience with her grief-stricken young friend. 'For goodness sake Kellie, pull yourself together. Every time I ring, you're in the same pathetic state. Are you going to live the rest of your life like this? I'm sure your parents would be disgusted to see you wallowing in such misery. Get a grip on yourself.'

The silence was long on the other end of the phone, then 'click'. Sam had hoped she could shock Kellie out of her present state and give her something to think about. Later that night, Sam's phone rang.

'W-what am I going to do?' Kellie's voice wobbled.

'Well, you need a change of scenery for a start. Why don't you come over here and stay at my place until you get yourself sorted. I can help you find a flat and a job. You'll have to sell your mum and dad's home. It holds too many memories. I'm sorry if I sound unfeeling, but I can't stand to see what you're doing to yourself.'

'It's all too hard,' mumbled Kellie tearfully. 'I feel numb and empty.

There's nothing inside of me, nothing at all.'

'Stop that! I want you to start thinking positive thoughts. Think about new places, new faces, and a new job. Sleep on these suggestions and see what tomorrow brings.' There was silence at the other end. 'I love you, girlfriend, and I want to help. Goodnight, Kellie.'

After a sleepless night, Kellie had decided to take Sam's advice. With a heavy heart, she organized the selling of her parents' property. The old house sold quickly, but there was very little money left over when everything was settled. Luckily, she had savings of her own to book a one-way ticket to Brisbane, in Queensland, Australia.

***

Kellie remembered how she had mixed feelings on the flight to Queensland. She hadn't been able to shake off the sadness that filled her entire being, but part of her was excited for what was to come. After she landed and passed through customs, she nervously pushed her trolley out into the public area not knowing what to expect.

'Kellie! Kellie! Over here.' Sam shrieked and waved her arms in the air.

Time stood still while they hugged each other.

Sam checked out Kellie's thin body and sunken face. 'Oh Kel, it's lovely to see you, but my dear friend, you look a wreck.' There were more tears.

'I'll help you,' Sam told the broken girl. 'Stay with me for as long as you like and when you're ready, I'll help you find a job and somewhere to live. In the meantime, you've got some living to catch up on.' Sam forced a laugh, 'Stick with me babe, and I'll show you around.' They both giggled amidst the tears.

They had been pals since primary school days and when the two girls were about to start College, Sam's parents moved to Australia in search of work. The two friends had kept in touch. Now they were together again and Sam had promised to help the stricken girl get her life back.

***

They had taken it easy for a few days, then Sam started her therapy by taking her to the hairdresser. Kellie's straggly ash-blonde hair was trimmed to a fashionable shoulder length bob. It looked fabulous, and after an appointment with a beauty therapist and some new clothes, she looked and felt a different person. This all took time and slowly, very slowly, the disheartened girl had come back to life.

Kellie remembered the turning point. 'Oh Sam,' she hugged her friend in gratitude one night after they had been to see 'Pink' in concert. 'I'm feeling heaps better thanks to you.'

'Nonsense, you're a remarkably strong person and you'll cope with whatever life dishes up. And I can tell you from experience, it comes up with some doozies.' They had roared with laughter remembering some of Sam's bad choices concerning old boyfriends.

It took a while to find a flat, but eventually Kellie found an old cottage in a quiet tree-lined street at Main Beach, near Surfers Paradise. Then she managed to fluke a job in a nearby coffee shop with a cheerful Aussie boss.

'Another Kiwi, ah?' He grinned. 'Although we do find you kiwi girls are good cooks, so here's your apron. Show us what you can do.'

Kellie fitted in well. The smell of good coffee and home-style baking drew plenty of customers into the busy café. The boss was happy and his cash register worked overtime. Kellie made good friends and settled down to enjoy all the coast had to offer.

***

The next few years had flown by. There were ups and downs, but she had never regretted the decision she had made to move to Australia.

One day, while wondering around a busy shopping centre close to where she lived Kellie noticed a job vacancy advertised in the window of a gift shop. She stepped inside and looked around. The shop had a nice atmosphere and a delicate hint of pot-pourri. It made you feel you'd like to linger awhile and browse. She walked up to the guy standing at the counter and asked if the job was still available.

As luck would have it, he was the shop-owner. 'Yes, it is. Drop your 'CV' in when you're passing and we'll take it from there.' She did and a few days later the chap phoned back to say the job was hers.

Kellie loved the work. Her boss, Jeff, grumbled most days about how bad business had become, but he was a good sort and the customers were a mixed bunch.

One night as they were closing the shop, her boss said, 'You're a great asset to this shop Kellie. Don't go running off with any slick guys now. You're needed here.' They both laughed, as men didn't seem to be interested in Kellie. Or so she thought.

Chapter Three

Barry

Various reps visited the shop on a regular basis. Barry Landgton, who Kellie thought was a heart-throb extraordinaire, represented a Sydney based firm and called in once a month to get an order from Jeff.

Kellie's heart did a little flutter each time he appeared. He arrived one morning when she was up a ladder changing stock around. Her boss was busy on the telephone so he made a beeline for her.

'Morning, Kellie. The shop looks good, are you the person responsible for all these great displays?'

Her heart missed a beat and for a moment, she was tongue-tied. 'M .. most of them. Why?'

'You have talent my girl...'

'I'm not your girl.'

'You could be.' He smiled up at her and she couldn't help but notice his eyes. They were a deep, dark blue and very intense.

'What does a lovely young girl like yourself do in the evenings for entertainment?'

'Watch television mainly, occasionally I meet some friends at the local pub.'

'I'll be going there for a few drinks myself later on. Would you care to join me?'

Kellie nearly dropped the glass vase she had in her hand. 'No thanks, I don't go out with men I don't know.'

'You could get to know me over a drink or two.' There was that smile again.

She wanted to go, but with her heart thudding like it was and the sensual fragrance of his aftershave she couldn't think straight so she just shook her head.

'Oh well, I'll be there around seven and I'll look out for you in case you change your mind.' The look he added to his invitation almost melted her insides. Jeff called out to Barry, and with a knowing wink, he walked over to do business with her boss.

Kellie had great difficulty focusing on what she was doing, and when he called goodbye to her boss she looked up and he sent another killer smile her way.

Of course, she had turned up at the tavern. Barry noticed her as she came through the sliding glass doors. They found a quiet corner in the noisy pub and chatted over a couple of drinks. Kellie's martinis went straight to her head and she became quite giggly. No male had ever been so attentive and she was like a blossom opening up to the warmth of the sun. They shared a plate of chilly nachos and he moved his chair closer to hers so that their thighs were touching. They talked and laughed. All too soon, the public address system announced the tavern would be closing in fifteen minutes.

Barry reached out for Kellie's hands. 'I want to see you again, can we meet here tomorrow night.' Her dazzling smile gave him his answer. He asked to give her a lift home, but she politely refused and ordered a taxi. Too much had happened too fast and her alcohol affected mind couldn't cope with making choices that could soon get out of hand.

***

The following evening, Kellie waited near the noisy entrance of the tavern hoping Barry would appear. Her nerves were playing up and she had gripe-like pains in her stomach. She had gone to a great deal of trouble with her appearance; tizzied up her shoulder-length blonde hair and put on her new red mini-dress with high-heeled red strappy sandals. She had even sprayed her perfume in a ring then walked through it, she'd read that in a book and thought it sounded a good idea.

Thirty minutes later, she still waited in the same place. The staff were starting to give her funny looks, as though she was a hooker or someone who was hoping to pick up a free meal along with a few hours of frantic frolicking.

'Sorry I'm late ...' Barry panted as he hurried in, 'my boss in Sydney called just as I was leaving and he wanted to go through some figures.' He heaved a sigh as though he'd just run a half marathon. 'Let's get a drink, then I'd like to take you somewhere nice for a meal.' He smiled and her insides almost dissolved. 'Are you okay with that?' She nodded, trying to appear cool and calm.

Later they went back to her unit and she made them coffee, but it never got touched as lust got the better of them. He passionately took her to heights she never knew existed and showed her a world she had not yet explored. When he left several hours later, she remained in a state of blissful euphoria, truly believing she had now found her one and only true love.

***

Barry returned to Sydney and Kellie felt lost. He phoned every night, whispering words of love and lust. Some things he suggested made her blush right to her core. She adored him and believed he felt the same way about her. He stayed at her unit whenever he came to the Gold Coast and treated her like a princess, showering her with gifts and making promises he had no intention of keeping.

A few weeks later she noticed her boobs were sore and getting bigger. Her skirts and trousers were tight and uncomfortable around her waist. She hadn't noticed the absence of her monthly period, but now realized it was over two months late! She had thought of going on the pill, but in her loved-up state had done nothing about it.

'Oh no!' Panic set in. She felt dizzy and thought she was going to faint. She took a couple of deep breaths and tried to think what she should do, but her brain wouldn't function. 'I'll tell Barry,' she whispered, 'he won't really mind. But what happens if he does?'

Kellie felt sick with worry. Barry was due back on the coast the next day. She decided to get a pregnancy test kit from the chemist to make sure of her condition. After work, she rushed home and did the test.

'It's positive. Oh my God!' She didn't know whether to laugh or cry. 'I'll do it again in case that one was faulty.' Positive again. 'How could I be so stupid and irresponsible?' She could not believe she had let herself get into this situation.

Nerves created havoc with her tummy. She couldn't sleep and couldn't concentrate. After work the next night, she rushed home and made lasagne. Barry loved Italian food. She tossed a salad and lit perfumed candles then did her make-up and put on a new dress.

He arrived early and kissed her passionately then handed her a beautifully wrapped parcel. Inside was a silver jewelry box. He knew she didn't have one. Kellie loved it and tried to stay calm as he poured their drinks. She picked at her meal. Then it all became too much for her and, stuttering with nerves, she blurted out her news.

Strangely enough, he didn't seem bothered. He kissed her and held her tight. 'A baby, wow! Let's celebrate and tomorrow night we'll discuss the serious stuff,' he said.

She felt such relief. She couldn't believe he was so calm about it all. They cuddled and chatted and then later with Andrea Bocelli singing romantic love songs in the background they made sensational love. Kellie felt truly blessed.

He left early the next morning taking his gear with him. 'I have an appointment with a new retailer this afternoon and I'll need to change before I meet him.' He blew her a kiss. 'See you tonight after work,' he called as he hurried out the door.

***

Three days passed and she didn't hear from him. Butterflies started up in her tummy. She phoned him. His mobile was turned off. Barry didn't normally do that, as he needed the phone for his job. A bad feeling crept over Kellie. During the long nights, panic gnawed at her stomach causing awful pains.

The next day she tried phoning him again, with no luck. *That's strange,* she thought, *what's going on?*

Panic turned to fear when two weeks went by and he still hadn't contacted her. Sick at heart, she spent many hours walking along the beach trying to clear her troubled mind. Heavy rain set in for several days, but she still kept walking. Life seemed unbearable and she was utterly miserable. She couldn't phone Sam, she was away on an overseas trip. She was the only friend who would understand and help her through this ordeal.

***

Barry was due to call into the shop that week and when he didn't turn up, Jeff commented. 'It's unusual for Barry not to call in for our order. There are several stock items we are running low on and his company are the only importers of that line.' He shook his head. 'I'll give his boss a call.'

Jeff phoned the office where Barry worked and found he'd resigned last week. Jeff relayed this news to Kellie; not knowing the effect such information would have on the emotionally troubled young woman.

'His supervisor said Barry handed in his notice. He found work closer to home with a local building firm in Gosford. Apparently, his wife's due to give birth in a couple of weeks. He never told us about that. What a strange bloke.'

When Kellie heard this, her legs shook and she clung to the counter for support. *Oh dear God, how did I ever get myself into such a mess!* She felt cheated and so stupid. She had trusted the guy. *What a fool I am!*

'You knew him fairly well, Kellie. Did he mention any of this to you?'

She shook her head and turned away, hoping he wouldn't see the tears she couldn't hold back.

After work, the rain had slowed to a drizzle, so she pulled on her coat and headed once more to the beach. In the diminishing light, the sea looked dark and foreboding. It seemed to invite her troubled soul into its watery depths. The frothy swell rose high like welcoming arms and under-foot she felt it try to pull her out towards the inky dark waves. For an instant she had an urge to drift with the tide, so deep was her pain.

Then a strong gust of wind blew in from the sea and pushed Kellie backwards, almost knocking her off her feet. The jolt somehow made her pull herself together and she turned away from the tempting, calling sea.

It was dark by now and with her life in tatters, she trudged back home.

Day after day, she struggled with deep, dark thoughts, fighting the hopelessness that weighed so heavy on her slim shoulders. She tried to focus on the small life growing inside her and decided she must make an effort to move on and find a way to look after her child the best way she could.

***

A few days later, while glancing through the local paper, she had noticed a live-in housekeeping position advertised. *I wonder*, she thought, *if that is a possibility. It would give me a job and a home.* A flicker of hope surged through her, the first one for a while. She went to bed feeling more optimistic about her situation.

The next morning, she called the phone number in the advertisement. A polite female voice answered.

'Central Health Centre, Rita speaking.'

'Hi, my name's Kellie Lund. I'd like to speak to someone about the housekeeping position advertised in yesterday's paper, please.'

Kellie was asked to hold the line.

A different voice came on the line. 'Good morning Kellie, this is Moira Grant. This job is for one of our doctors. He lives out in the country, about one hour's drive from Miami at a place called Wonglepong, does that bother you at all?'

'No, that's not a problem.'

'Good. Would you be able to come for an interview tomorrow at the Copper Kettle café? It's next-door to our surgery here at Miami. Shall we say ten o'clock?'

'Yes, certainly.'

'Good. Dr Harvey will meet you there. Oh, and please bring your resume.'

'I will. Thank you.' Kellie's hand shook as she put the phone down. It all seemed to be happening so fast, but she knew this opportunity might not come again.

***

The next morning she caught a bus to Miami and found the Copper Kettle. She ordered a cappuccino while she waited at a table near the door. A tall, well dressed guy came in at ten past ten and came over to where she sat. All the other tables were empty.

'James Harvey.' He reached out to shake her hand.

'Hi, I'm Kellie Lund.'

He pulled out a chair and sat down. 'Sorry I'm late. Did you bring your resume?' Kellie passed her folder across the table. While he studied the two pages, she took a good look at him and wondered if she could trust this man. His dark hair had sprinkles of grey at the temples and small furrows in his brow made him look older than he probably was. She guessed his age to be around late thirties. He finished reading the document, asked a few more questions, then stood up.

'Do we have your phone number?' Kellie nodded and got to her feet. 'If you need to check my details, call the surgery and ask for the practice manager. She will fill you in.' He picked up her resume. 'We'll be in touch.' Then he walked off.

She felt he wasn't the friendliest person she had ever come across, but so far, he seemed all right. To be on the safe side, she called the practice manager to make sure he was legit. The details given to her by the doctor all checked out.

Later that afternoon, her mobile rang. 'Kellie this is Moira Grant speaking. I work at the Central Health Centre with Dr Harvey. I'm calling about the housekeeping position. It's yours if you would like to have the job. Are you able to start next week?'

Kellie had to stop and think for a moment. 'Um, yes I can.'

'I'll e-mail you the address and work details. If you have any queries, please call here any time between eight am and five pm and ask for me.'

'I will thank you, bye.' Kellie sank down on a nearby chair. The enormity of what she'd done had started to sink in.

She prayed, feeling ashamed, as she only seemed to pray when she needed help. 'Please God, let me be doing the right thing for me and the child I'm carrying.'

***

Kellie resigned from the gift shop. Jeff let her go straight away as his niece desperately needed work and could start immediately. He knew she was pregnant and had a pretty good idea of who the father might be.

Two days later, she finished up and Jeff gave her holiday pay and a small bonus. 'Kellie love, make sure you call in and let us know how you're doing.' He produced a gift bag. She looked inside and found a hand-knitted white baby shawl and a card. 'Keep my phone number handy in case you need help of any kind.'

She thanked him and they shared a hug. He'd been a good boss and she would miss him. Then she went home and sorted out what to take and what to give to the Salvation Army's opportunity shop.

As she sorted through her belongings, Kellie wondered what the doctor would say when he found out about her pregnancy. She desperately hoped he would let her stay on after the baby arrived. What other possibilities were there? How would she cope? How could she look after a child and work at the same time? These questions turned over and over in her mind as she packed her suitcase.

'Bloody Barry, I wish I'd never met him.'

By Monday, she was packed and ready to go. One large suitcase held all her worldly goods. Feeling somewhat apprehensive, she ordered a taxi to take her to the bus that would transport her out to Wonglepong.

Chapter Four

James

In the last few years, 36 year old Dr James Harvey had been through sheer hell. Serena, his wife, had left him two years ago taking their one-year-old son Harry with her.

He had first met Serena Morris five years before, while working in the accident and emergency department of a large Brisbane hospital. She had recently arrived from Sydney and worked in the X-Ray department. James had spotted her when he checked on a patient there. For him, it was love at first sight.

Friday nights after work, a thirsty group from the emergency department met at a nearby tavern for a couple of drinks before heading home. Inside the noisy pub, James would watch Serena out the corner of his eye. He quizzed the guys around him trying to find out if she was attached to anyone in particular.

'James mate, why don't you go and talk to the woman instead of standing there drooling. She won't bite.' Gavin his work-mate tried to hurry him, but James had to give the situation some thought. Serena chatted with many different guys so maybe, he thought, she wasn't dating anyone special. It took a few weeks to build up enough courage to ask her out.

Then one day, the opportunity arose. It happened at the end of a busy day. He called into the X-Ray department to sign a couple of forms. Serena had just wiped down the equipment and the place reeked of methylated spirits. She noticed him walk in and went over to her desk to find the paperwork that required his signature.

'Hi, Dr Harvey. Here are the forms for you to sign.'

He checked them then scribbled his name on each one and passed them back. 'Are you enjoying your work here?'

Serena looked startled. 'Yes, I am, although we're short staffed, so it's quite busy.' She smiled at James, while quietly thinking, *He's cute, he's really cute and I bet he's loaded!* Serena had been on the look-out for such a man. She had expensive tastes and great plans for her future.

James was completely taken in. 'Would you care to join me for a drink after work?' he inquired then held his breath as he waited for her answer.

Serena checked her watch, hiding her excitement. 'I can meet you at the local pub in half an hour if you like.'

James nodded. He couldn't get to the pub fast enough.

From that night on, they were inseparable. They shared dinners in romantic settings, danced cheek to cheek in the moonlight, and spent weekends away together where they could love in private.

Serena had a selfish personality and always looked after number one. She had big plans, but until she actually became Mrs. James Harvey, she was keeping them to herself.

After six months, James proposed. He took her to a fabulous Italian restaurant where a guy serenaded diners in Pavarotti style and there he popped the question.

'Marry you? Oh James, yes,' gushed Serena. He produced an engagement ring – a huge solitaire diamond set on a wide gold band.

Three months later, they married and spent their honeymoon in Paris. Life seemed perfect and everything was going along as Serena planned. She convinced James to buy an apartment in a trendy residential block by the side of the Brisbane River. It had breathtaking views of the city and a balcony with gardens of magnificent flowering plants that bloomed most of the year round. Life was perfect – until Serena fell pregnant!

'Pregnant! How the hell can I be pregnant?' She shouted at James and then stopped.

She put her hand up to her mouth. 'Oh no, I forgot to take that damn pill with me when we spent the week-end in Noosa a couple of months ago and now look what's happened.' Angry tears spilled down her cheeks. 'This is all your fault!' She shouted and threw a vase at him, narrowly missing his head. Starting a family this early in their marriage did not fit in with Serena's plans. James, absolutely devastated by her attitude, discovered a side of his lovely bride he never knew existed.

'What can I do,' she shrieked. 'I don't believe in abortion. You've ruined everything. Don't come near me or touch me again. Not ever!'

Shocked, James shook his head in disbelief and heartbreaking despair.

***

Seven miserable months later, Serena gave birth to a baby boy. They named him Harry. She suffered serious post-natal depression and after a frightening psychotic episode was admitted to hospital and sedated. James took sick leave and looked after the needs of the little boy. With drug therapy and rest, her condition improved and two weeks later, she returned home. James had enjoyed time spent with the baby, but that all changed as Serena took over.

She reprimanded him whenever he went near the infant. 'Leave him alone, he's supposed to be sleeping,' or 'Leave him be, I'm going to feed him.' James loved them both and found her mood swings and selfish attitude difficult to cope with.

He worked longer hours, reluctant to go home where he was no longer welcome. When Harry was twelve months old, James arrived home to a quiet house. Serena had left, taking the child with her. There was no note, no forwarding address, nothing at all to tell him where they had gone.

Inconsolable, James hired a top-rate solicitor. 'I want you to locate my wife and son,' he pleaded, 'if you can't, please find someone who can.' The lawyer felt sorry for the heart-broken doctor and promised to do his best.

He found Serena had transferred a large amount of money into her bank, withdrawn the money, and then closed the account so she couldn't be traced. James found it hard to believe what she had done and didn't know how he would survive without them in his life.

He sold the apartment, resigned from the hospital and applied for a position at a Health Centre in Miami on the southern end of the Gold Coast. Close by, he found a flat with beach access where he could walk along the golden sand morning and night. The Health Centre was always busy, which suited him as he tried to blot out the misery that filled his heart and soul.

Time passed, nothing changed, and before long, James felt he would like to live somewhere quiet and maybe find a place to renovate. He enlisted the help of a real estate agent who suggested looking at a rundown home on their books out at Wonglepong.

'Wonglepong,' he said to the agent, 'are you serious. Where on earth is that?'

'It's a lovely, small, country area about fifty kilometers from Surfers Paradise, near Canungra,' she replied. 'If you like solitude, growing your own vegies, gum trees and wild life, you would love it out there.'

Intrigued, James checked the place out. It had possibilities. He made a quick decision, signed the contract, and within a month moved out there.

Eager to get stuck in, he set about renovating the old house. This was just what he needed. With his work at the surgery combined with hard physical work at home, he slept better, undisturbed by troubled dreams.

The office staff at the medical centre knew nothing about Dr James Harvey and his private life, although they did wonder what caused the haunted look in his sad eyes.

'It would have to be a woman,' he overheard one of the receptionists say during their morning tea break. 'Maybe he lost a patient and it was his fault.' They made up all sorts of different reasons for his wistful look and stand-off attitude.

'Maybe he won the lotto and lost his ticket,' piped up the not so bright junior, there for the week doing work experience.

James made good friends of the other two doctors at the centre. They knew nothing about his past. His qualifications were brilliant and his work was excellent. They often invited him to their homes for dinner. James enjoyed these visits. The home cooked meals were a welcome change from his own basic efforts and their wives and children made a big fuss of him.

Driving home one Sunday, after lunch at the home of one of his partners, Dr Richard Wilkinson, James noticed a small dog limping awkwardly along the side of the road. He stopped and went over to check it out. The poor animal cringed when James touched him. He gently felt the dog's hind leg and noticed dried blood around a nasty wound, as well as many other injuries. His badly matted fur was alive with fleas and he stunk something shocking.

'You poor old thing,' James murmured softly not wanting to scare the frightened animal. 'You'd better come home with me and I'll clean you up.' James carefully lifted the terrified dog and gently laid him in the back of his station wagon.

Over the next two weeks, James put three advertisements in the 'lost and found' column of the local newspaper but didn't get one reply. It seemed that no one had lost a dog.

He looked at the poor creature with his leg in plaster. 'It looks like it's just you and me mate. I think I'll christen you Charlie, somehow that name seems to suit you.'

The dog with the broken leg and the man with a broken heart became great mates and helped comfort each other.

Chapter Five

Moira

Moira Grant, head receptionist at the health centre where James worked, kept a motherly eye on all the staff. She was in her late fifties and excelled at her job. Don, her devoted husband was semi-retired. He mowed lawns and did odd jobs.

The patients loved Moira, sensing a sympathetic ear when they phoned the surgery. They knew she would do her best to get them in to see one of the doctors.

James and Moira often had morning tea together. They chatted about this and that. She had been watching over this quiet sad man ever since he came to work at the centre. She liked the kind, dignified way he treated elderly and sick people. Sometimes he sounded off at the staff when they made silly mistakes that upset patients, but in general, he seemed a nice but solemn guy.

***

Two years passed without too many hiccups, and then one morning during their coffee break in the surgery kitchen, Moira noticed how tired and worried he looked.

'What's up James? Why the long face and tired look?' She didn't pussy-foot around.

He sighed and rubbed his eyes. 'Oh… I'm struggling to keep on top of things. The housework and gardening is never ending…'

'For crying out loud man, get some help. Get a housekeeper or a cleaner.'

He looked sideways at her. 'Oh, I don't know.'

'Maybe you could have a live-in housekeeper. Your home's big enough that you wouldn't get under each other's feet. You can certainly afford it.'

James looked stunned. 'Mm, maybe something like that's the answer. I like my privacy, but as you say it's a big house. One thing though, the person must like dogs.' He sat and chewed over the idea for a few minutes.

Moira sipped her tea then put her cup down. 'You'd need a small car to go with a job like that, seeing you live out in the sticks.'

James grinned. 'All right, sounds good to me. Let's do it.'

'Okay, I'll scribble something for the job's wanted column in the local rag.'

They chatted about it for a few more minutes and decided Moira would be in charge of finding a suitable person. And so the advertisement appeared in the local paper.

Only four women replied for the position of housekeeper. Two of them were not interested when they found that he lived so far out of town. They thought 'out of town' as the ad read, meant on the edge of town. The other woman had a voice like sandpaper. James knew straight away that if she lived under the same roof as he did, he would end up taking to the evil drink! No, that woman was definitely not going to live in his house even though she told him she was a great cook and a meticulous cleaner.

Chapter Six

Sydney N.S.W.

The morning after Kellie's arrival James caught an early flight to Sydney. He picked up a hire car with a child seat installed then called Child Services and spoke to Heather McFarland, Harry's case manager.

'Good morning, this is James Harvey speaking. I think you're expecting me.'

'Oh yes, Dr Harvey,' she said. 'Can you be here around 11am?'

'Certainly. I'll see you then.' James jumped in the hire-car and headed for downtown Sydney to find the address he had been given.

He arrived at an old red brick building that housed several government departments. Heather McFarland was at reception when he arrived. After introducing herself, she invited him into her office and asked him to take a seat. The room was small and cluttered with thick folders piled high on overflowing shelves. A shriveled up flower in a drinking glass added a musty smell to the untidy office.

She pulled out her chair and sat down. 'Thank you for responding to us so quickly, Dr Harvey. Harry has been with a foster-carer since he was brought in a few days ago. The sooner he's settled in a stable environment, the better it will be for him. We've run several checks on you with the information you supplied and everything checks out. We appreciate your co-operation in getting us those details so quickly. When you leave here with Harry, we will keep in contact. Someone from our department will call every month, checking your son's progress and seeing regulations are being adhered to. Also, a nominated doctor will check the child every three months.'

'My colleague, Dr Richard Wilkinson, at the surgery where I practice, will monitor Harry's health and report back to you.'

'That will be fine,' she replied.

'I have searched for my son and his mother since they left over two years ago. I even hired an investigator.' James swallowed to get his emotions under control. 'These last two years have been extremely difficult.'

'I understand, Dr Harvey.'

'My housekeeper, Kellie Lund, lives in. (He hoped he'd be forgiven for that small fib, as Kellie had only arrived the previous night). She's good with children and will care for him while I'm at work. I intend to spend a great deal of time with Harry as we have a lot of catching up to do. Also, I have a small dog named Charlie who will be a great companion for the lad.'

'I see you know the way of small children, Dr Harvey.' Heather smiled then continued. 'We haven't been able to trace your wife; all our efforts have come up against a blank wall. Evidence from a reliable witness living in the same apartment block indicates that Serena was on drugs and worked as a prostitute to fund her habit.'

James shook his head in dismay. 'She struggled with post-natal depression after Harry was born and received psychiatric treatment. There were indications in the months leading up to her disappearance that she had become dependent on valium.'

'How tragic,' Heather murmured. 'However, you need to know all these details so you have some understanding of what Harry's been through. That young boy has seen things no young child should see and lived in conditions no one should ever live in.' Her phone rang. Heather excused herself and left the room, taking her mobile with her.

She returned a few minutes later. 'Sorry, but it was important. Now, moving on – you know about Harry's physical condition, but we are worried about his emotional state. He is very fragile. This young boy has not spoken a word since he was found. With your medical knowledge, you'll understand he needs a lot of help. We are relying on you to judge what is needed to get him back on track and enjoy life like a normal three-year-old. With tender loving care and a good diet, he should become a happy, healthy young boy. We are sure he will speak when he's ready, so we'll leave that for the time being. Help is available if you think it's needed.' She paused and wrote something down. 'Are there any questions you would like to ask before you collect your son?'

'Can my ex-wife try to get him back?' He held his breath.

'For Serena to even apply for a supervised visit, she will have to prove to a judge that she has been free of drugs for the last twelve months. We will keep you informed. Is there anything else?'

'No, not at the moment. Where do I find Harry so I can take him home?'

'He's waiting in the next room.'

'Thank you, thank you very much.' James stood up and they shook hands.

Chapter Seven

Harry

James walked across the hallway and quietly opened the door. Over by the window, a small boy watched children playing in the park next door. The child turned and James stood still, paralysed by the flood of emotions that surged through his body. He quickly pulled himself together, not wanting to frighten the boy. The child looked emaciated, as though he had come straight from a concentration camp.

Harry had only been twelve months old when James last saw him, now at three years of age his features had changed. His face was elf-like and his brown shoulder length hair had a few curls. His skin was a pale unhealthy colour, made worse by dark circles under his haunted eyes, and he was thin. *So terribly thin,* James thought, his heart breaking.

A middle-aged lady in a well-worn green coat stood close-by. She smiled and reached out to shake hands. 'Hello, I'm Kay Peters, Harry's foster-carer. It's nice to meet you.'

James shook her hand and nodded in acknowledgement. He couldn't speak; words failed him, he felt shocked to see his son in such a pitiful condition.

He went over to the young boy and crouched down. 'Hi there, Harry. I'm your dad. I've come to take you home.' James reached down for his son's small hand and was startled to feel how fragile that little hand felt. The foster-carer said goodbye to James then bent down and gave Harry a farewell hug.

The small boy walked at a slow pace beside his dad as they left the building. Once they were outside, the warm mid-day sun created a rosy glow in the child's pale cheeks as they headed towards the hire car.

Passing a department store, James realised the child had nothing to wear apart from what he had on. 'I think we'll go into this shop and get you some clothes and a teddy bear. All kids need a teddy. Come on, we'll go and have a look.' Automatic doors glided silently open and they went inside. A young woman helped James with what Harry needed and then they found the soft toys. He encouraged the boy to choose something, but the child showed no interest. James found a suitable teddy, paid for it and then they left the shop.

On the drive out to the airport, James chattered away to Harry about his new home. He told him about Kellie and the dog. The child sat expressionless in his car seat.

During the flight home, the young boy sat rigid in his seat and fell asleep as they were coming into land. James phoned Kellie from the Coolangatta airport to let her know they were back and should be home soon.

***

The late afternoon sky had clouded over and a few drifting leaves lazily landed on the windscreen as James turned into his driveway and brought the station-wagon to a stop beside the house. He glanced back at his son, secured in his new car capsule, and saw fear registered on his small face as he clutched tightly to the new teddy.

'Harry, we're home now,' James murmured softly. 'Look here's Kellie and our dog Charlie.' Kellie held firmly to Charlie's lead, as he barked madly, wondering what was going on. James lifted Harry out of the car and carried the small boy inside to the kitchen. The room was warm and from the oven came the mouth-watering smell of roasting chicken.

With one hand, he pulled out a chair and sat down with the child on his lap. Charlie spun around in circles looking for attention.

'Kellie, would you get us a glass of milk and maybe a biscuit each please? We shared a milkshake around midday at the airport, but we've had nothing since.' She placed their milk and some chocolate chip biscuits on the table, then knelt down and gently rubbed the small boy's hands.

'Hi Harry, I'm Kellie and this here's Charlie. Isn't he a cute dog?' Charlie's tail wagged madly and he laid his head on the child's leg. 'He loves kids. When you've finished your snack you can pat him if you like.' Harry looked at the dog and said nothing. He sipped the milk, but didn't touch the food. James lifted him down.

'Maybe we'll have a walk around the garden. What time's dinner?' James glanced at the clock.

'There's time enough for your walk and maybe a warm bath.'

James grinned. 'Sounds good doesn't it, mate?' He reached for his son's hand. 'Come on, we'll get some fresh air.' Charlie followed close behind them.

***

Kellie set the table in the kitchen and dished up dinner. She gave Harry a little piece of chicken, a few tiny carrot sticks, and some bread topped with vegemite cut into squares. She and James tucked into their roast chicken and vegetables while Harry slowly ate the bread and finished off his milk. *Oh, well,* she thought, *whatever's left, we'll put in Charlie's bowl.*

The little boy's eyes struggled to stay open.

'Time for bed I think,' said James. He lifted Harry from the cushion Kellie had put on a chair and carried the tired child to his new bedroom. Kellie followed, with Charlie close behind. James tucked the little boy in and placed the new teddy by his pillow, while Kellie switched on a bedside lamp and left it glowing softly. They didn't want Harry to wake during the night, frightened in the dark.

She returned to the kitchen and turned on the television, keeping an eye on the news while she cleaned up the mess from dinner.

A few minutes later, James came in. He looked tired. 'Thank you for your help today.' He rubbed his eyes. 'If you're making coffee later on, I have mine black with no sugar. I'll be in my study.' With that, he left the room.

When the kitchen was clean and tidy, she set the percolator going and set out two mugs. Carefully, she carried his coffee down the hallway and knocked on the study door.

'Coming,' he opened the door and reached for his drink. 'Thank you. By the way, I'm taking the next two days off. Do you think by Thursday you'll be able to cope with Harry by yourself?'

Kellie grinned. 'I think so. I'm quite used to small children. A lady I worked with had two young boys and they often stayed weekends with me. Having Charlie around will be a big help as little kids usually relate to animals.'

'Good, I'm sure he'll soon settle down,' he answered as he closed the door.

'Oh, a man of few words,' muttered Kellie. Later she heard him call the dog to go for a walk.

When they returned, he came into the kitchen where Kellie rested on the window-seat. She was propped up with comfy cushions and totally absorbed in a movie.

'Sorry to interrupt…'

She sat up and grabbed the remote to turn the volume down.

James cleared his throat. 'I forgot to mention that Harry hasn't spoken a word since they found him. His case-manager thinks his emotional state is rather fragile. We'll wait and see what progress he makes and take it from there. Tonight, I'll leave my bedroom door ajar in case he wakes. Goodnight.' He softly whistled Charlie and they left the room.

***

Kellie hadn't been asleep long when the sound of heart-wrenching cries woke her. Realising the noise came from Harry's room; she grabbed her dressing gown, throwing it on as she ran to his bedside. The young boy was sobbing as though his little heart was breaking. Making soothing noises, Kellie gently lifted him up in her arms then sat down in the rocking chair next to his bed. She held him close and whispered comforting words as she gently rocked. There was a rug on the end of his bed, she reached for it and draped it across his shoulders to keep him warm. He cried and cried and Kellie kept rocking. Before long, they both fell asleep. She woke to a hand softly shaking her shoulder.

'I'll take him now. You go back to bed,' James whispered.

Kellie gently passed over the sleeping boy. 'I woke and heard him sobbing,' she told him quietly, 'and he's cried himself to sleep.' She left James to it and returned to her bed.

The following nights followed the same pattern. There was no consoling the small boy when he woke during the night and his gut-wrenching sobs almost broke Kellie's heart. Each night, James held him in his arms and rocked him until he fell back to sleep.

***

They muddled through the next couple days trying to establish some sort of routine. James took Harry shopping as there was so much he needed and Kellie went to the local supermarket for supplies.

She drove in to Canungra, a small country town about ten minutes away. In the newsagents, she found a few books and puzzles suitable for Harry, then bought a coffee and sat in the green leafy park opposite the shops surveying her surroundings. There was a well maintained monument in the park with names of the brave young soldiers killed in the last two world wars. Kellie felt a deep sorrow as she remembered the sacrifice of these courageous young servicemen and women.

***

Thursday morning, the noisy rooster woke Kellie again. He let everyone know he was out there and awake. Now a family of kookaburras joined in laughing raucously, their cackle building up to a noisy crescendo. She opened one eye and peered at her radio alarm clock, 6:15am. The fog of sleep cleared quickly as she remembered James would be going to work soon, seven o'clock he'd told her. Kellie showered and dressed at high speed then tiptoed in to check on Harry. He was still asleep making little snoring noises so she quietly left his room.

Time for a quick cuppa, she thought and filled the kettle. James had cooked himself bacon and eggs before he left, and the greasy fry pan lay soaking in the sink.

Suddenly, her tummy did a flip and she had to sit down. Then vomit started to rise! 'Oh no.' She covered her mouth with both hands and quickly took off, only just making it to her loo where she threw up and kept dry retching. Then her nose started to bleed so she staggered to the basin and pinched the bridge of her nose until the bleeding slowed then stopped. She looked in the mirror. 'Bloody hell.' Her face was a terrible mess. *Just as well the good doctor can't see me right now*, she thought. *I think he'd soon send me packing.* In the next room, Harry had started to grizzle so she quickly cleaned herself up, put a smile on her face, and went in to see him.

Feeling a little better, she helped the young boy get dressed then made his breakfast. He didn't eat it, so she sat him down with crayons and a colouring book while she started the housework. Her mobile phone began to vibrate on the kitchen bench. She could see her girlfriend Sam's name come up on the screen.

'Hi, Sam, are you checking up on me?'

'I certainly am. Anything could happen to someone who takes off to work and live in the bush with a complete stranger. How's it going out there and when do you have days off?'

'I'm doing okay, the jobs a bit different to what I expected, but I'll fill you in when I see you.'

'What do you mean a bit different – is that doc ridgy-didge or not?'

'Of course he is. I can't chat now, but I'll call you at the weekend.'

'Make sure you do or I might report you as a missing person.'

Kellie laughed. 'I'll definitely give you a ring. Please don't worry about me. Love you, bye.' With another chuckle, Kellie ended the call. Sam was such a sweetie.

Harry soon got bored with his colouring book and crayons so Kellie brought out a bucket of Lego that James had bought. She helped him build a couple of simple things and he seemed content, even when Charlie became excited and knocked them both over. James rang at lunch time to see how they were. He spoke quite sharply over the phone.

'H-Harry's fine' she informed him, 'there's no problems.' She became tongue-tied because he was so abrupt.

'Good, I'll be home later.' He ended the call, just like that. He was such an unfriendly man.

After lunch, Kellie felt the young boy needed a rest and tucked him into bed. Charlie jumped up next to him and they snuggled down. She hugged them both then sat on the rocker next to the bed and read 'Hairy McClairy from Donaldson's Dairy' out loud. Harry soon fell asleep with one arm around the dog, who almost smiled as he snored like an old steam train.

Kellie tiptoed out and went to her room for a short rest. She lay on the bed with her book and a Mars Bar, enjoying every mouthful. *Funny how chocolate gives you such a good feeling*, she thought and quietly drifted off to sleep.

They were both up and out pottering around in the garden when James arrived home.

'Hi, mate,' he called as he ruffled the boy's hair. A small change came over Harry's face and he ran inside and returned with Charlie's lead. James laughed and hugged him. 'Thanks, Harry. What a clever lad you are.'

After dinner, Kellie made a mug of hot chocolate, carried it outside, and sat on the verandah steps. Stars sparkled brilliantly in the dark velvet sky and a delicate perfume wafted across from the nearby rose garden. The fragrance reminded her of Barry and the many times he'd brought her roses. Pain filled memories of his deceit and betrayal caused silent tears to slide slowly down her cheeks.

She pulled herself together, came back inside, and switched on the percolator. When James' coffee was ready, she carried the steaming hot drink to the study and gently tapped on his door. There was a scraping noise then the door opened.

He reached out to take his mug. 'Thanks Kellie. Come in. I'd like a quick word.'

Tentatively, she stepped inside the room.

He picked up a credit card from his desk and handed it to her. 'This card is for all household expenses including your petrol and anything Harry might need. It has a limit in case of loss or theft, but there will always be sufficient funds there to run this house. Your name is on the card, but the account will come to me. Make sure you sign the back straight away.'

She nodded. 'Sure, can I borrow your pen?'

He handed her his biro then perched on the corner of his desk while she signed her name. 'How was your day? Did Harry cause you any problems?'

Kellie shook her head and handed back his pen. 'No, he was fine. It's just so difficult to get him to eat. He drinks plenty of milk and today he ate a small amount of cheese.'

'That's good to hear. His sleeping hasn't improved. He's like an emotional roller-coaster during the night, poor kid.' A strained look crossed James' face. 'By the way – about your days off. How does Saturday afternoons and Sundays sound to you?'

Kellie nodded. 'Great, those days suit me fine.'

'All right, we'll start this weekend. Goodnight.' He stood up and went back to his desk.

She was dismissed – just like that. *Oh well.* 'Goodnight,' she answered politely and returned to the kitchen.

Chapter Eight

Early Saturday morning Kellie made meat pies for James to heat up for their dinner, hoping it might be something Harry would eat.

After lunch, she changed her clothes, grabbed her handbag, and headed for Tweed Heads to look around. She wandered through the local shopping centre and bought a pirate book for Harry, then she smelt coffee. Turning a corner, there was a large café.

Across the front window was an Italian alfresco scene. 'That looks my sort of place,' she muttered and went inside. After studying the display cabinet for a good few minutes, she ordered a slice of caramel banana tart, with a skinny cappuccino. When she'd finished eating, she phoned her girlfriends. They all got a quick update on her job, but wanted to find out more about the "mysterious doc". 'What a nosey lot they are,' she said and laughed as she gathered up her shopping.

In an alleyway, she found a bookshop and bought a couple of new titles, then further down a swinging sign caught her eye, 'Death by Chocolate'. Since she'd been pregnant, Kellie had become an addict. As she went inside the shop, she took a deep breath, letting the sweet chocolate smell invade her nostrils.

'Wow, I feel like I've died and gone to heaven,' she exclaimed seeing the magnificent display. She then realized she'd spoken out loud. The cranky looking sales assistant stopped talking on her mobile and gave her that "she's lost the plot" look. Ignoring the insolent girl Kellie looked around the shop, picked up some goodies, then went to the counter.

The girl carelessly shoved her purchases in a bag. 'Have a good day,' she mumbled rudely then went back to her phone-conversation. Kellie left the shop shaking her head. Next, she spotted a video shop. She bought a couple of new movies then decided that was enough for one day – her shoes were hurting.

The sun was setting as she drove home through Canungra. Vibrant red and orange streaks filled the horizon, making a brilliant contrast to the deepening blue sky. Safely back home, she collected her shopping from the car and struggled to her room where she flopped on the bed completely worn out.

Later, propped up with pillows, she scoffed chocolates as she watched one of her new movies. There were all sorts of noises coming from the kitchen as James organised dinner for himself and Harry. She could hear James chatting away, but the only one answering him was Charlie with an occasional bark.

When the clatter from the kitchen died down, Kellie ventured out. She could smell burning and hoped it was not the meat pies she had left them. As she made herself cheese on toast she heard footsteps. She turned and saw James holding a bottle of red wine and two glasses.

'Would you care for a glass of wine?'

Would she ever, but she politely refused him. 'Thank you, but no. I have a bottle of mineral water opened.'

He nodded, called Charlie, and went into the lounge room, closing the sliding door behind him.

Kellie could hear the television going in there with some rugby game on. She made herself comfy on the window seat and ate her snack as she watched George Clooney in one of his early movies. Later as she showered and got ready for bed, she had a strange feeling that things were going a little too well.

The next morning she woke feeling very sorry for herself. The chocolates she'd eaten the previous night combined with morning sickness caused her serious feelings of remorse. Her head ached something shocking and she felt awfully sick. Covering her mouth, she dashed to the loo and vomited. That made her head hurt even more. She tried to vomit quietly so James wouldn't hear, but that was hopeless. Feeling like she was at death's door, Kellie cleaned herself up and struggled back to bed then slept until lunch time. The house was unusually quiet so she got up and checked the garage. James's station wagon wasn't there. Thank goodness for that. Still feeling poorly, she had a shower and gave her hair a good wash, massaging her scalp well to help ease her aching head. She got dressed and made a coffee then grabbed one of her new paperbacks and went outside to enjoy her hot drink on a lounger by the pool.

The late autumn sun peeped through wispy clouds as Kellie relaxed under the large umbrella that shaded her recliner. She started to read but soon fell asleep. She woke when a car door slammed. Charlie came bounding over, followed by Harry, who tapped her on the arm. He pointed towards James who was struggling to carry a cumbersome carton.

'We bought a swing and slide set,' the doctor called out, 'but I'm not very good at assembling this sort of thing.' He placed the box on the ground near Kellie. 'There are two more to come,' he grumbled as he turned away.

She put her book down and gave Harry a hug then patted Charlie. 'It shouldn't be too difficult. Let's have a look.' She waited until he'd brought over the three cartons then looked for the one marked "instructions inside".

'First of all,' she informed him, 'we find the directions, and then we follow them.'

James unpacked the parts. He looked at each one individually as though it carried smallpox or some other chronic infection. Kellie studied the instructions. She had successfully assembled kit-set furniture many times and this didn't look too difficult.

Two hours later, with some hiccups and James whacking his thumb a couple of times then uttering a few mild swearwords under his breath, the swing and slide combination was assembled and ready to go.

James lifted Harry onto the swing seat. 'Hold tight, mate,' he said and pushed the child a few times. Harry loved it. Charlie couldn't work out what was happening so he barked madly and ran around in circles.

Kellie started to pick up the rubbish and James came over.

'Thank you for your help, but I'll clean this mess up later.' With that, he turned away and walked back to where Harry waited on the swing.

'Oh well,' Kellie muttered as she picked up her book and walked inside, 'he wouldn't win a personality contest that's for sure.'

The afternoon had turned chilly so Kellie decided to run herself a hot bath. She added lots of fragrant smellies to the water then relaxed amongst dried rose-petals and bubbles. Using one foot, she turned the hot tap on every few minutes to maintain the temperature.

'This is the life,' she told herself. 'James Harvey with his boorish personality can go and get lost.'

***

Harry made slow but definite progress. His little cheeks soon picked up a hint of colour, but his eating was a worry and every night terrifying dreams still surfaced cruelly through his sleep.

Weather permitting, they spent each afternoon outside. Kellie tackled the overgrown garden while Harry and Charlie searched for lizards.

The next few days went by uneventfully and Thursday night after dinner, James came into the kitchen. 'Kellie, Harry is due to have his first medical check with my colleague, Richard Wilkinson. He has a spare appointment tomorrow morning at eleven. Does that time suit you?'

She thought for a moment. 'Yes, that's fine. Afterwards we might go to Maccas for lunch.'

'I'm sure he'd like that. Do you remember where to find the surgery?

It's next-door to the coffee shop where I met you for the interview.'

Kellie nodded. 'Yes, I know where to go.'

'Good. When you arrive at reception ask for Moira and she'll call me.'

***

A patient in the waiting room sneezed loudly just as they walked into the Health Centre. Kellie cringed inwardly and headed for the reception desk where an older lady looked up with a friendly smile.

'Good morning. Do you have an appointment?'

'Hi, this is Harry Harvey. He has an appointment at eleven o'clock with Dr Wilkinson.'

'You're Kellie?' The receptionist looked a little taken back.

The younger woman nodded. 'Yes'. The place was all white and sterile. There were a few pictures of beach scenes on the walls and the chairs were red with chrome legs. It all looked very clean and smelt of antiseptic. Kellie felt queasy.

'I'm Moira Grant. We've spoken on the phone. It's nice to meet you both. Hi Harry, come on through.' She spoke softly to the small boy as she led them down the hallway. Harry quickly hid behind Kellie, clinging tightly to her hand.

Moira Grant had been keeping an eye out for these two. Kellie looked lovely. Her ash-blonde hair was tied back in a pony-tail and she was dressed in smart white trousers and an emerald green top. She looked so pretty that a question ran through Moira's mind, *Why on earth was such a good-looking young woman working way out at James' place as a housekeeper?*

She knew James was pleased with Kellie. He'd told Moira she ran the house well and seemed genuinely fond of Harry. Moira felt in her bones that there was more history to this attractive girl than what they knew.

The trio entered a small sterile room where a red-haired freckly guy sat working on a computer. He stood up and with an out-stretched hand, introduced himself.

'Hi Kellie, I'm Richard Wilkinson. Hello there, young Harry,' he ruffled the child's hair causing the frightened boy to cling to Kellie's leg. 'I'm going to be keeping an eye on this young fellow, watching his weight, height and so on.' They heard a knock on the door and James came in.

Harry started to cry and ran over to his dad. James picked him up and sat on the doctor's chair with the child on his knee. As the stethoscope moved over his skinny little chest, Harry cried louder. The noise was terrible. James's face went bright red and the doctor just carried on. He spoke soothing words to the boy as he weighed and measured him, but the tantrum continued.

Eventually, it was all over and James picked him up. Harry clung tightly to him and sobbed into his shoulder.

The doctor made some notes then turned back to them. 'He's doing ok, quite underweight for his age, but I'll keep an eye on that and see him again in three months. It was nice to meet you both.' He smiled at Kellie and opened the door.

They left the consulting room and she gave James her car-keys so he could carry the distraught child out to the car.

Kellie followed and as she passed reception, Moira leaned over. 'Is everything all right, Kellie? The poor little mite's terribly upset.'

'He's okay, just frightened. This is all out of his comfort zone. We'll be back in three months and hopefully he'll cope better next time.'

'Good, we'll see you then. It was nice to meet you both.' Moira smiled warmly then returned to her work.

Out in the carpark James buckled the upset child in his car seat. 'See you tonight, mate.' He ruffled the boy's hair and nodded at Kellie then went back to the surgery.

Harry was still sniffing loudly when they arrived at Maccas. She ordered a Happy Meal for him and a milkshake for herself. That did the trick. He calmed right down and ate most of his chips. Kellie ate his cheeseburger and he had some of her drink. They did the grocery shopping then went home.

She put Harry down for a short nap then made herself a coffee and carried it out to the verandah, feeling somewhat guilty. 'I also should have seen the doctor, but maybe some other time.'

***

She had arranged to go to the pictures with her friend Mary the following weekend. It was a long drive into Surfers Paradise, but it was nice to catch up with her old mate. The movie was a real tearjerker and they cried their eyes out. As they left the theatre, they laughed at themselves for being such sooks.

They found a rustic-looking brasserie where they ordered a meal and caught up with all things important – like Kellie's living arrangements with the grumpy doctor and Mary's drunken husband. Then they decided to call it a night. Kellie drove her friend home, then pushed in a country music disc, and sang all the way back to Wonglepong.

Sunday morning, she woke feeling worse than usual. She dashed to the loo and tried to vomit quietly, but it was hopeless.

Feeling like death warmed up, she washed her face then made a coffee and carried it outside to sit on the verandah. It was a brilliant morning, the fresh blue sky promised a sunny day and the lawn glistened with droplets of sparkling dew that added a touch of magic to the fragrant garden.

'I wonder if James realises how lucky he is to have this fabulous back yard, probably not,' she muttered grumpily and then decided she had better do something to shake off her gloomy mood.

'Mm...maybe, I'll check out the markets.'

The area around the Scenic Rim and Mt Tambourine was well-known for its craft and produce markets and Kellie enjoyed poking around their stalls.

Just as she headed back inside she heard the crunching sound of footsteps on the driveway. She peeped out a nearby window and saw James and Harry coming home with the dog dawdling along behind them.

'Oh, thank goodness. At least he wasn't here to listen to me bringing up everything I've eaten in the last few days,' she muttered, 'Phew that's a relief.'

***

Two weeks passed and nothing much changed – except, one night, Harry slept right through without waking.

The following morning, Kellie lay in bed and listened to the birds as they twittered and tweeted, welcoming in the new day. She badly needed to go to the loo and thought she'd check on the young boy. He was still fast asleep with one arm clutching the dog. Usually Charlie slept on James's bed, but here was this scraggy bundle of fur snoring loudly next to the sleeping child. The sweet-tempered dog had become an anchor in Harry's insecure world and from that day on the small boy's night-terrors were never so bad. Kellie felt a big step on the child's road to recovery had been taken.

James left for work earlier than usual that morning and Kellie took her time getting out of bed. She didn't feel very well and it was a real effort to get Harry dressed and fed. After giving Charlie his dry food, she went back to bed taking the child with her to watch Sesame Street while she rested. He soon became bored and threw a tantrum, accidently knocking the lamp on Kellie's bed side table. It fell to the ground and the glass shade smashed as it hit the floor.

'Oh no!' Kellie struggled off the bed and saw all the broken glass.

'You naughty little boy,' she yelled, 'get outside!' Angrily, she pushed him towards the back door. Then, as she cleaned up the mess, tears of guilt and frustration welled up and overflowed. She felt terrible for being so mean to the young child.

She showered and dressed, then made a coffee and took it out to the back verandah. Feelings of shame and regret overwhelmed her when she found him sitting on the swing crying. She knelt down and held him until his tears stopped. Then she tried to distract him by telling him about the nest of baby doves in the nearby tree. Kellie lifted him up to have a quick peek at the squawking nest of featherless babies. Fascinated, he soon recovered. A few minutes later, he wriggled away from her and ran over to the trampoline. He climbed up and showed off some new tricks his dad had recently taught him.

The day passed slowly. Later in the afternoon, she was helping Harry put a puzzle together when James arrived home.

He glanced at his mail then looked at her. 'Are you feeling all right, Kellie? You look very pale?'

'I'm a bit off colour, but I'll be okay.'

Harry ran out of the room and returned with Charlie's lead and they set off for their afternoon walk. Kellie found the rest of the afternoon a challenge, but managed to muddle her way through.

Many times in the next few days, she caught James staring at her, as though he had a question, but nothing was said.

Friday afternoon, she called her friend Shirley Goodwin, desperate to talk to someone about her how sick and depressed she felt. Her friend had twice ended up in hospital on a drip with morning sickness.

'Oh Kellie, you poor love. Come and spend the weekend with us, we'll look after you.'

'I'm not f-fit company for anyone at the moment.' Kellie blubbered.

Shirley's husband Bob grabbed the phone.

'Get yourself in here for a couple of days. You either drive in or we'll come and get you.' Finally, Kellie agreed. After checking with James, she packed a bag and left early Saturday morning.

Chapter Nine

Shirley and her husband lived near the ocean beach at Currumbin about twelve kilometers from Surfers Paradise. They had a lovely old wooden home. The only problem was their neighbour's two bull mastiff dogs. They stood guard not far from Shirley's front gate baring their teeth and snarling at strangers. They had never hurt anyone, but Kellie was dead scared of them.

Bob heard her car and came out. The dogs barked and growled. Saliva dripped off their jowls.

'Shut up you mongrels. Get home, go on. Bloody dogs.' He yelled and they took off.

'Why do your neighbours keep such dogs?' shouted Kellie. She was still hiding behind her car, terrified.

Bob shook his head. 'God only knows. Come on in. Shirley's making coffee.'

Kellie loved their unique house. As you stepped through the ornate front entrance, threads of sandalwood scented smoke spiraled up amongst lush indoor plants and crystal-clear water trickled over rustic water features. Sofas with masses of cushions invited you to sit and relax and glass doors opened onto a concrete terrace. Outside, large terracotta pots filled with red bougainvillea gave a Mediterranean look to the old house.

The couple cheered her up with their pregnancy stories, which often had Kellie in fits of laughter. Bob did all the cooking and produced scrumptious mouth-watering meals. Being Italian, he yelled and shouted a lot, issuing instructions to Shirley, who in turn yelled back. Kellie watched the goings on, as she lay propped up with pillows on one of the sofas. They were really entertaining. Sunday evening she returned to Wonglepong feeling a whole lot better.

James was in the kitchen making a hot drink when she walked in. 'Hello,' he greeted her. 'You obviously enjoyed your break.'

'Hi, yes. I had a great time, thanks.'

'Good. Now tomorrow morning, Joy Brennan from Child Services is coming here to check on Harry. She's his local case manager. Are you okay with that?'

'Sure, I'll watch out for her.'

'Thank you. Also, don't make a meal for me tomorrow night as I have a dinner meeting. I should be home around nine-thirty.' He picked up his coffee, wished her goodnight, and left the room.

The next morning, she finished the housework and then sat on the lounge floor with Harry, helping him build a service station with his Lego. Charlie became terribly excited over something and jumped on their half-finished building. They both roared with laughter. As Kellie wiped the tears from her eyes, she heard the front-doorbell ring.

She got up and opened the door. A stout middle-aged woman stood there, wearing dark trousers and a grey jumper. She had an ID card displayed on her chest.

'Good morning. I'm Joy Brennan,' she announced. 'Would you be Kellie?' Her breath stunk of smoke and her raspy voice sounded a touch masculine.

'Yes, I am. Please come in.' Kellie led the way to the lounge-room. 'This is Harry. The dog just wrecked a garage we built.'

'So I see. I'm not keen on dogs. Hello Harry, my name's Joy.'

He looked at her and turned away, kicking at his ruined building. Charlie took refuge behind the coffee table.

'Kellie, can I speak to you privately?'

'Sure,' she replied and turned to the young boy. 'Harry you try and make the service station again by yourself. We'll be back in a moment.' His bottom lip dropped and again he roughly pushed at the Lego with his foot.

She led Joy through the dining room to the kitchen, closing the sliding door behind them. Earlier, Kellie had made a fruit loaf. It was nearly cooked and the room smelt of delicious spices.

'Would you like a coffee?' she politely asked Joy.

'No, thank you. I'm here to do an assessment.' Joy pulled out a chair and sat down at the table. 'From what I read in his report the boy doesn't speak. What's happening there?'

'Well, we offer plenty of encouragement, but, no nothing yet.'

'He's very thin. Is he being offered good nourishing meals?'

'He's just not interested in food, but he's improving. We're getting there slowly.'

'That's a worry. He's very underweight. You stay in here. I want to observe him playing by himself.'

Kellie pottered around waiting for the woman to return. A few minutes later, she was back.

'My next visit will be in one month's time.' She put a card on the table. 'If you have any queries please call me. I think the boy prefers the dog's company to mine. He wouldn't leave that animal alone even when I asked him to. I'll see myself out. Goodbye.'

Kellie waited until she heard the front door close then muttered, 'Miserable old cow.'

She was ironing and watching a movie when James arrived home.

'Hello. How did you go with the case-worker's visit?'

'Hi. All right, but she was a bit different. I think she's a man in women's clothing and she reeked of smoke.'

A slight grin appeared on James' tired face. 'What did she have to say?'

'She asked about his eating and sleeping habits and watched him for a short time then left. Said she'd be back in a month's time. She wasn't the friendliest person I've ever met.'

'Well, we just have to go along with what they say and do. Everything's black and white to that department. How was Harry when she left?'

'He didn't seem bothered at all.'

'Good, I don't want him upset by her visits.' He turned to leave the room. 'I'll have a coffee when you have time.'

Shortly afterwards, Kellie knocked on the open study door and put the hot drink on his desk.

'Thank you, goodnight.' He didn't even bother to look up from his paperwork.

***

Each afternoon, Kellie continued her work in the back garden. Autumn was her favourite time of the year. Leafy trees changed colour and new buds sprouted from dormant plants. The neglected roses bloomed in abundance with a gorgeous mix of colours and fragrances. Harry and Charlie played while Kellie gardened. They were awfully rowdy and Kellie hoped they didn't upset the elderly lady who lived a short distance up the road. After lunch, she planned on taking Harry and the dog over to say hello.

Before they left, she put a small leg of pork in the oven to roast for their dinner. They set off to walk the short distance to where Betty Thompson lived.

James had a great deal of time for the elderly lady. He said she was a wonderful cook. She used to bring him soup or fresh scones, biscuits and lovely fruitcake before Kellie came on the scene.

Turning into Betty's driveway, Kellie heard 'I'm over here in the garden.' They wandered over to where an elderly lady waved a gardening fork.

'I'm so pleased you came over. James told me you'd arrived. It's lovely to meet you both.' Betty wore an ancient straw hat with a faded red striped frock and gumboots. She proudly showed them around her garden with its neat rows of vegetables, flowers, and fruit trees.

It took a while as she walked slowly with a pronounced limp. 'I had polio as a small child and it left me with one leg shorter than the other,' she explained.

They wandered past an old shed covered in masses of flowering jasmine. Next to it was a wooden table with bench seats that had seen better days. 'Sit yourselves down and I'll bring out some ginger beer. I won't be long.'

Betty limped away and they sat down. It was lovely sitting in the shade, annoying wasps buzzed around Kellie, she chased them off, but they were very persistent. The old lady returned with a tray of cold drinks and a plate of homemade jam drops.

'They look yummy, Betty. James said you were a great cook. What a lovely place you have here,' sighed Kellie. 'It's so peaceful and relaxing.'

'Ten years I've been here,' she informed them. 'It's like a small slice of paradise. I used to live in Brisbane, but when my husband passed away I bought this place.'

The two ladies chatted away while Harry and Charlie sat gazing into the fish pond. They watched as fat goldfish glided lazily through rocks and swaying green weeds. They stayed for an hour or so, then Kellie thanked Betty for the delicious afternoon tea and promised to visit again soon.

Back home, she unlocked the back door and caught a whiff of the roasting meat. Her tummy did a flip. The smell made her feel ill.

With difficulty, she made it through to dinner time, and managed to serve the pork-roast with crisp crunchy crackling and vegies. James made short work of his meal, Harry picked at his, and Kellie only managed a few mouthfuls. She felt light-headed as she collected their dirty plates and carried them over to the bench. Suddenly, a black wave roared through her head and she dropped to the floor unconscious.

'Kellie! Kellie!' James knelt above her patting her cheeks as she came to. 'Kellie, speak to me.' He felt for her pulse as she started to move her head.

'I feel sick.'

He waited a moment then helped her off the floor and into her bathroom where she vomited nosily into the toilet. James didn't say a word. He waited patiently until she had finished then helped her to her bed.

'Lay down and I'll fetch you a glass of water.' He moved Harry and Charlie out of the way, as they both stared wide-eyed at the distraught Kellie.

James returned. 'Sip this slowly.' Gently, he helped Kellie sit up. She was a mess and tears streamed down her cheeks. He reached over and pulled a handful of tissues from a box next to the bed.

'Here,' he put them in her hand. 'We'll leave you to rest. Call out if you need me.'

She nodded and wiped her eyes. Oh! She felt terrible and so embarrassed.

Later, James knocked on her door and came in. 'Is there anything I can get you?'

'No thanks.'

He wished her goodnight and closed the door. Feeling miserable and so very alone she quietly sobbed into her pillow.

Later, she got up, brushed her teeth, and changed into pyjamas. When she was back in bed, she wondered about James, and what he might be thinking. Being a doctor, he probably had his suspicions. She was too woozy to think straight, so she gave in to the weariness that overwhelmed her and fell asleep.

She slept until a noise from the kitchen woke her. She glanced at her bedside clock. *8.00 am, oh no*! It was Friday and James should have left for work.

'Oh, dear God, what else can go wrong?' She showered and dressed then took a deep breath and braced herself to face the music. James was frying mushrooms when she went into the kitchen. The smell almost sent her running back to the toilet.

He looked up. 'You're looking a little better this morning. Your colour has improved.' He hesitated a moment then looked her straight in the eye. 'Are you pregnant?'

She expected the question, but actually hearing it from him caused the fragile grip she had on her emotions to slip. 'Y-yes.' She searched for a tissue in her trouser pocket as her eyes watered.

His voice changed, it grew harsh. 'I thought you might be. How far along are you?'

'Four months.' Where was that flaming tissue?

'Have you seen a doctor?'

By now, the tears had overflowed and with both hands over her face and no tissue, she miserably shook her head.

James could hardly contain his anger and spoke through clenched teeth. 'I've made an appointment for you at one-thirty this afternoon with Richard Wilkinson. Harry will stay here with me.' Shaking his head, he pushed the frypan to one side and stomped off. Kellie heard him mutter, 'Women, you can never trust them.'

She stayed out of his way for the rest of the morning and arrived at the Health Centre in Miami five minutes before her appointment. Moira asked her a few details to start her file.

'Now, that's all done so if you'd like to have a seat, Dr Wilkinson won't be long.'

Kellie nervously sat in the waiting room and pretended to read an out-of-date magazine. A scruffy man who smelt like he needed a good wash, came and perched on the seat near her then proceeded to cough and sneeze without putting a hand over his mouth. She turned away in disgust, hoping she wouldn't catch whatever he had.

Moira didn't know what the young woman's visit was all about, but something seemed to be brewing. Before long, Dr Wilkinson came out to reception, picked up Kellie's file from the desk, and called her name. Nervously, she stood up and followed him down the hallway into a consulting room.

'Have a seat, Kellie,' he closed the door. 'I understand you're around four months pregnant. Let me check your blood pressure and weight to start with.'

After he'd done that and made some notes he asked her some very personal questions, which made her feel quite uncomfortable.

'Hop up on the bed and I'll check the baby's position and heartbeat.' He pulled up her top and she could smell a touch of garlic on his breath as he poked around her tummy. Then with his stethoscope, he picked up the beat of the baby's heart.

He looked up. 'Would you like to hear it?'

Kellie nodded and he put the instrument to her ears. He watched for her reaction as she heard the first faint k-thump of the baby's beating heart.

Her sad face burst into a beautiful smile. 'Oh, that's lovely, thank you.'

'You can get down now.' He walked over to his desk. 'The baby's an average size with a healthy heartbeat. Your morning sickness should ease up in the next few weeks. I can't give you anything to settle the nausea, but try nibbling a dry biscuit – that often works.' He did some calculations. 'We're looking at a due date around September the twenty-fourth. I'd like you to have a scan sometime this week. I'll organise that and get in touch. Now, your next check-up is due in four weeks' time, but contact me if you have any worries.'

She thanked him and went back to Moira at reception, signed the Medicare form, and made an appointment for her next check-up.

Moira quickly guessed that Kellie must be pregnant. *Holy hell,* she thought. *What's going to happen now?* James had phoned this morning and asked to speak to Richard Wilkinson, he sounded mad as hell. All along, she couldn't work out why an attractive young woman like Kellie would take a housekeeping job out in the wop-wops – now the reason was crystal clear.

Chapter Ten

Meanwhile, back home, James was livid. He had wondered why Kellie looked pale and unwell, but in his wildest dreams, he never guessed she was going to have a baby.

'Who on earth is the father and why isn't he on the scene?' he asked himself shaking his head. 'This could be a real problem.'

The dilemma kept turning over in his mind. 'Harry's making excellent progress and he's fond of Kellie. Changes in his life at this stage could set his progress back considerably.'

He scratched his head. He had no idea what to do about his housekeeper being pregnant. 'Women are such deceitful creatures; I should never have trusted her in the first place.'

Kellie returned home to an empty house. *Thank goodness,* she thought. She dreaded facing James. Tomorrow and Sunday were her days off and she had decided to go into Broadbeach and stay with Sam. She found her mobile phone and pressed Sam's number.

'Kellie, I was just thinking of you isn't that strange. How are things going out at the doc's?'

'Um, will you be h-home tomorrow?' Kellie struggled to get the words out.

'Sure, are you coming to visit?'

'S-something's happened….'

'What, what's happened? No, wait 'till tomorrow when you get here.'

'T-thanks Sam, I'll be there after lunch.' Kellie finished the call, wiped her eyes, and went to rest on her bed.

***

James, Harry and the dog arrived home later in the afternoon. He bathed the young boy while Kellie prepared dinner. She had bought fresh flounder on the way home and cooked it in butter. They all liked fish. She made tasty potato wedges to serve with salad greens.

When they had finished eating, James turned to Kellie. He looked like a wound up coil about to spring loose. 'What did Richard have to say?'

'Not a great deal. He thought my faint was due to morning sickness and said it should ease up shortly. He booked me in for a scan next Wednesday at eleven.'

'What due date did he give you?'

'The end of September.' No more was said. It was as though a blind had been pulled down over James's face. He left the table taking Harry with him. A few minutes later she heard his car start up.

Kellie cleaned up the kitchen then pulled out the ironing board and ironed like there was a demon inside her. 'You'd think I'd committed bloody murder or done something terrible. Honestly, of all the insufferable obnoxious bosses, he'd take the prize. Oooh!' She was so angry she couldn't think of enough bad words to describe him.

James had gone out when Kellie woke up the next morning, so she showered and dressed then went about her work as though nothing had happened. He was coldly polite when he returned, but didn't ask any more questions. Being Saturday, Kellie's time off started after lunch and she couldn't leave fast enough when they'd finished their meal and she'd cleaned up.

***

Sam watched out for Kellie and when she arrived, she held her as she listened to the predicament her friend was in.

'Oh, Kellie. Leave it all behind you for the moment, Darl,' she consoled her. 'James Harvey doesn't know when he's on to a good thing. He'll never find a better housekeeper than you. Just give it some time and see what happens, but for now, it's all about us. We're going to do what girls do well and that's have a great time.' Before long, she had Kellie laughing and forgetting all about her job at Wonglepong.

They went to a comedy movie. They laughed so much Kellie nearly wet her knickers. She made a mad dash for the lady's and only just made it in time. They were still laughing when the movie finished, then hunger got the better of them and they looked around for somewhere to have a meal. An Italian brasserie caught their attention.

'This will do,' Sam announced and nudged Kellie in the ribs. 'Have a peek at the spunky Italian dude serving at the counter, whipty-doo! I'd like him in my Christmas stocking or knickers!' Kellie cracked up and had to run to the loo again.

The meal was great. When they had finished Sam suggested they head for the casino.

As they walked in, people milled around and the noise of chatter filled the air. Kellie stood and stared. There were so many people. Some were scantily clad, tottering on heels they could barely manage, and others poorly dressed, while some were dressed to kill. It was such a strange mix of people. Kellie watched a woman at the roulette table put her hand into a brown paper bag and bring out a pile of one hundred dollar notes!

'Fancy keeping your money in there and not bringing a proper handbag,' she innocently remarked to Sam.

'Easy come, easy go. Some of these people look pretty dodgy to me,' Sam remarked.

They wandered around then played the poker machines for a short time. Kellie tired of them quickly as they gobbled up her money and gave her nothing back in return.

Sunday morning they went to the beach. The flat sea sparkled in the winter sunshine and the breeze had a tangy salty smell. The loud thundering surf and screeching seagulls were like soothing music to Kellie's frazzled nerves.

'This is a wonderful change from the squawking crows and noisy roosters I get every morning,' she told Sam.

Later, they had brunch in a crowded restaurant on the side of the Nerang River, watching fast boats tow water skiers up and down the shimmering water. Kellie felt great. James Harvey and all problems associated with him ceased to exist.

She drove back to Wonglepong in a better frame of mind. She had decided to play it by ear and deal with challenges as they arose. Her tummy had settled down and she maintained an attitude of 'things can only get better.' Or so she thought!

***

The atmosphere in the house had changed considerably. James was polite, but never asked how she was or how her day had been as he used to. He uttered a quiet 'hi' when he came home from work and thanked her after meals. He chatted with Harry, but didn't engage in any conversation with Kellie.

He spent most his spare time with his young son. He researched the child's problem and consulted with people specializing in juvenile trauma. They all said the same thing, "time and a safe loving environment".

Tuesday night, James walked into the kitchen where Kellie ironed as she watched television. His nose wrinkled at the fishy smell remaining from the grilled perch they had eaten for dinner.

He picked up the remote and turned down the volume. 'Tomorrow when you go for your scan, drop Harry at the surgery. I'm taking him to have his hair cut and then he can have lunch with me. You can collect him around one o'clock. He should be ready to go home by then.'

Kellie nodded without looking at him and kept ironing. 'Okay, I'll do that.'

James returned to his study and Kellie thumped the iron down a few times on the trousers she was pressing, shook her head, and turned the volume back up.

Wednesday morning she went for her scan. After giving her name at reception, she sat down on a long divan. The waiting room had that sterile medical smell. The grey walls were softened by some colourful frangipani prints. A vase of artificial flowers shared a small table with a few well-thumbed magazines. Kellie crossed her legs. She desperately needed a wee, but for this procedure her bladder had to be full. Her name was called and she went into a cubicle to undress and get into a paper gown. By now she was about to burst, but hung on with great difficulty.

A radiographer called her into a small room. 'Hi Kellie, come in and hop up on the bed?' Nervously she did as instructed and watched as the young woman rubbed cold gel on her tummy then maneuvered a wand type gadget over her abdomen. Soon a dark mass appeared on a nearby monitor screen and the gentle pulsing of the baby's heartbeat could be clearly heard in the quiet room.

'There you are,' the lady said, 'that's a good strong heartbeat.'

Tears welled up and spilled over Kellie's cheeks. She wished she had someone special to share this moment with.

The radiographer pointed out a few details and clicked away while moving the instrument over different areas. Measurements were calculated, then she wiped the gel off Kellie's tummy.

'You are eighteen weeks into your pregnancy and by my calculations the baby's due on the twenty-sixth of September. Your doctor will let you know if you need to come back. You can go to the loo now, then get dressed. It's nice to have met you Kellie, goodbye.'

As she drove to James's surgery, she felt overwhelmed by what she had just seen. Before, *baby* had just been a word. Now it was real.

She arrived at the medical centre just before one o'clock and hoped Harry was ready.

Moira looked up, smiled, and came over. 'Hi Kellie, they aren't back yet. Would you like to have a coffee and share some fruit bun with me?'

'Yes thanks, it does seem a long time since I had breakfast.' She followed Moira out the back to a small cluttered kitchen. Someone had just eaten a meat pie and the smell lingered from the unwashed plate.

'Have a seat and I'll make our drinks.' Moira soon placed two steaming mugs of coffee on the small table, pushing newspapers and other paraphernalia out of the way.

'Sorry about the mess. The place is clean, but untidy.' Kellie sat down and Moira handed her a piece of fruit bun on a plate. They chatted about the scan and babies and the older lady recalled her pregnancies, telling Kellie how she used to wet her knickers every time she sneezed or coughed. They were having a good laugh when James and Harry came in.

'Kellie,' the doctor glanced at the coffee and the half eaten bun, 'Harry's ready to go home and I have patients waiting.' He spoke sharply and Moira glared at him.

Quietly fuming, Kellie put down her unfinished coffee, left her piece of bun on the plate, and stood up.

'Thanks for the lunch, Moira.' She grabbed Harry's hand and left the room. As she walked out to the car, she struggled to keep her temper in check. 'What a rude pig of a man,' she muttered after Harry was safely strapped into his car seat and his door closed. 'One of these day's he'll go too far and I'll let him have it with both barrels!'

***

Meanwhile, back at the surgery, Moira was ready to do battle on Kellie's behalf.

'James!' Angrily Moira followed him into his consulting room and closed the door. 'What the hell are you thinking of speaking to Kellie like that? You didn't have to be so bloody rude!' She stopped for a breath and shook her head. 'I can't understand you. She's a lovely girl, good with Harry and a great housekeeper. What's your problem? She hasn't shot anyone. She's having a baby, get used to it.'

He thumped his fist on the desk. 'Kellie deceived me by not admitting she was pregnant when I interviewed her. If she hid that, what else is she hiding? Who's the father? Where the hell is he? She should have come clean in the first place.' Wearily he rubbed his forehead and mocked,

'Women and deceit go hand in hand.'

Moira's fingers itched to slap him. 'Would you have hired her knowing about the baby?'

'No and I didn't want a housekeeper I couldn't trust either.'

She shook her head in disgust. 'You have a lot to learn, James Harvey. Life isn't always perfect and you could try being a bit more tolerant of those less fortunate than yourself.' Moira retorted then stormed out of the room slamming the door as she left. 'Men,' she snorted, 'sometimes I could shoot the whole bloody lot of them.'

Exasperated, James dropped down into his chair. He couldn't work females out. First, there was his wife who turned against him then left, taking their only child with her and now his new housekeeper had deliberately deceived him during her interview by not telling him she was pregnant.

'And now Moira's ticked me off and all I've done is give the girl a job. I really think her reprimand was uncalled for.'

He took a long deep breath then buzzed for the next patient to be sent in.

Chapter Eleven

Life out at Wonglepong muddled along. Kellie did her job and tried to ignore James' bad attitude and Harry slowly became more confident and trusting.

He spent a great deal of time outdoors, watching birds collect bits and pieces for their nests, and each morning he fed a small family of wallabies who came to their back fence. Sometimes, he came inside with caterpillars crawling up his arms, Kellie always pretended to be frightened, and he would giggle. Together they walked Charlie and enjoyed the sounds and smells of the Australian bush with its spectacular wildlife and fragrant eucalypt and gum trees. Harry gathered treasures along the way. Once it was a dead stick insect.

'No, Harry, I'm not carrying that home. Throw it away.'

He shook his head and added it to his other bits and pieces that he carried in a small bag. As for James, he stayed coldly polite.

***

Sunday came and Kellie went to the beach at Burleigh Heads. Dark clouds threatened rain and the usually vivid blue sea was a dull uninteresting grey. She read magazines and munched on chocolate bars then dreamily paddled along the water's edge. By the end of the day, she felt ready to face another challenging week. She tried not to let James's attitude upset her, but there were times when she felt like decking him one.

After lunch on the following Tuesday, Kellie put Harry down for a nap then started preparing dinner. The telephone rang. She moved quickly to answer it before the noise woke the young boy.

'Moira here, Kellie, listen carefully. There's been an accident and James is injured. He went out to buy his lunch and a car mounted the footpath and knocked him down. They think the driver had a heart-attack. James has a nasty gash on his head where he hit the concrete and his left leg is badly c-crushed.' Moira was crying and difficult to understand. 'H-he keeps slipping in and out of consciousness and the paramedics said that's causing them some concern. They're taking him to the Southern Cross Hospital at Southport. I'm going with him in the ambulance. I'll call you later when I know more about his c-condition. Bye for now.'

Kellie's hand trembled as she put the phone down and looked for the nearest seat. She felt sick. Outside a lone crow squawked, an irritating monotonous call. Suddenly, the nausea building in her tummy erupted. She ran but wasn't fast enough. With both hands over her mouth, she caught some of the vomit and the rest spilled over onto the immaculate hall carpet. Her head started to spin and she dropped down onto her knees and rested back against the wall.

'What will we do if he dies?' she whimpered amongst the sticky mess. 'What about little Harry. Oh dear Lord, what will happen to me?' All these thoughts spun around in her troubled dizzy head.

It took nearly an hour to get the carpet back to its near-perfect state. By then, Kellie's energy had fizzled out and the whole house reeked of disinfectant, making her feel sick again. Harry woke from his nap in a cranky mood. 'Bloody hell,' she muttered, 'that's all I need.'

Moira rang as she dished up their dinner. 'Kellie, they think James is going to be all right. He has concussion and is in intensive care where they're watching him closely. They said tomorrow he'll go to theatre where they'll stitch the cut on his forehead and repair his leg. He has a couple of nasty breaks below his left knee and his ankle's badly damaged.' She started to cry. 'Oh Kellie h-he looks such a mess, the poor man. I feel so sorry for him.' She sniffed a couple of times. 'Is e-everything all right out there?'

'Yes, Moira, thanks for asking. We're fine. You must be tired, what a terrible day you've all had. By the way, how is the person who drove the car?'

'We haven't heard. I'm off home now. I thought of ringing James' parents, they live on Bribie Island, but they're elderly and I don't want to frighten them. When he's feeling better he can phone them himself.' Her voice broke again. 'G-give young Harry a hug from me. He'll miss his dad not coming home tonight. I'll talk to you in the morning. Night-night love.'

Kellie wished Moira goodnight and put the phone down. 'Oh dear God, what next?'

She rubbed her tired eyes then went back to the dinner table. Harry ate a fraction of his meal and Kellie picked at hers then pushed it to one side.

She bathed him and tucked him into bed then read him his favourite pirate story. He lay with one arm around Charlie and kept glancing towards the window as though waiting to hear his dad's car come up the drive. Kellie bent down and kissed him gently. He smelt of baby soap and shampoo. She left a lamp glowing softly and couldn't help but wonder what would become of him if James didn't recover.

Squabbling lorikeets woke Kellie early the next morning. A few minutes later, Harry crept into her room. He looked a bit lost so she lifted the blankets and let him hop in for a cuddle. Not one to miss out Charlie jumped up, scratched himself a few times, and then settled down. She switched on her television set and the three of them snuggled up to watch The Wiggles.

They were having breakfast when the phone rang.

'It's Moira here Kellie. I've just heard from the hospital, James is back from theatre. It all went well and a CAT scan showed no permanent injury to his brain. Thank God for that.' She sniffed and continued. 'He's sleeping now and probably won't wake until tomorrow. I'll pop up later and sit with him.' Her voice broke. 'It's h-hard to believe this has happened. What terrible bad luck that poor man's had.'

'He's in good hands Moira. Make yourself a strong cuppa and sit down for a few minutes. This has all been a terrible shock to you.' Kellie thought for a moment. 'Maybe I should take Harry in to see him tomorrow and then we can take his pyjamas and toilet gear in. He'll be pleased to see Harry and know everything's okay out here.'

'That's a great idea, thanks Kellie. I'm sure he'd like to see the young fella. If you need help, anything at all love, please call me. James put my mobile number in his address book out by your phone.'

'Thanks Moira. Harry keeps searching for his dad. He's looked in James' bedroom and the garage a number of times, even though I've explained that daddy's hurt his head and needs to stay in hospital. Anyhow, I'll stop chatting. Call us when you get home. Bye for now.'

Moira phoned later that afternoon sounding gloomy and tearful. 'There's no change in James' condition. They said he's caused a few anxious moments, but by tomorrow he should be more stable.'

Kellie couldn't sleep that night. She tossed and turned. Her mind kept coming up with questions she couldn't answer! When morning came, her head ached from lack of sleep.

After breakfast, she packed a small bag with gear she thought James might need then dressed Harry. She looked in her walk-in-robe. Her choice of going out clothes was very limited. Most things were too tight. She sucked in her stomach and squeezed into a pair of white trousers leaving the waistband undone and covered it with an emerald green shirt that hung long and loose. She desperately needed some maternity clothes.

***

As she drove in to the hospital, Kellie switched from being near hysterical to feeling sick. She wasn't at all sure about facing James. 'Would he want to see his housekeeper? Especially one he wasn't fussed on.' Getting a car park was very frustrating until, luckily, a van pulled out right in front of her.

They made their way into the hospital past groups of smokers in hospital pyjamas and nighties. One guy hooked up to a drip had a cigarette dangling from his mouth.

Several people were in the queue under a sign saying 'Enquiries' so she joined the line and waited her turn.

A frosty-faced, overweight woman sitting in front of a computer grunted, 'Next!'

'We'd like to see Dr James Harvey, please. Can you tell me where to find him?'

The woman punched something into her keyboard and without lifting her head barked, 'He's in a private room on the fourth floor. There's a nurse's station up there, ask them.'

Kellie thanked her and looked around for the lifts. The sterile hospital smell upset her tummy and she started to felt squeamish. Harry grizzled and pulled on her hand. He wasn't happy in the unfamiliar surroundings.

Up on the fourth floor, they found the nurse's station, but they were all busy. Harry kicked at the side of counter and kept sniveling. Eventually a nurse came forward, frowning at the noise.

'Sorry, but we're really busy at the moment. Were you looking for someone?'

'Could we see Dr James Harvey, please?'

The nurse scowled. 'Are you family?'

'Yes,' Kellie lied. Harry stopped bawling and hid behind her.

The nurse came around the counter. 'You're allowed ten minutes. Follow me.' She walked to a nearby door and opened it quietly. The room had large floor to ceiling windows with a view out over the Gold Coast hinterland and it smelt of antiseptic and other indescribable things. Nervously, they approached James' bed. He looked terrible. He had drips and drains connected to various machines and a large dressing covered his forehead. The rest of his face wasn't too bad. His arms had a few neatly stitched cuts plus some angry looking grazes and his left leg was plastered and hoisted up to a metal stand. Harry whimpered in horror and wrapped himself around Kellie's legs.

'Hi, James. It's me, Kellie' she murmured softly. 'I've brought Harry to see you.' She lifted the little boy up and held him gingerly on the edge of the bed. James' good eye partially opened and a slight smile moved his lips when he saw his son.

The nurse checked his chart then returned it to the end of the bed. 'Please don't stay longer than ten minutes. He needs to rest.' Then she quietly left the room.

James lifted one hand and laid it on Harry's arm. 'Are you being good?' he slowly whispered, then stopped and took a breath. Harry grinned and nodded his head.

'I'm p-pleased.' James paused. He struggled to get the words out. 'Look after Charlie.' His hand dropped and his eye closed. Harry looked up at Kellie, his bottom lip dropping ready to burst into tears.

'Charlie,' Kellie laughed trying to cheer James up. 'He brought a lizard inside. We both nearly had a heart-attack! I had to pick the poor thing up. Its tail was missing. We think Charlie had bitten it off, as there was a lot of blood on the floor. We growled at him, didn't we, Harry?' The small boy nodded and looked up at his dad with a nervous giggle.

To James this was a wonderful sound. He felt reassured his son was in good hands.

Then Harry became restless, grabbing at his crotch and Kellie saw that 'alarmed look' appear on his face and knew she needed to find a loo quickly.

'I think we'd better go now James and come back tomorrow.' She lifted Harry up so he could kiss the small part of his dad's cheek that was undamaged. When she stood the small boy down on his feet he started to cry, then she saw a puddle form around his sneakers. She quickly grabbed some paper towels and cleaned up the mess. By now, Harry bawled at full volume. Extremely embarrassed, she grabbed his hand and they made a quick exit.

'I think we might go to Macca's for lunch. Would you like that?' He quickly forgot about his dad and skipped along the corridor while Kellie tried to remember where she parked the car. After they had shared a milkshake and hot chips at McDonalds, they headed home.

Later in the afternoon, as dark clouds gathered slowly in the distance, Kellie hooked Charlie's lead on and they walked up to see Betty to let her know about James.

The old lady cried. 'I knew something had h-happened as I haven't seen his station wagon around.' She wiped her eyes with her apron. 'What can I do to help you? Would you like me to look after Harry?'

'Thanks for the offer, but we're managing all right at the moment.'

Tearfully Betty limped over to the kettle and switched it on to make them a cuppa.

***

The next day they went back to the hospital. Kellie wore a pair of dark-blue trousers with the button undone at the waistband and a safety-pin holding it together. She covered the gap with a loose white top and Harry wore cute new jeans with a checkered shirt. He liked dressing up.

When they stepped out of the hospital lift, James' door was still closed. Kellie opened it cautiously and peered inside. The room was dark and the curtains were pulled right across.

They tiptoed in. 'Hi James,' Kellie whispered. 'We've just called in to say hello.'

He grunted something she didn't catch.

A nurse came bustling in. 'He's had a bad night. You can only stay a few minutes.'

Kellie nodded. A few minutes suited her fine. The room had a funny smell. She thought it must be something to do with the drains and plastic bags hanging out from under his blankets.

Harry clutched her legs.

'It's all right love. Daddy's head is sore, so we'll only stay a couple of minutes.' Kellie lifted the small boy up so he could kiss his dad.

James briefly caressed Harry's head and whispered, 'Sorry, son.'

'We'd better go.' Kellie did feel sorry for James. She could see he was really suffering. 'At least Harry's seen you, and hopefully tomorrow you'll feel a bit better.'

The next day they went back and peeped around the door before venturing in to his room. 'Is it okay to come in?'

He managed to open both eyes. The swelling was going down but the bruising looked terrible. 'Yes, do come in. I'm feeling better than I did yesterday.' He still spoke slowly. 'Hello Harry.'

Kellie lifted the child up so he could sit on the side of the bed. Then the boy reached over, kissed his dad, and handed him a container. James carefully opened it and sniffed the contents.

'Wow, banana cake. That's my favourite. I'll save it to have later on.' He smiled and patted Harry's hand and then looked up at Kellie. 'How are you managing?'

'Good, no hassles,' she replied. 'Charlie's fine. We take him for lots of walks. He likes that.'

A nurse bustled in to check on James, told them they could stay a few minutes longer today if they wanted to and then she left.

'How's the morning sickness, is it settling down?' James inquired politely.

'It's okay. Odd smells upset me and my appetite isn't great,' she sighed. 'Some days it's worse. I'm totally over the whole thing.' She looked at him and grinned. 'Sorry, but you did ask.'

James changed the subject. 'Moira and Don came to see me last night; she brought me up to date with the latest gossip from the surgery,' he rolled his eyes. 'It's like a soap opera hearing what the girls in reception get up to over the weekend. One had her boyfriend's name tattooed on the side of her neck! Can you believe that? What if they break up, what happens then?'

Half an hour into their visit Harry became cranky. He accidently tipped over the water jug and then squashed a plum on the bedspread.

'Oh Harry...' James wailed.

Kellie grabbed the young boy and lifted him up. 'Quick, give Dad a kiss. It's time we left.'

She quickly stuffed James' washing in her carry-bag. 'If there's anything you want, just give me a call.'

'Thanks. Will I see you tomorrow?'

Kellie nodded. 'Sure, I'll bring Harry back in. Goodbye.'

James felt quite miserable as he watched them leave.

***

Kellie had prepared a picnic lunch so she drove to Main Beach and parked the car under a shady palm-tree. It was a beautiful day. The sky was picture-book blue with puffy white clouds and she could smell the heady mix of salty sea air and sun-tan oil. She took a deep breath to enjoy the moment before she unclipped Harry from his car seat.

'Come on mate, help me find a picnic spot,' she called. Kellie covered him in sun-screen and plonked his floppy hat on, then they sat on the beach and ate their lunch. They spent a lovely couple of hours constructing sand castles and paddling at the water's edge. Harry giggled as water splashed up his skinny legs and his little face beamed.

Later, they packed up and Kellie drove home singing along to 'The best of The Eagles' while Harry fell asleep in his car seat.

Her mobile phone rang as she walked into the kitchen.

It was James. 'Kellie, I want you to bring my lap-top with you when you come tomorrow?'

She got a shock to hear his voice. 'Should you even be turning it on?'

'Sure. See you in the morning. Is Harry all right?'

'Yes, we've just this minute arrived home. We've been to the beach.'

'Tell him I called. Goodbye.' With that, he finished the call. *He must be getting better*, Kellie thought, *he's starting to sound like his normal bossy self.*

***

Meanwhile back at the hospital, James had a lady visitor. She wore a white coat and was tall and slim with short dark hair and very captivating features. Her face glowed with good health.

'Good afternoon, Dr Harvey. I'm Ruth Simonds your physiotherapist. I'm here to start a few exercises to get your damaged body moving again. Do you mind if I call you James?'

'No. What did you have in mind?' Gingerly he sat up and took notice. Ruth explained that while his injured leg must not be disturbed, his good leg and the top half of his body needed to work out. After outlining a plan for his therapy, she gently began his treatment.

Afterwards, they chatted for a few minutes then Ruth picked up her paper work. 'That's enough for today. Tomorrow we'll increase the pace. I'll see you in the morning.'

The following day, James had just finished his morning tea when Kellie and Harry arrived. Harry held a small bunch of pansies and ran to the bed holding the flowers up to his dad.

'Are they for me?' James asked and made a big deal out of smelling them. 'Thank you, Harry.' He glanced at Kellie who carried his laptop. 'Here, there's space on my bedside cabinet.' She put the computer down and lifted the child up onto the bed.

'Are these flowers from our garden, Harry?' The small boy shook his head.

Kellie answered. 'No, Betty next door brought them over for you.'

They heard a quick knock. 'Morning, James.' A tall, good-looking woman wearing a white coat glared at Kellie and Harry. 'Is it visiting time already?'

Kellie became flustered. 'We can come back later, James'. She looked at him for guidance.

He nodded. 'That might be best. See you later, Harry.' Kellie lifted the bewildered boy down off the bed. He couldn't work out what was happening and started to kick and scream.

'For heaven's sake,' complained the woman in the white coat. 'This is a hospital,' her mouth puckered as though she had just sucked a lemon.

'Come on, Harry,' Kellie whispered to the young boy, 'We'll go and have a milkshake then come back.' He stopped crying and sniffed loudly as he stomped out of the room following Kellie.

Chapter Twelve

Still smarting from the woman's bitchy attitude, Kellie and Harry left the hospital and headed for the local shopping centre.

They sat in a café, shared a milkshake and a toasted sandwich, then looked for warm boots to fit Harry. She bought them and let him keep them on so he could show his dad.

A couple of hours later, they made their way back to the hospital. Kellie held the child's hand firmly as she peered around James' door, making sure no one else was there. He looked to be asleep.

He must have had visitors as a vase of cream freesias stood on his bedside table giving the room a fresh tangy scent. A pleasant change from the usual antiseptic, bleach and bed-pan smells.

They tip-toed in. He stirred and opened his eyes. No welcoming smile there.

'Where have you two been?'

As though he didn't know, Kellie thought. 'After we were all but kicked out of here we went to the shops, had lunch, and bought Harry some new boots.' She glanced at the young boy. 'Show your dad.' The child grinned from ear to ear as Kellie lifted him up to sit on to the bed.

'Watch out!' James bellowed as Harry accidently kicked his good leg.

The doctor groaned. 'I've just had an hour of physio and my body's aching all over,' he grumbled. 'Please be careful!'

The small boy turned to Kellie, his bottom lip dropped and he turned on the tears.

Kellie lifted the distressed child off the bed and a spark of temper flashed in her eyes. 'It was an accident, for heaven's sake.'

James screwed up his face and rubbed his leg, making a big deal of it.

Kellie shook her head, thinking, *You great big sook.* She pulled out a chair and sat Harry on her lap. He buried his head in her shoulder and gave a few loud sniffs.

Feeling inquisitive, she asked, 'Who was the rude woman in a white coat that barged in here earlier on?'

James eyed her with contempt. 'Ruth is the physio here. She's in charge of getting me up and about and I'm finding her exercise programme difficult to cope with.'

He glanced at his son who was touching things he shouldn't be. 'Harry, don't press that buzzer!' Too late. In came a nurse to see what James wanted.

His face turned bright red. 'I'm sorry – my son accidently hit the button.' He glared at Kellie and snapped, 'Can't you keep your eye on him?'

The nurse didn't speak, just shook her head, and left the room.

Kellie didn't know whether to laugh or cry. He was unbelievable. What he really needed was a good swift kick up the backside to stop him feeling sorry for himself.

Well, she'd had enough for one day and wasn't going to be part of all this nonsense. She jumped up. 'Harry we'd better get going.' Quickly she gathered James' laundry.

Brutal thoughts raced through her mind. *Let me get me out of here before I throw this bloody washing right at his miserable dial.*

She drove home practicing her deep breathing and thought that James had better be in a more reasonable frame of mind tomorrow or else he would miss out and they would go to the beach. Infuriating man!

She found it a long drive each day, but worth the effort to see Harry's little face light up when he saw his dad.

***

Back at the hospital, Ruth continued her tortuous daily treatment. After each session James' pale face dripped with sweat, the exercises were so intense. Kellie and Harry timed their visits to allow James plenty of time to recover from his morning physio sessions.

Soon they had him out of bed and struggling on crutches, it was slow and painful. He didn't go far, just to the bathroom and back.

Two and a half weeks after his accident, Kellie and Harry arrived at the hospital to find James with a grin on his face. Kellie wondered if he'd won the lotto!

'Guess what?' he said, 'I'm allowed to go home tomorrow as long as you can manage to look after me. What do you think?' Harry started to jump up and down clapping his hands.

'I'm sure we'll manage,' she lied with a forced smile, quietly thinking, *Oh dear God what have I let myself in for?* They discussed arrangements for how best to get him home. Kellie was to drive his station wagon to the hospital so he could lay his plastered leg across the back seat. It all sounded good in theory.

'Can you be here by eleven o'clock tomorrow?' James asked.

Kellie nodded, still in shock.

'And bring me something suitable to wear home.' He didn't even say please. She was totally over this whole hospital thing. Then Harry wet his pants so thankfully she had an excuse to leave.

When they got home, Kellie made a coffee and sat on the back steps dreading the next few weeks. She could cope with James when he was well, but since he'd been injured, his fuse was noticeably short. She took a deep breath and the delicate fragrance of the violets flowering near the verandah helped calm her over-stretched nerves.

Charlie barked loudly and ran around in circles, then, Harry, who had slept all the way home suddenly became full of beans and copied him. They made a terrible racket.

'Come on you two, we'll walk over and see Betty.' Harry raced inside to fetch Charlie's lead and the noisy trio made their way up the road.

Betty heard them coming and met them at her front gate. 'How are you all?' She limped over and gave Harry one of her bear-hugs. He giggled and pretended to be shy. 'And how's James doing?'

'He's coming home tomorrow. I wondered if you could look after Harry and Charlie while I fetched him from the hospital.'

The old lady's face broke into a huge smile. 'I'd love to have them. Harry can help me clean out the fish pond.' The child's face lit up, he was fascinated with those goldfish. They went inside. Betty had been baking and a freshly iced chocolate cake sat on the bench. They devoured two large slices each, then Harry accidently dropped his on the floor. Before Kellie could clean up the mess, Charlie ate it.

'Oh no,' she growled, knowing dogs aren't allowed to eat chocolate. 'It's time we went home. Come on Harry.' She grabbed Charlie's lead and hugged the old lady. 'Thanks for the afternoon tea, Betty, it was delicious. I'll bring these two over just before ten in the morning. See you then, bye.'

They went home and she put fresh sheets on James's bed, opened the windows, and gave his bathroom another clean.

***

The next morning, James had his last physio session with Ruth. He knew it was thanks to her he'd made such good progress. Over the past few weeks, they had become good friends. She had a weird sense of humour and he liked that.

'I drive through Wonglepong every now and again,' Ruth informed him, 'visiting an uncle out that way. Would you like me to stop by your place and see how you're coming along?'

'That would be great,' James replied with a smile. 'You'd be very welcome. Give me a call when you are out my way.'

She beamed as she left the room, leaving a lingering hint of Chanel No. 5.

***

After breakfast, Kellie took Harry and Charlie over to Betty's then drove to the hospital.

'Good morning, Kellie.' James sounded his normal arrogant self. 'How's Harry this morning?'

What about me? Kellie thought, *or don't I count?* 'When I left Betty's, he was scoffing hot pikelets. He had butter and jam all over his face.'

As she spoke, Kellie unpacked the clothes she had brought for James to wear home. He had pyjamas on and Kellie wondered if she should leave him to get dressed or stay. Opting to play safe, she asked, 'Shall I call a nurse to help you get changed?'

'No, if you don't mind giving me a hand, I think we can manage.' James undid the buttons on his pyjama top as he spoke. Kellie felt panic rising and hoped her face wasn't bright red. *Does he have undies on under those pyjama pants or not?* She helped him put a polo-shirt on his top half.

'Pass me the shorts you brought in.' He'd noticed Kellie's red cheeks and added 'I am wearing boxers underneath these pjs.' Trying to overcome her embarrassment, Kellie bit her lip and gently edged the pyjama pants down then picked up the shorts. James had lost weight and Kellie gingerly pulled them up over the cast to his thighs. Before she could stop them, her treacherous eyes strayed to his 'man bulge'. She knew those boxers had a front opening and was petrified in case his privates were visible. *I will just die if that thing's poking its head out,* she stifled a nervous giggle.

'I can do this part thank you.' He lifted his behind to wriggle the shorts into place then fastened them and glanced over at Kellie. She looked extremely flustered and kept her head down as she frantically packed his gear into the carry-bag. James suppressed a grin.

The door opened and in came the smiling white-coated figure of Ruth Simonds. 'All set to leave us are you James?' she asked, once more totally ignoring Kellie.

'Yes, I'm looking forward to some peace and quiet. No banging around in the middle of night. Don't forget to drop in when you're passing Ruth, we'll open a bottle of something nice and catch up.'

'That'll be great. I'll be in touch.' She flashed her piranha like smile at her latest conquest.

Then she actually noticed Kellie and the smile vanished. 'Make sure you take good care of him. We've all worked jolly hard to bring him this far.'

Kellie steadily met her gaze. 'I'm his housekeeper not his nurse,' she replied in her most flippant tone then turned to James. 'I'll see about a wheel-chair.' She left them to it and resisted the urge to kick the door as it closed behind her.

A pleasant faced young nurse approached with an empty wheelchair.

'Here we are. This is for Dr. Harvey. Is he ready?'

'Yes, he's all set to go.'

'He's had a pain-killing shot to cope with the ride home and here's his medication.' She handed Kellie a plastic bag with tablets, a script, and instructions. 'The exact doses are important, times and so forth. Our phone number is there. Don't hesitate to call us if you're worried. He has an appointment at an outpatient clinic in two weeks, there's an appointment card in the bag. Good luck.'

Kellie raised an eyebrow. 'I'm beginning to think I'll need it. Thanks for all this.'

The nurse opened James' door, clicked it right back and then helped him into the wheel-chair. After making sure his plastered leg was in a comfortable position, they set off.

'Right, let's get this chair rolling.' The nurse pushed and Kellie followed with his weekend-bag over her shoulder, the laptop under one arm, and his flowers in her spare hand.

Getting him into the backseat of the station wagon was hard work and his face turned a pasty grey.

The nurse checked his pulse. 'That's fine. Goodbye Dr. Harvey. Please be extra careful with your injured leg.' She glanced at Kellie. She thought the housekeeper looked pregnant, although the good doctor seemed to be smitten with the physio. *Mmm*, she thought, *this is all a bit strange. I wonder who the father of her child is.*

'Bye,' she smiled at Kellie. 'It was nice to meet you. Drive safely.' She left them and pushed the empty chair back into the hospital.

Kellie got in the car, pushed in a disc James liked, then started the motor, and headed for home. The flowers at the back of the car had an overpowering scent and she opened the windows to let the stink out, hoping James wouldn't catch a chill. Every few minutes, she glanced in the rear-vision mirror making sure he was all right. She tried to drive extra carefully so she didn't cause him any discomfort, but when she braked sharply at a pedestrian crossing near the casino, she heard a quick gasp of pain.

'I'm so sorry,' she apologised. 'A lady just stepped out onto the crossing!'

***

Finally, they were home. She drove up to the garage, got out, and unlocked the side door into the house. Helping James get out of the car was a massive effort. He was so heavy. She put the crutches under his arms and slowly and painfully, he hobbled forward. He stumbled, so she took away one crutch and brought his arm across her shoulders, putting her arm firmly around his back. Eventually, they made it to his bedroom where he sank down heavily on the side of the bed. Kellie lifted his plastered leg up on top of the bedspread so he could lie down. She closed the curtains leaving the windows open just enough to catch the soft breeze that carried a hint of the eucalypts that grew nearby. She checked that he could reach his water bottle then left the room leaving his door slightly ajar.

Tired and exhausted, she still needed to bring those stinking flowers in from the car and she was desperate for a cup of tea.

A short while later, Harry rushed in followed by Betty and the dog.

The old lady looked flustered. 'We couldn't wait any longer.' She handed Kellie a large jar of home-made jam drops. 'How's James?'

'These look yummy, thanks Betty. Well, he's been asleep since we came home but by now, he may be awake. Come on, we'll go and see.' Kellie quietly led them down the hall-way and peeped around his door. He was awake, having a drink as he swallowed some tablets. Charlie bounded in ready to leap upon the bed.

'No, Charlie,' Kellie called and caught hold of him just in time.

James looked terrible. 'Hello Betty,' he mumbled. 'Thanks for minding these two this morning. Harry, come up here for a few minutes.'

Kellie lifted the boy onto the bed and he gave his dad a gentle hug then quickly reached behind his father's back and grabbed a bottle of pills.

'Put those down,' James roared and Harry instantly dropped the bottle on the floor. A look of intense shock registered on his young face and he started to cry. James covered his face with both hands and didn't utter a word.

Kellie quickly lifted Harry down. 'Come on, we'll leave daddy to get some rest. You get the Lego out and I'll help you build a helicopter, or maybe a boat.' His crying stopped and he sniffed loudly as he tucked his head into her shoulder.

Betty was halfway out of the room. 'I'll pop down again soon, James. I'm pleased you're home.' She followed Kellie back to the kitchen shaking her head. 'He's very touchy isn't he? The trip home seems to have taken the stuffing out of him.'

Betty looked at Harry who still whimpered as he clung to Kellie's legs. 'I think I'll be off love and leave you to it. Don't forget to ring me if I can help.' She limped off through the back door.

Later, Kellie made a chicken pie and cooked some fresh asparagus. It smelt delicious. She put James' meal on a tray and carried it to his room then gently knocked on the door.

'Dinnertime,' she called. He sat up and she placed the tray across his knees. 'I wasn't sure how hungry you'd be. Just eat what you can.' He didn't bother to say thank you. She went to leave then turned back. 'I put a non-slip mat and a stool in your bathroom for when you feel like having a shower.'

'I'll have one later,' he grumbled.

'Do you need to cover the plaster on your leg?'

'Yes, but I can shower myself,' James barked. He watched Kellie's face turn bright red as she left the room.

'Insufferable pig of a man,' she muttered after she closed his door.

After dinner, Kellie bathed Harry and it was a real struggle to get his pyjamas on. He squirmed and carried on, impatient to go to see his dad. He got away from her and took off at high speed down to James' bedroom. Kellie flew after him and stubbed her big toe on the corner of the bathroom vanity.

'Ohhh,' she groaned as she ran. He was quick and had leapt up onto James' bed before Kellie could catch him. 'Sorry,' she mouthed to James. 'Kiss daddy goodnight Harry, it's your bedtime.' He didn't want to leave and pushed Kellie away. She reached over to get hold of the child and he threw an almighty tantrum. One wild kick caught her right in the stomach and she gasped in pain. James yelled at the boy. Harry bellowed and jumped down from the bed. He ran to his room bawling at the top of his voice and Kellie quickly went after him.

He sprung onto his bed and continued to shriek and lash out. Charlie hid under the dressing table and Kellie tried but she couldn't pacify the small boy. Eventually, he cried himself to sleep.

Feeling totally inadequate, she returned to James' room to help cover the cast on his leg with plastic cling wrap. 'Do you need a hand to get this off after your shower?'

'No, but you can fill up my water jug, I have more tablets to take.' Kellie did as he asked then she left the room without saying a word.

Tears blurred her eyes. She was bone weary and sick to death of taking the crap being dished out to her.

'I don't need all this,' she whimpered as she walked to the kitchen, 'but what can I do? Where else can I go?' She reached for the box of tissues on the bench. 'Who's going to want a pregnant housekeeper? Nobody. I'm stuck out here with these two dysfunctional demanding oddballs.' She pulled out a chair and sat down then let the tears of self-pity run freely down her cheeks.

A while later, she pulled herself together and went to look for Charlie, he needed to go out to the toilet before she went to bed. As she lifted the dog off Harry's bed, she could hear knocks and bangs coming from James' bathroom. His ensuite wasn't very big, and would seem even smaller when using crutches. She shook her head and chased Charlie out the back door.

During the night, she checked on James. He lay on his back snoring loudly, with his mouth wide open. 'That's not a very attractive look,' Kellie muttered with an impish grin.

The next morning, she woke to the sound of rain that sounded like rapid drum beats hammering on the tin roof. When it slowed to a drizzle, she could hear the television going in James' room. She slipped on her dressing gown, made a cuppa for herself, and took him a coffee.

She knocked and went in. 'Morning James, how did you sleep?' She put his mug on the bedside table then drew back the curtains and opened some windows. The room had a stale airless smell.

'Patchy,' he mumbled. 'Thanks for the coffee.' Using the remote, he turned the volume down. 'I'll be having my shower in thirty minutes and I'll need your help to cover my cast.'

'Okay, I'll come back then.' His attitude always reminded her that she was only his paid employee.

She gave Harry a hand to get dressed, fed Charlie, then returned to James, and wrapped the plastic film around his damaged leg. 'That should do', Kellie said as she finished. 'I'll take Charlie for a quick walk while it's not raining.'

Harry and the dog waited by the back door. The child already had the lead clipped onto Charlie's collar. 'Good boy, Harry,' Kellie commented and his little face lit up. 'Come on, let's get cracking.'

On their return, they found James dressed in a loose track-suit, lying on the sofa in the lounge room watching the news, his crutches propped against the coffee table.

This was Kellie's favourite room. It spoke of simple elegance, but still felt cosy and welcoming. A dark chestnut lounge-suite and matching floor length drapes stood out boldly against a carpet and walls that were the colour of whipped cream. An antique sideboard and coffee table were in a light shade of walnut. They smelled of beeswax from Kellie's frequent polishing. A light breeze drifted in through the wooden doors that opened onto a terrace where red geraniums bloomed in tall pots.

Harry ran in and handed James the newspaper. He had it delivered each morning.

'Kellie,' the doctor called, 'I'm ready for my breakfast when you have time.' Then he turned his attention to the paper. Kellie hated being spoken to like that and felt like telling him to get his own flaming breakfast. She made scrambled eggs on toast with coffee then carried his through to him.

He looked up, then folded his newspaper while she stood waiting. He glanced at the nicely presented meal. 'This certainly looks more appetising than hospital food.'

Grrr, thought Kellie, *you could at least say thank you.*

She grabbed Harry's hand. 'Come on, we'll go into the kitchen and have ours.'

Chapter Thirteen

The day flew by. She cleaned James' messy bedroom and bathroom, made scones with soup for lunch and dried endless loads of washing. He kept calling her, as though she didn't have enough to do, and the phone rang several times with people inquiring after his health. It rang so many times that in the end she took the mongrel thing into the lounge-room and almost threw it at him.

'Keep this in here with you. Half of the Gold Coast wants to know how you are!' James grinned. She had a streak of something dark down one side of her face, flour on her chin and her ponytail had lost most of its hair. Charlie started to bark.

'What's he barking at now?' Kellie grumbled. Then the front doorbell chimed. 'Oh, that's all I need.' She stomped down the hallway and opened the door and there stood the rude physio cow from the hospital, Ruth Simmonds.

Ruth looked Kellie up and down and seemed to focus on her belly. 'Hmm' she exclaimed rudely. 'I was passing and thought I'd check on James.' She walked straight past Kellie as she spoke and her perfume was so potent it nearly knocked the over-worked pregnant girl out.

Ruth could see into the lounge-room where James was laying on the sofa. 'Hello there!'

'Ruth, this is a nice surprise.' James raised himself up and smiled. 'Come in and have a seat. Is this your rostered day off or are you doing house-calls?'

Ruth smiled and kissed his cheek. 'I wanted to check on you and see that you're being properly looked after.'

Kellie was speechless.

James gave her a fleeting glance. 'Kellie, will you rustle us up some coffee?'

Ruth parked herself down near James. 'I've had a really busy week, so this is a nice change for me,' she gushed.

Kellie shook her head as she left the room and went back to the kitchen. 'I think they deserve each other.'

While the coffee perked, she ran to the loo. When she washed her hands, she caught a glimpse of herself in the mirror. 'Oh my Lord!' Frantically she scrubbed her face and tidied her hair. 'Trust that bitchy tart from the hospital to come here and catch me looking like this.'

Tired and cranky, Kellie returned to the kitchen where the smell of perking coffee somehow helped to revive her. She filled two mugs and placed them on a tray, added sugar and milk, along with some biscuits, then carried it through to the lounge.

'Thank you,' James said as she laid the tray on the table next to him, 'that'll be all.'

Quietly seething, she left the room.

She called Harry to fetch Charlie's lead and they took off up the road. The young boy had to run to keep up with her as she walked off her anger. 'All jobs have their ups and downs and this one certainly has its moments!' she told herself as she stepped up the pace.

Ruth's car had gone by the time they returned, which was a blessing as Kellie felt like a wreck and her hair was once more all over the place.

Early the next day, Moira phoned. 'Morning love, can you cope with a couple of visitors? I've made some date scones to bring out for morning tea.'

'Oh, visitors would be lovely, especially ones with scones.'

'Don thought he'd come out and give you a hand with your lawns and the gardens.' The young woman sighed with relief as she thought of the long grass out the back.

An hour later, they pulled up the driveway.

Kellie and Harry went out to meet them. 'Hi Moira, and this must be Don. I'm so pleased to meet you.' He shook her hand and Moira gave her a hug. They made a big fuss of Harry, patted Charlie, then went in to see James.

He perked up when they walked in. 'Hello. Visitors, that's good.' Then he turned towards the kitchen and called out, 'Kellie! Is the kettle on?'

'She has it all under control James, so stop shouting.' Moira said as she sat on the sofa next to him and proceeded to bring him up to date with the ongoing dramas at the surgery.

Meanwhile, out in the kitchen, Kellie made the tea, warmed the scones, and put raspberry jam on the table with a dish of soft butter. 'Come and get it,' she called. Don and Harry hurried in and sat down. They waited for James, who struggled in on his crutches with Moira hovering at his side.

Moira glanced at him as she buttered her scone. 'Don's going to mow the lawns when he's had morning tea, aren't you love?'

'Yep, and I'll tidy up out there. Kellie can't be expected to work outside when she has so much to do in here.' He winked at the younger woman. 'James,' he eyeballed the grouchy doctor, 'you should be really grateful that a treasure like Kellie came along when she did.' Don nodded at Kellie as though to say 'that's telling him.'

She turned bright red and bent down to pick up an imaginary crumb off the floor. James sipped his tea and made no comment. The next minute, Harry spilled his milk as he leaned over to pat Charlie then toppled off his chair. He burst into tears and bawled at the top of his voice.

'Oh dear me,' Moira pushed her chair back and picked him up. She cuddled him better, then he got down from her knee, and ran outside with the dog following close behind him.

She looked at the tired young housekeeper, 'Come on Kellie, I'll give you a hand to clean up.'

The two women worked well together. Moira didn't stand any nonsense from James. They had been friends for years, and there were times when she really got stuck into him.

The men left the kitchen, but Moira stayed to chat. 'This is a lovely home isn't it Kellie? I'd give my eye teeth for a beautiful place like this, and you keep it so nice.' She felt quite protective of the young pregnant girl and wanted to help her.

'I've got a bassinet, cot and baby clothes at home for you if you'd like them. They're from my daughter. She doesn't need them anymore. They're like brand new.'

'I haven't got any baby things. That would be lovely.'

'If you like, I'll keep them at our place until nearer your time.'

'Thanks that's very kind. I don't know what's going to happen here.'

Moira thought, *I don't know either, but please God give this girl a break.*

Kellie went outside to see if Don needed a hand. She breathed in the pungent smell of freshly cut grass then noticed he'd also trimmed back some trees.

'Struth Don, you certainly don't muck around. Ohhhh!' she screamed as a small green snake slithered silently past, very close to her feet.

'It's all right,' called Don. 'He's harmless, must have been in those trees I cut back.'

Petrified, Kellie dropped down on to the verandah steps, her heart thumping as though it might jump right out of her chest. 'Oh, oh, my God!' She took a deep breath and tried to calm herself down.

Unperturbed, Don gathered up the trimmings. 'Now, Kellie love, don't you go picking up these heavy branches. Next Saturday I'll bring the trailer out and take away all this rubbish.'

'Okay, thanks Don,' she replied still trembling.

She turned around and went back inside. *He's such a dear man,* she thought tearfully, *much like my own dad.*

***

In the lounge room, Moira was having a go at James over his treatment of Kellie. 'I want you to stop all your nonsense and start treating that young woman with some respect. Who looked after young Harry all the time you were in hospital, ah? You tell me, she did, and drove your son to the hospital and back every day, you ungrateful bugger.' James pulled a face. 'And you needn't pull a face like that either. I'm telling you James, you either start to treat her better or you'll lose her.' Moira stood up to leave the room then turned back. 'And, I want you to give her a bonus.'

'A bonus? What the hell for? I already pay her.'

Moira shook her head. 'Just do it James. That young woman hasn't had a day off in over three weeks!'

'All right, if that's what it takes to get you off my back.' With a frown, he turned his attention to the nearby newspaper. 'Women!' he muttered rudely under his breath.

Don and Moira ended up staying for lunch. Kellie knew Moira had spent a great deal of time in the lounge-room with James. She couldn't hear what they were talking about as the sliding door was closed. She concentrated on getting the meal ready.

Harry helped Don out in the garden. When he came back inside, his little cheeks were flushed pink, and his smile went from one ear to the other.

They left mid-afternoon. Kellie put Harry down for a nap then checked on James. He was asleep with an open magazine in his hands. The house was quiet, so Kellie lay on her bed to read her book. She soon fell asleep.

An hour or so later, she tip-toed in to check on him and he was chatting on his phone. *I bet it's that witch from the hospital,* Kellie thought. *She's got her sights set on him, that's for sure.*

When Harry woke up, they went for a walk up to Betty's place.

'Hello there,' she greeted them as she trimmed the front hedge. 'You had a real toiler at your place this morning, Kellie.'

'That was Don, Moira's husband. She works at the surgery with James and keeps a motherly eye on him. Don worked hard. He's mowed all the lawns and trimmed some trees. They were both such a big help.'

Betty put her clippers down and invited them inside for a drink. 'You needed a hand. It's not easy nursing someone and James wouldn't be an easy patient. Make sure you look after yourself as well. How far along are you?' Betty asked as she filled glasses with cold homemade ginger-beer.

Kellie blushed, she didn't realise Betty had guessed. 'Five months. I'm starting to get a bump.' She showed Betty who laughed.

'I think that bump has a bit of growing to do.'

***

When they came home, James ate a light tea then picked up his crutches. He said goodnight to his son and hobbled off. Kellie bathed Harry and tucked him in bed. He fell asleep with one arm around the dog in the middle of a pirate story. Kellie cleaned up the kitchen and hopped up on the window-seat to watch the news.

Suddenly, there was a loud bang followed by a crash. 'Oh shit!' she exclaimed, 'that's James.' She jumped up and took off down the hallway, knocked on his door and pushed it open. A light shone under the ensuite slider so she ran over and called out. 'James, are you all right?'

Another bang. 'I'm fine,' he barked, 'I dropped my crutches.'

'I thought you might have fallen over.'

'I didn't,' he snarled, 'so go away.'

Kellie pulled a rude face and went back to watch her show. 'Why do I bother?' she mumbled. 'He's like a bear with a sore head. I'll give him a sore head shortly, grumpy old coot!' She ripped open a bag of pineapple lumps and stuffed two in her mouth.

The next afternoon, she thought she'd let James have some peace and quiet. He had spent the morning grumbling about almost everything – from the price of fuel to their power account.

Kellie was fed up. 'I'm taking Harry into Canungra for a while. We'll go to the park and then we might get a milkshake.'

'Good,' muttered James, 'and take that damn dog as well, I need some peace.'

***

Canungra looked a picture at this time of the year. The well-maintained park had gardens bursting with colour and some of the lovely old trees now wore their vibrant autumn coats. The fresh clean air smelt of cut grass and jasmine from a massive bush that covered the public toilet block with its heady white flowers.

Kellie and Harry looked around the information centre; a delightful shop with today's weather forecast and other interesting tit-bits on a notice board out the front. Inside, there were amazing old photographs and documents showing the hardships of the early settlers in the Canungra area. Harry soon became bored so she bought a carton of hot chips and they ate them sitting on a bench-seat in the sun drenched park. He enviously watched a group of children as they giggled and played some ball game with a spunky-looking bloke. *Probably married with children,* Kellie thought wistfully.

Harry looked at Kellie as though to say, 'Can I?'

She nodded. 'Off you go.' Shyly, he joined the youngsters and the guy encouraged him to join in their game. After a few minutes, one sour looking kid didn't want Harry to get the ball so he gave the youngster a good shove. Harry fell and landed face-first on the grass. Bravely he hopped back up, wiped his face, and then got back into the game. The nasty brat looked up and saw Kellie watching him and he gave her the finger.

'Rotten little sod,' she muttered. 'Come on Harry, we're going to get a milkshake now. Wave goodbye to your friends.' He huffed and puffed as he ran over to Kellie with a huge grin on his face. His babyish cheeks were a healthy bright pink.

Later, when the evening chores were finished and Harry was tucked up in bed, James called out to her from the lounge-room. 'Kellie, would you come in here a moment?'

She wondered if she was in trouble.

'Please,' he gestured toward a chair, 'have a seat.' She sat down and could smell the potato chips he'd been nibbling. He'd spilt a few on the coffee table.

He looked across at her and frowned. 'I realise you haven't had any time off these past three weeks. To compensate I've deposited an extra week's pay and a bonus into your bank account.'

Bloody hell, she thought, but politely said, 'Thank you.'

'You don't have to thank me, you deserve it. In hospital, I never worried about Harry, as I knew he was in good hands. Next weekend, I want you to have three days off. Moira and Don are coming out Friday morning and staying until Monday afternoon.'

'That's awfully kind of them. I might go and stay with one of my friends in town.' She hesitated a moment. 'Um, today at the park Harry enviously watched other kids mucking around and having lots of fun. I let him join in and he had a great time. I wondered how you felt about enrolling him in some type of preschool activity.'

'I think that's a great idea. He's been bored lately and a couple of days a week socializing with other children will do him good. But whatever facility we choose needs approval by his caseworker and the department.'

'Well, I had a quick look in the local business directory and there is a kindergarten in Canungra. There's a child care centre as well...'

'No, not a child care centre, but I'll make inquiries into that kindergarten.'

'Good.' Kellie nodded, pleased with the outcome. 'Was that all?'

'Yes, and if you're making hot chocolate I wouldn't mind a cup.'

'Sure, I'll make it now.' Kellie got up and left the room. She returned a few minutes later with his hot drink and placed it within his reach.

'Thank you,' he said. 'By the way, I managed to put the plastic wrap around my plaster cast by myself this morning so I won't need to bother you again. Goodnight.'

'It wasn't any bother, goodnight.' Kellie felt she'd actually got somewhere. He was being polite, which made her feel so much better.

***

Moira and Don arrived after lunch on Friday towing a trailer. Harry ran out to meet them and rushed up to Don with his arms held out for a hug. Kellie knew it was the sort of moment the man treasured.

'Don's got a real little friend there. How come he gets a hug before me?' Moira called out.

'Because I'm better looking, aren't I mate?' Don cuddled the young boy then hugged Kellie.

'Watch him you two. He's got tickets on himself,' Moira declared. 'Hello, Kellie love, can you give us a hand with these containers. I pre-cooked a few things to make my life a bit easier out here.'

Charlie tried to jump into the car. He smelled food and wanted to get at it. 'Get down, Charlie.' Kellie growled as she looked inside the vehicle shaking her head. 'Moira, we do have food here you know.'

Don laughed. 'You can't tell her. I reckon she thinks we'll all going to starve.' He laughed as he carried bags and cartons inside. James had made it to the front door and stood there propped up on his crutches.

'Hi, come in. How long are you staying?' He commented watching all the provisions coming into the house. 'You've brought enough for a month or more.'

'Stop moaning James and do something useful. Can you put the kettle on? We'll have a drink before Kellie goes. On second thoughts, go back to the sofa and rest, I'll put it on.'

Kellie had earlier packed what she needed to take for a couple of days, so she joined them for a coffee then left.

Don carried her bag out to the garage. 'Now we want you to have a nice time. It's not been easy for you cooped up way out here with no girly company. You know what they say about all work and no play. Now drive carefully and we'll see you sometime Monday. Don't rush back we'll be fine.'

'You are both darlings, Don. James is so lucky to have such wonderful friends. Bye.' She hugged him then got in the car and drove off.

Chapter Fourteen

The percolator was whistling and the coffee mugs were set out when Kellie arrived at Sam's Broadbeach apartment. Her kitchen smelt yummy; much like the local bakery.

Kellie hugged her friend warmly. 'Thanks so much for having me to stay. What can I smell? My taste buds are driving me crazy.'

'I made a weight-watchers chocolate caramel slice, especially for you.'

'Weight-watchers? Do we watch the weight go on while we eat it?' They both giggled.

Sam brought over the hot drinks and they sat at the table. 'You need to take things easy, my girl, so sit down and tuck in.'

Kellie sighed. 'It's so nice being pampered. Keep this up and you'll never get rid of me.'

Later, Sam made her have a rest as she had plans for them to have a fun night out.

When darkness fell, they walked to Broadbeach to check out the restaurants. The Mall looked stunning by night; relaxed diners sat outdoors chatting while they sipped sparkling wines. Buskers sang and some juggled, all adding to the exciting atmosphere of the place. The girls chose Mazola's Fine Italian Cuisine where the mouth-watering smell of garlic drew them in like a magnet. Their spicy veal cutlets were everything the gorgeous Italian waiter said they would be. He flirted with them outrageously.

Next, they boarded the monorail. It glided between the Oasis and the casino twenty-four hours a day. After dark, it gave passengers a spectacular view of Broadbeach with its masses of bright lights sparkling from gigantic high-rises.

They stepped off at the casino. Sam led her through a massive crowd to a small trendy pub off to one side; with its bright strobe lighting and musty smell of spilt beer.

'How's this, Kel, I bet it doesn't rock like this out at Wonglepong!'

Sam bragged.

The usual pop music was cranked up, as the band sorted out their sound-system. Sam bought the drinks – mineral water for Kellie, and a Vodka Chaser for herself.

Then the show started. They sang and rocked along with the crowd and when space permitted, they joined the masses on the dance floor gyrating and shaking.

Suddenly, a fight broke out. Loud angry voices disturbed their fun. Then 'crash' the terrifying sound of breaking glass! A bloodcurdling scream pierced the air. It came from a nearby table.

'She's been glassed,' a voice cried out, 'Phone for an ambulance, quickly!'

A panicked male voice bellowed, 'Where's security. Get the police.' All hell broke loose. Girls screamed, guys yelled and the band stopped playing and ran for their lives. A guy serving behind the bar grabbed a towel and ran towards the injured girl. Kellie saw her holding her cheek with both hands. Thick blood oozed through her fingers.

Sam shouted, 'Quick, let's get out of here,' and grabbed her friend's hand, yanking her along at high speed. 'Hurry!' she yelled. They almost collided with security guards racing towards the distraught woman. Sam kept hold of Kellie as they ran out the side door towards the safety of the stationary monorail.

'Quick, run, jump in, it's about to leave!' They made it and gratefully flopped down on to some empty seats.

The silence inside the monorail was a welcome contrast to the noise and bedlam they had left behind. They looked at each other and shook their heads in disbelief.

Back in Sam's flat, they made hot chocolate and relived the horror they had just witnessed. Knowing it would be difficult to sleep, Sam pulled the couch out into a double bed and the two girls snuggled up to watch late night television.

When daylight crept into their lounge room, they showered and dressed, then headed to the beach. The day was overcast and the waves had frothy white tips. Seagulls screamed as they searched the empty beach for food and the fresh sea-air had a strong salty smell. They walked and talked trying to rid their minds of last night's frightening incident.

***

Back at Wonglepong, things weren't going so well. James' head ached badly and any loud noise caused shards of pain to shoot through his temples, a lingering reminder of his accident. Harry had the grizzles and a touch of diarrhea and poor Moira found it all difficult to cope with. Don worked outside. He knew when to keep out of the way.

Betty limped over with a plate of hot apple muffins for afternoon tea. She noticed how frazzled Moira looked and saw that the kitchen was in a mess. 'Shall I take Harry home with me for a couple of hours to give you a break?'

'Oh, yes please, then I'd be able to catch up on a few jobs and get the dinner ready.'

'I'll take Charlie as well. Come on Harry, get the dog's lead and we'll be off.'

'Phew,' Moira breathed a sigh a relief as they left. She made a pot of tea and buttered the muffins, then called out to the men. James didn't reply so she put his on a tray and took it into the darkened lounge room where he lay with his plastered leg propped up on a cushion and ice-packs across his forehead.

'Sit up James, here's a cup of tea and one of Betty's fresh muffins.'

'I'm not hungry,' he grumbled, 'and you know I'm not fussed on tea.'

'You can't drink coffee all day. She made these especially for you, so please make an effort!'

'All right,' he moaned, 'Leave it on the table.' *Ungrateful wretch,* Moira thought then went outside to join Don and enjoy their afternoon tea in peace.

After dinner, Moira tucked Harry up in bed and Don read him a pirate story, performing all the actions.

'Stupid old fool,' Moira muttered as she watched him from around the corner. Once the boy had fallen asleep, Don made them all hot chocolate. He took his cup out to the back steps where he liked to sit and gaze at the sky. The soft breeze carried an earthy smell and the country sky was a deep dark-blue, dotted with bright twinkly diamonds.

Moira carried two mugs into the lounge-room and put one beside James. 'How's the head?'

'Much better tonight. Thanks for the drink.'

'I want to talk to you, James.'

A bored expression crossed his face. 'What about? What have I done now?'

'No, it's more what you haven't done.'

'Like what?'

'Well it's to do with Kellie.'

'Oh,' he snorted and turned his head away. 'What about her?'

'Are you going to keep her on after she's had the baby or not? She needs to know.'

He waited a few moments before answering. 'I have been giving that some thought.'

'And what conclusion have you come to?' She wanted to kick him. He was deliberately making her squirm. 'You know jolly well that you will never find another housekeeper like Kellie. I think Harry's missing her, that's why he's grizzly and his little tummy's upset.'

James sipped his drink. 'She's good at her job, but the fact remains, she lied to me.'

'Oh, for heaven's sake, don't get on that band-wagon again. Can't you move on? When she applied for the job, she needed a roof over her head and a home for her child. Surely you can understand that.' Moira shook her head in disgust. 'Just give the girl a break James.'

'Well, where's the father – who is he?'

'That's none of our business.'

'It is my business when she's living in my home.'

Sparks started to whizz through Moira's brain and she stepped up a gear. 'Don't you argue with me, James Harvey, at work you might be my boss, but I'll not stand around and watch you to treat a vulnerable young girl this way.'

She put her drink down and angrily stabbed a finger at him. 'Don't forget who kept this house running when you had your accident and took young Harry to visit you every day as though she didn't have enough to do...' She stopped to take a breath and James just stared at an imaginary spot on the ceiling.

'All right, all right. Don't go down that road again. I've heard it all before. I'll go a bit easier on her. Now will you please get off my back woman and let me enjoy my hot chocolate. It's probably gone cold by now.'

Moira was still irate. 'Well it's not before time. You should have said something to her before this.' She stood up and glared at him. 'Right now I'm going out to sit with Don on the back steps. If I stay in here much longer, I'll throw something at you.' With that, she stomped out of the room.

James sat back and shook his head. 'Women!'

Harry's grizzly mood continued on Sunday making everyone a bit edgy. James had another headache so he stayed on the lounge sofa with the curtains closed and didn't touch any of the breakfast Moira put in front of him.

When she went in to collect the tray he could hardly keep his eyes open, such was the pain in his head. 'Close the sliding door and keep the noise down.'

She opened a couple of windows and left him in peace.

Mid-morning there was a knock on the back door and Betty limped into the kitchen with a batch of hot cheese scones tied up in a clean tea towel.

Moira's tummy rumbled in delight. 'Betty you're a lifesaver they smell scrumptious. Cheese scones, gosh I haven't had one for ages.' She sat down on a chair by the table looking awfully weary.

'How's it going?'

'James isn't well this morning. His head's giving him gip again.'

'Would you like me to take Harry and keep him for the day? He's no bother. We had a great time yesterday pottering around doing odd jobs.'

'I feel awful, it's as though I'm not able to cope anymore.' Close to tears Moira rubbed her eyes.'

'You're doing a great job. You aren't young like Kellie. She does this every day so it's much easier for her.'

'I thought I'd cope much better than this.'

Betty called out to Harry. 'Would you like to come home with me and help clean out the goldfish pond?' His little face beamed and he quickly put Charlie's lead on ready to go. Where one of them went, so did the other.

***

After lunch, James felt a little better and turned on the TV to watch a rugby union test match between the Wallabies and the All Blacks. While Don repaired the back fence that had been badly damaged by an adventurous kangaroo, Moira caught up on the ironing.

The front door-bell rang and she stood the iron up and went to see who was there.

A dark-haired, poshly dressed woman stood impatiently tapping her foot. She gave Moira an odd look. 'Oh hello, I'm Ruth Simmonds, a colleague of James. I've called to see how he's doing.'

Moira looked her up and down. 'He's resting at...'

'Thank you, I know the way.' She pushed past the open-mouthed woman and walked straight in. 'James,' she gushed, 'how are you making out?'

Her voice alone made Moira want to puke. 'Who the hell is she and how come I've never heard of her before?' she muttered as she returned to the ironing.

An hour or so later, there was a rowdy commotion outside. Betty puffed her way through the back door almost dragging Harry behind her. He held one hand up and bellowed at the top of his voice. His grubby cheeks had strings of snot stuck there mixed with smears of blood.

'What the hell?' muttered Moira as she secured the iron.

The poor lady was almost out of breath. 'He jammed his finger in the old shed door!'

Moira sat down and lifted the screaming child onto her knee. He stopped yelling and cradled the injured finger close to his body.

'Show it to me, there's a good lad.' He shrieked and smacked her hand away.

'Oh, this isn't going to work.' She looked at the old lady. 'Can you call his father?'

Betty met James hobbling towards the kitchen. 'What on earth…?' Then he saw the boy's injury. He propped his crutches against the buffet, sat down, and pulled the child onto his lap.

Harry's high-pitched screams made James' ears ring.

'Hold still, son.' The squirming child was so upset he fought, and coughed, then vomited over his father's trousers. 'Oh no. Hold him firmly, Moira, so I can see what he's done.'

James pulled the boy's arm down and levered open his fingers. 'Shh, Harry. Let me see where all this bloods coming from.' The noise stopped, replaced by the child's loud sniffs. A snot-bubble appeared at the end of his nose and seeking comfort, he rubbed his face against his dad's shirt.

Ruth, still waiting in the lounge room, didn't appreciate being cast aside and decided to leave. *I can't tolerate spoilt brats and this kid's obviously an attention seeking little sod!*

She poked her head around the kitchen door with a forced look of concern. 'I'll let you get on with it, James. Take care and give me a call sometime.' She blew him a kiss and behind his back sent the two women a filthy look, jangled her car-keys then left.

James inspected the damage. It wasn't too bad. The child's distress was worse than the injury. He hugged the boy and kissed his forehead. 'When your finger has been cleaned and covered it will be fine. Go with Moira, she'll fix it up and put a plaster on it.' Harry's tears stopped and a watery smile appeared on the child's filthy face.

Betty looked nervously at James. 'I'm sorry about this. I do watch him, but he wandered into the old garden shed looking for the dog and the door banged shut, catching his finger.'

'Don't worry about it. These things happen. He's all right and his vocal cords have had a good work out.' He reached for his crutches. 'When Moira's finished attending to Harry, tell her a coffee would go down well. We could all do with one.'

Out in the kitchen Moira couldn't wait to bail up Betty. 'Who was that dark-haired piece?' Moira whispered as Betty filled the kettle.

'I don't know. I was going to ask you the same thing. I've never seen her before.'

'She's latched on to him that's for sure and I didn't like her manner. She's a nasty piece of work.'

Betty nodded. 'I'll ask Kellie about her and let you know.'

They both couldn't wait to get the low-down on James' stuck up visitor.

***

Driving back to Wonglepong Kellie pondered over her weekend. The shocking incident on Saturday night had frightened them. The next day they relived the dramatic scene many times over – that poor girl, she would probably be scarred for life.

Earlier in the day, Sam had taken her to Myers, shopping for maternity clothes. Kellie found tops and trousers she liked and a knee-length red jacket that looked great over her new pants. She already had good black boots and hoped they would team up nicely with the gear she had just bought. Then they found a lingerie shop with lacey maternity bras and knickers. She liked nice underwear.

Growing up, her mum told her many times, 'Always make sure you have nice undies on in case you have to go to hospital.' Her mum would be ecstatic to see the gorgeous pile of unmentionables she had just bought.

Sam blinked back tears when it came time for her friend to leave, but Kellie wanted to get home by mid-day.

Turning into James' driveway, she noticed Don's car-trailer piled high with clippings and rubbish. 'My word, he's been busy,' she muttered as she parked the car.

The front door flew open and Harry and Charlie came charging out.

'Hi Harry. Get down, Charlie, you rascal. Get down.' The dog was impatient for her attention.

She hugged Harry and patted the dog. 'I missed you, young man. Have you been helping Moira look after your dad?' He nodded and held up a plastered finger.

'My goodness, what have you been doing to yourself.' Kellie made a big issue of kissing his injury.

Moira came out, wiping her hands on her apron. 'He jammed it in Betty's garden-shed door yesterday and nearly brought the house down.' She put a hand over her mouth to hide her smile, and kissed Kellie on the cheek, then grabbed a couple of shopping bags to take inside.

'Nice to have you back, love.' Eyeing the Myers bags, she looked at Kellie.

'Are there any clothes left in Myers or are they all here in these bags.' They both laughed.

'Have you had a good time?' Moira asked.

'Different, but I had a lovely break thanks to you and Don.'

The older lady smiled. 'I'll put these in your room.'

'Thanks Moira. I'll see how James is doing.' Kellie went into the lounge-room where James lay on the sofa. He'd been asleep and woke-up as she walked in.

'Hi James. How's it going?' She smiled and sat on the edge of nearby chair.

'I'm all right. How did you find life in the big smoke?' Looking sorry for himself, he struggled to a sitting position.

'Busy. I'm pleased to be away from all the traffic and impatient drivers. How's your leg, is it still troubling you?'

'Yes and no, but I've had terrible headaches.' He rubbed his eyes and looked very tired.

'You rest and I'll go and see what Don's been up to in the garden. Judging by the amount of rubbish loaded on his trailer, he's worked his butt off.' She left him and headed out the back door.

Well, Don had certainly been busy. Trees were trimmed back, the lawns were cut, and garden beds were weeded and tidy. The backyard looked a picture and smelt earthy and fragrant.

'Oh Don, thank you very much. This all looks wonderful, you must be worn out.' Kellie hugged the older man.

'I've enjoyed doing it and Harry here has been a great help, haven't you mate?' He ruffled the boy's hair. Harry screwed up his face and clutched Kellie's leg, a healthy glow lit up his little cheeks.

Kellie took his hand. 'Come with me, we'll go inside and help Moira get the lunch ready.'

In the kitchen, Moira had the table set and she'd dished up pumpkin soup with hot scones. The mouthwatering smell caused a loud rumble in Kellie's hungry tummy.

Moira filled the teapot and put out cups and saucers. 'Call Don in for his lunch, would you love?' Kellie met him at the back door heading for the laundry to wash his hands.

James hobbled out on his crutches and sat down next to Harry.

They all wanted to know about her weekend and Kellie felt like she'd come home to her family. It was a good feeling.

When lunch had been cleared away, Moira and Don left. Kellie's eyes watered as she waved them goodbye. Both of them were bone weary and pleased to be going home, but she would miss them, they were wonderful friends.

Chapter Fifteen

James slept most of the afternoon. He'd taken medication for his aching head. After checking on him, Kellie closed the lounge door quietly and grabbed Charlie's lead then went outside to find Harry.

'Come on, we'll walk up and see Betty.'

The old lady saw them coming. 'Good timing. I've just put the kettle on.' Betty grabbed the young boy and gave him a big hug. He giggled out loud and she whispered in his ear. 'There are fresh-baked chocolate-chippies on the bench, Harry. Take two and you can go and see the new babies in the goldfish-pond.' He grabbed the biscuits and raced off, followed by the dog.

She gave Kellie a quirky smile. 'I think you were missed while you were away. His nibs out there jammed his finger in my old shed door, it's a wonder you didn't hear him in town. Also, a dark-haired piece from the hospital called to see James, but she high-tailed it smartly when Harry hurt himself. Squawking kids weren't her cup of tea, that's for sure.'

'Ruth Simmonds is her name. She's James's physiotherapist.'

'She might well be, but mark my words, she's out to get him.'

Kellie laughed. 'She usually arrives when I'm looking really scruffy and she looks like she's come straight off the cat-walk of some fashion house.'

'Don't you worry about her love, she's all show. We'll just wait and see what she's up to.' With a knowing nod, Betty poured the tea, cut some cake then they settled down for a natter.

Outside, Harry and Charlie were having a great time. They loved this old garden. Apart from the pond, there was so much to see. There were all different kinds of wonderful butterflies and wild birds in the most amazing colours. Harry held tight to the dog's collar as they watched pink and grey galahs squabble noisily over some berries that had dropped off the creeper, running along the rickety back fence.

When they went home, James was still asleep so Kellie bathed Harry and cooked him a boiled egg with dippy fingers of toast. He was cranky, overtired and knocked the runny egg on the floor then upset his milk. She tucked him into bed, cleaned up the mess and then once more checked on James.

He stood leaning heavily on his crutches as he stared through the glass doors into the inky darkness of the frosty night. He looked lost in some unhappy thoughts.

'James.' He turned as she spoke. 'Do you mind having your dinner on a tray in here?'

Frowning, he shook his head. 'No, that's all right, but just something light. And I'd like a glass of red wine with my meal.'

He spoke sharply and Kellie thought, *Well nothing's changed around here.*

When dinner was over and she'd tidied up, she made hot chocolate for them both and carried his mug into the lounge-room. He had the remote in his hand and was channel surfing.

'Thank you Kellie. Are you having one as well?'

'Yes, but I'll have mine in the kitchen.'

'Could you bring yours in here? I'd like a word with you.'

'Okay.' Feeling like a naughty schoolgirl about to be ticked off, she returned to the kitchen and picked up her drink then headed back into the lounge-room.

He nodded at a chair. 'Make yourself comfortable.'

Kellie sat down wondering what this was all about. She could smell chocolate from a freshly opened box on the table next to James.

'How is the morning sickness?'

She sighed. 'In the mornings, it's not so bad, but the nausea lingers all day. Different smells set it going.'

'Yes, I never worked out why they call it morning sickness.' He took a sip of his hot drink then carefully placed the mug back on the coffee table. 'Now, I'd like to discuss your future.' He glanced at Kellie. She'd turned pale.

'I'm pleased with your work and to say Harry is fond of you would be an understatement. You've given him the stability which he badly needed in his young life.'

'Having Charlie's helped,' Kellie mentioned, 'Harry gets a great deal of comfort from that dog.'

'That's true, quite recently I read where they're using dogs more and more to assist with childhood issues.'

He took a few sips of his drink. 'Now getting back to you, late September I think you said your baby was due.' She nodded and her heart almost stopped beating as she waited for her notice to quit.

'I do wish you had told me about the baby when I interviewed you, however I've had plenty of time to think about the situation.'

She bent her head and focused on the red enamel polish chipping off her toenails while he finished his hot drink.

'When your child's born, I'd like you to stay on here as the housekeeper for Harry and myself.'

Kellie took a couple of nervous gulps from her mug and then very carefully put it down as her hands shook uncontrollably. For a moment, she couldn't get any words out and then couldn't think of what to say.

'T-thank you,' she stuttered, trying not to let him see how worried she had been.

'Now we have that sorted, help yourself to the chocolates. I noticed you eying them up before.'

She blushed. 'I've had this terrible craving for chocolate since I've been pregnant and these ones smell so good, thanks.' She took one and he shook the box under her nose, so she helped herself to two more.

She slept much better that night knowing she still had a job and a roof over her head; indeed the future looked promising.

***

Tuesday morning, Kellie was busy catching up with the housework when she heard the front doorbell ring.

'Who on earth can that be?' Charlie barked and ran in front of her as she opened the door. Standing there were two police officers. Kellie nearly died of fright. A police-car was parked in the driveway close to the house. They were never the bearer of good news. One took off his hat and held out identification.

'Good morning, I'm Senior Constable Trevor Wright and this is Constable Brian Anderson. We are looking for Dr James Harvey. We have this as his address.'

Kellie somehow found her voice. 'Please come in. He's in the lounge.' They wiped their feet on the door mat then followed her into the room.

'James, these police officers would like to speak to you.'

The older cop stepped forward and introduced himself and his partner.

'Please have a seat,' James offered as he struggled to a sitting position. 'This is my housekeeper, Kellie Lund.'

They nodded in her direction. 'Kellie,' the senior constable said, and sat down.

She turned to James. 'I'll be in the kitchen if you need me.'

'No,' he instructed, 'Please stay.' Kellie perched on the arm of the sofa next to him.

The senior constable cleared his throat. 'Do you know a Serena

Harvey?'

James' face turned a pale shade of grey. There was silence then...'Yes, she's my estranged-wife.'

The police officer looked at his notes. 'We are sorry to inform you that she passed away in a Sydney hospital two weeks ago.' He waited a moment for this news to sink in. 'We had trouble tracing her next of kin and then, searching amongst her belongings, we found your name.'

A light wind blew in through the open sliding doors, bringing with it the sweet smell of flowering jasmine and the sun disappeared behind small fluffy clouds causing an instant chill in the quiet room.

Kellie glanced at James. His eyes were tightly closed. For a few moments, the room stayed silent apart from the constant ticking of the grandfather clock.

'H-how did she die?' James asked.

'An accidental drug-overdose. The ambulance responded to a triple zero call and found her unconscious. One of her flat-mates apparently phoned in then took off.'

'What makes you think it was accidental?'

'An autopsy revealed she'd been using a bad batch of heroin. The substance added to make the drug go further was contaminated. Normally the amount of heroin found inside her body wouldn't be fatal, but it was a crook lot.'

Overwhelmed by all this, Kellie stood up. She needed to get away for a few minutes. 'I'll make James a coffee. Would you men like one?'

'Yes please, black with no sugar.'

She left them talking and escaped to the kitchen. James looked dreadful. He was in a state of shock and needed something strong and sweet. She made the coffees and carried them through to the lounge-room. She placed them on the low table in front of the police officers.

Betty had left a jar of fresh-baked jam drops by the back door earlier in the day. Kellie placed the biscuits within reach of the guys and told them to help themselves.

The next minute, Harry and Charlie rushed inside like a whirlwind.

Kellie jumped up and got two biscuits for the child.

'Harry, here take these. I want you to go to your room and make me a big red bus with your Lego, there's a good boy.' He screwed up his face and kicked the carpet then dramatically dragged one foot as he left the room, followed by the dog.

The older cop smiled at the boy's antics then picked up his notes. 'Now, getting back to your estranged-wife, James, what about her parents, what was her maiden name?'

'Morris, Serena Morris. I never met her family. They're Jehovah

Witnesses. Serena was brought up strictly within the confines of their religion. At eighteen, she rebelled and left the church. Her parents were unforgiving and told her, to them, she was dead. I don't even know where they live.'

The police officer shook his head. 'Finding you wasn't easy either, the deceased's neighbour told us of a small boy, your son, who was found in the same flat and how he'd been taken away by the Sydney police. We followed up on this and traced you through Child-Welfare.' He checked his notes again. 'Now we need you to do a formal identification.'

Horrified Kellie gasped. 'James isn't up to travelling.' She explained about his accident.

'Sorry.' The older cop shook his head. 'This has to be done.' He wrote something down then glanced at James. 'We'll use an ambulance to get you to and from the airports. When you arrive in Sydney, you'll be taken straight to the mortuary. Once the identification has taken place, you'll be brought back home.'

James fell back on the cushions, completely stunned.

The young police officer went outside and made a phone call then returned a few minutes later. 'The ambos will be here at 4-30 tomorrow morning to take you to Coolangatta. You'll catch the early flight to Sydney and return late in the afternoon. Once again, we are very sorry.'

The two men gathered up their paper-work and put on their hats. 'We'll be back in the morning.'

The young cop nodded at Kellie. 'Thanks for the coffee and jam drops. They were good. My gran makes those.'

While they let themselves out, James and Kellie sat in silence, trying to take in what they had just been told.

A quiet few minutes passed, then Kellie stood up. 'I'll check on Harry and see what he's up to.'

James' head slumped onto his chest and his face turned a ghostly grey colour. 'Get my tablets, then close the door.'

Kellie fetched his medication then drew the curtains and quietly left him to grieve for the woman he had loved, searched for, and so tragically lost.

***

For the rest of the day, James refused the tempting light meals she prepared for him and lay on the sofa in the lounge-room with headphones on and his eyes closed.

Before she went to bed, Kellie checked on him, lightly touching his arm. 'James, can I get you anything?'

'No!' he snapped. Exasperated she turned to leave. 'I'll set my alarm for three-thirty in the morning. I want to be ready well before those men arrive.' He waved her away and adjusted his headphones.

'Dear God,' she muttered, 'give me strength.'

She woke with a fright and looked at her clock radio, three am. Her alarm was set for three-twenty-five so she turned it off and switched on the radio, finding a talkback show. She listened for a while then checked the time, three-thirty-five and no movement or sound from James' room. Trying not to wake Harry, she tiptoed down the hallway and listened outside his dad's door. Still nothing, so she flicked on the hall light and gently knocked. No answer. 'Bugger,' she whispered then quietly pushed it open and went in. In the half light, she could see him lying on his back, dead to the world.

'James,' she called. No response, so she gently shook his shoulder. 'James!'

Slowly one eye opened. 'What, what do you want?' he grumbled.

'It's time to get up. The ambulance will be here at four-thirty!'

Roughly, he shook off her hand and stared at the bedside clock. His eyes were bloodshot. *Probably from swallowing too many tablets,* she thought. Still half asleep, he struggled to stand up, so she went to help him.

'Leave me alone.' Angrily he pushed her away.

Shocked at his attitude Kellie stepped back. 'I'll make the coffee while you shower and get dressed.' In the kitchen, she switched on the percolator and put out two mugs.

A slamming noise came from his bedroom followed by a couple of loud knocks. 'Kellie,' he yelled, 'Where's my navy shorts?' She knocked and went in. He was sitting on the bed in his undies looking lost and his good pants lay in a heap on the floor. 'My blasted trousers won't fit over this cast!'

She opened the wardrobe door and found his shorts, a matching polo shirt, and a pair of deck shoes, then put them next to him on the bed. 'You get dressed and I'll go and pour your coffee.'

From the kitchen, she heard the thump-thump of his crutches as he came down the hallway. He managed to get to the table and sit down, dropping his crutches on the floor next to him.

She poured a drink for herself and sat opposite him. 'I had a look at your clock-radio and you'd set the alarm for pm not am. It wouldn't have gone off until this afternoon.'

Bewildered, he shook his head. 'I've done that before and missed an important appointment.'

'Would you like me to get your denim jacket, it may be cold in Sydney?' He nodded. She fetched it and sat down again. His freshly showered male smell wafted across to her. It was nice.

'Kellie, I...' the front doorbell rang and she never got the chance to hear what he wanted to tell her. It was the two police officers. She invited them in and asked if they'd like a coffee. Just then, they heard the ambulance turn into the driveway.

'No, but thanks for the offer,' the senior cop replied. Then he briefly caught a glimpse of Kellie's tummy as she turned around. *Struth*, he thought, *someone's knocked up the hired help! What's going on here? We've got the doc losing it because his estranged wife karked it, and now this so called housekeeper is obviously pregnant. He must have fringe benefits, the lucky bugger, and she's a good looking honey.* He scratched his head, deep in thought as they followed Kellie down the hallway to the kitchen.

'Morning, Dr Harvey,' the police officers addressed James. He didn't return their greeting, but reached for his crutches and adjusted them under his arms.

Kellie passed him his painkilling tablets. 'You might need these.'

James hobbled outside where two paramedics waited by the back door of the ambulance.

He handed the ambos his crutches and turned to find Kellie just behind him. 'I'll see you later,' he mumbled.

'Okay.' She stepped back. The guys helped James up the step and onto a stretcher. Kellie passed his jacket to one of the cops as he hopped in the back with him. James gave her a brief nod and they closed the doors. The other police officer hopped in the front with the driver. She watched until they turned onto the road then went inside. Quietly, she opened Harry's door and peeped in, he was still asleep with one arm across Charlie. The animal looked at Kellie as though to say, 'Look at me, how good's all this?' She shook her head at the spoilt creature and tiptoed away.

***

It was still early so she decided to go back to bed. So much had happened so quickly that Kellie's head began to spin, then her tummy rumbled and a queasy feeling came over her.

'Oh no. Not again!' Covering her mouth with her hands, she ran to the loo and threw up. Afterwards, she sat on the floor by the toilet, holding her head in her hands as she wept in frustration. 'When will all this stop?'

She pulled herself together and grabbed a flannel to clean her face. The nausea continued and she couldn't shake off a feeling of despair and loneliness. At six o'clock, she rang her friend Sam.

'M-morning, Kellie' Sam stuttered half asleep as she viewed her caller ID with only one eye open. 'Are you okay?' She heard Kellie sobbing. 'What is it, what's happened? Tell me.' She waited a few moments.

'I'm s-sorry, Sam, to be a nuisance this early in the morning, b-but I'm feeling lousy and needed to talk to someone.'

'I'll tell you what love,' Sam recognized real desperation in her friend's voice. 'I'll pull a sickie today and come and spend some time with you.'

'Really, you'd do that for me?'

'My oath I would. You and I are mates and that means a lot to me.'

'Thanks, Sam, I'd really appreciate that. H-how soon can you get here? James is away. There's only me and Harry.'

'In time for breakfast! Now you go and have a shower and put one of your new tops on and I'll see you soon, bye.'

Kellie showered and found one of her new preggy tops they'd bought at Pacific Fair. She pulled it on with new maternity jeans. Harry woke up and she helped him get dressed. While she was waiting for Sam, they took Charlie for a long walk.

On their return, she prepared breakfast. Harry started to whine so she let him have his while she waited by the front door, hoping Sam would be able to find the place.

Finally, her blue Barina turned into the driveway and Kellie ran out to meet her. There were lots of tears amongst the hugs.

Sam held her tight then stood back. 'Nice to see you, love. The new clothes look really good.'

'Oh Sam, thanks so much for coming...' at that moment, Harry and Charlie appeared. 'This youngster is Harry,' announced Kellie, 'and this cute dog is Charlie.'

'Hello Harry,' Sam hugged the small boy. 'Hi Charlie,' She tickled the dog under his chin and his tail wagged faster than ever.

Sam looked around. 'Man is this out in the sticks or what. It's a long way from the city, but the scenery's lovely.' She put her arm across Kellie's shoulders and they went inside. 'Nice place. The old doc must have a bob or two,' she commented as she peeped into the rooms while following her friend along the hallway to the kitchen.

After breakfast, Sam gave Kellie a hand to tidy up then they piled into her small car and headed to the beach at Burleigh Heads.

The late morning sun cast a golden glow over the shimmering sand and a gentle breeze skimmed along the top of the waves. Seagulls screamed up and down the water's edge on the lookout for something to eat and Kellie relaxed as the salty sea-air cleared her head and settled her badly frayed nerves. They bought fish and chips then helped Harry make sandcastles. While he paddled at the water's edge, Kellie opened up and poured her heart out to Sam.

'I don't know about this doc,' Sam shook her head. 'He's a bit of a worry. Even though I haven't met him. He's just got too many issues. You can always come and live with me, remember that.'

'Thanks, Sam, you're a sweetheart. I know you mean well, but I'm hoping things will improve. He's made my job permanent now so I'm going to try and stick it out.'

'It's up to you, but you know where I live if you ever need a bed and a roof over your head.'

Sam yawned as Kellie pulled into James' driveway. 'I've had a great day, love, but I'd better be on my way. You take it easy and keep in touch.' She hugged Kellie and Harry then hopped in her Barina.

Sam didn't like leaving her friend, she felt the doctor had far too many problems and they were getting Kellie down. 'Bye, girlfriend!' She called cheerfully through her car window.

'Thanks for everything,' Kellie replied. 'I'll phone you tomorrow night, bye.' Kellie brushed away a tear as she waved her best mate goodbye.

***

The ABC's seven o'clock news bulletin had nearly finished when Kellie heard the revving of an engine. She opened the front door and watched the ambulance back up close to the front steps. Harry and Charlie came tearing down the hallway to see what was going on.

'Harry, sit next to the door and stay there,' Kellie directed him firmly. 'Keep your hand on Charlie's collar and do not let him go.' Harry pouted in disgust as he dropped down to the floor and clung to the nervous dog. They didn't like strangers and these ones looked scary.

The back door of the ambulance opened and a paramedic stepped down. The driver came around and they helped James get down from the vehicle. In the porch-light Kellie could see his chalk-white face, with frown lines deepened by pain. They assisted him up the front steps into the house and he nodded towards his bedroom. Kellie opened his door and turned on the light.

The men sat James on the bed and a paramedic took his pulse and blood pressure. Then he laid James down and looked at Kellie. 'Give him two of his painkillers now then leave him to sleep. Ring your GP if you're worried.'

She nodded, 'Thanks, I will.'

The ambulance left and she closed the door. She went over to the frightened boy. He sat on the floor clinging to the nervous dog, with quiet tears streaming down his face.

'Daddy will be okay. He's had a big day and is very tired.' She lifted Harry up and hugged him. 'Come on, it's getting late. I have a special pirate story to read tonight, so go to the toilet then hop into bed. I'll come and tell you all about Captain Hook!'

Kellie made a growling noise and the boy laughed through his tears and ran flat-out down the hallway, pulling his pyjama pants down to his knees as he went.

He fell asleep halfway through the first chapter. She kissed his rosy cheek, patted the spoilt dog that was snuggled up to the sleeping boy, and then left the room.

She went back to check on James. He hadn't moved. She gently took the shoe off his good leg then found a thick woolly sock to put over the toes sticking out from his plaster cast, they were blue with cold.

His painkillers were on the bedside table so she removed two and poured a glass of water.

'James,' she gently shook his arm and he stirred. 'Take these tablets. They'll help with the pain.' Still half-a-sleep he managed to get them down. Kellie covered him with a warm rug, turned off the light, and left the room.

Exhausted by the day's events, she made herself a hot drink and took it to bed.

Chapter Sixteen

The next morning she was up early. Harry was still asleep so she closed his door, flicked the switch on the kettle, and then checked on James. She knocked, but there was no reply so she poked her head around his door. He lay staring at the ceiling with a vacant look on his face. The room smelt stale and airless.

She tiptoed over to his bed. 'Morning, James. Would you like a coffee?'

He mumbled something she couldn't hear.

Kellie returned to the kitchen, made the coffee, and took one to him. She carried hers outside and sat at the table on the back verandah. The day was sunny but cold, and steam rose from her coffee mug. She shut her eyes for a moment and breathed in the early morning perfume drifting across lawn from the rose garden.

Lost in the moment, she didn't notice James hobble out through the door. She jumped with fright when he hooked a chair out with his good foot then sat down. His eyes were bloodshot, he hadn't shaved, and still had yesterday's clothes on. He looked a mess.

'Are you okay?' she asked gently.

'I...' his voice caught on a sob and he stood up, grabbed his crutches, and quickly stumbled inside, as though chased by demons.

He locked himself away in his bedroom. Kellie called him for meals, but he didn't answer or come out.

She felt useless and didn't know what to do. 'Maybe if I leave him alone he can deal with his grief and move on.'

***

Kookaburras and roosters were in full voice the next morning and woke Harry earlier than usual. Kellie read to him for a while then helped him to get dressed.

Concerned about James, she tapped on his door. 'James, would you like some breakfast?' He still didn't answer. Kellie shook her head and walked away.

Lunch time came, she called him, but he didn't reply or come out.

Harry had a rest then she took him and Charlie for a long walk. It was four o'clock when they returned and James' door was still closed.

Once more she made him coffee and knocked on his door. 'I've brought you a coffee James,' no answer. 'I'll leave it on the hall table.' She felt frustrated, as she didn't know how to cope with this sort of behavior.

Later she heard the toilet flush. *At least I know he's still capable of moving around,* she thought.

Dinner time came and once again, she called him, hoping he would be so hungry he would come out of his room. He didn't answer so she covered his meal in cling wrap and put it in the freezer.

Later, Kellie bathed Harry. He giggled and squealed as though he didn't have a care in the world. She really enjoyed this part of her job and hoped his childish giggles might make James realise he had a lovely young son who needed his father's love and attention, but no, nothing happened.

That night Kellie woke around midnight and heard the toilet flush in James' bathroom. 'At least he's okay,' she told herself sleepily.

She couldn't get back to sleep so she got up and made a hot drink. *Maybe I'll take James one*, she thought as the milk heated.

Kellie tapped on his door. 'James, I've made you some hot chocolate.' She waited – no reply.

'I'll leave it on the hall table.' She gave up and went back to bed, listening to see if he came out to get the drink.

Daylight eventually came. Kellie hopped out of bed and went to check if the mug was still there, sure enough it was in the same place with a yucky skin formed across the top. She stood outside his room not knowing what to do next.

Harry woke up with the grizzles. He threw one tantrum after another. She helped him put his clothes on. He wouldn't eat any breakfast and then wet his pants. The angry child fought and yelled at the top of his voice when she made him change his trousers. Eventually, he calmed down. Kellie thought he knew something was up, something to do with his dad, but he couldn't work what the problem was.

Kellie struggled through the morning, doing her chores, but all the time wondering what to do about James. He had water in there, but had not eaten for two days.

Maybe he's got a stash of food in there that I don't know about, she thought and carried on working and worrying.

After lunch, Kellie heard a loud commotion in the hallway. It was Harry. He was outside James' bedroom, screaming and yelling as he hit and kicked the wooden door.

She hurried to stop him. 'Daddy needs to rest. He isn't well.' She grabbed the child but he lashed out. 'That's enough!' she growled and seized his arms in an attempt to lift him up. Angry tears streamed down the boy's red cheeks and he fought her off. A vicious kick caught her right in the stomach. 'Oh...' it brought tears to her eyes. She put him down and rubbed where his boot had connected with her tummy. 'That's it,' she whimpered as she stumbled back to the kitchen. 'I've had enough. I wish James realised the problems he's causing. He can't just lock himself away like this; it's all too much. We need some help.'

She grabbed her mobile phone and sent a text off to Moira. She didn't want James to overhear her conversation.

A reply came back ten minutes later. *I phoned Dr Richard Wilkinson and he will come out to see James in the morning, but call him if the situation becomes urgent. Love Moira.*

The doctor and Moira arrived after breakfast and Kellie showed him to James' room.

He knocked. 'James, its Richard. Open the door, mate.' He waited, nothing happened. 'James, open this door now!' A few moments later, he heard the thud of crutches and a click as the lock turned.

He went in. 'Pooh...' The stench in the room hit him straight away and he could hardly breathe. Quickly, he pulled back the curtains and pushed open the windows then gulped in some fresh air.

'What the hell...' James was back on the bed rubbing his bloodshot eyes.

'It's me, Richard. What have you been doing to yourself mate? Look at the state you're in.'

The troubled man broke down. 'I don't care, I just don't care anymore.'

'Oh mate, you have a three-year-old son who's been to hell and back, he needs you. You must stay strong and carry on for him as well as yourself.'

'I can't. I'm tired, so tired.'

'Tell me about going to Sydney?' Are you sure it was Serena, the woman you identified?'

'Yes,' he whispered. 'Not the beautiful girl I remember, but a terrible shrunken shell...'

'You're positive it was her?'

'I checked. She lost the tip of her left index finger in an accident when she was young and had a t-shaped scar on the back of her neck. Yes, it was her, but it didn't look anything like her....' Deep gut-wrenching sobs shook his tormented body.

Richard put a comforting arm across his friend's shoulder. 'Oh mate, I'm so sorry. Would you like to come and stay with me for a while? My family has gone to the U.K. for a month visiting Lindy's parents. Her dad hasn't been well and she wanted to spend some time with them.' James lifted a tear-stained face and the doctor felt alarmed at the blank expression in his eyes.

Richard continued. 'A chap I know does grief counseling and you would benefit from a few sessions with him.' He gave up then, as he realised James was in a place where nothing registered.

'You sit there, mate. I'll have a word with Kellie and get Moira to pack your gear.'

Richard hurried to the kitchen and went over to Kellie. 'He needs professional help. I'll take him back to my place and see he gets the right sort of care. Moira's just packing a few of his things.'

Just then, Harry ran inside to see who had arrived, followed closely by the dog. The boy ran straight for James' bedroom where he saw Moira filling a suitcase with his dad's clothes. He screamed and threw himself on the floor. He couldn't understand what was going on.

Kellie knelt down and took his squirming little body firmly in her arms. 'It's all right, Harry, Daddy isn't well, and he's going to stay with his friend Richard for a while. You want him to get better don't you?' The small boy nodded and rubbed his tear-filled eyes as smudges of black dirt ran down his little cheeks. He looked around and saw Richard pick up his dad's suitcase then help him hobble out to the car. This was too much for the poor child and he went hysterical.

Moira looked at Kellie and shook her head. 'This is like a bad nightmare. Will you be okay?'

'I'll manage. Please let us know how James is doing.'

'I certainly will. You go back inside with Harry. It might be easier if he doesn't watch us leave.' She gave Kellie a quick hug. 'Take care, love. I'll be in touch.'

After they left, Kellie eventually calmed the distraught child and the frightened dog came out of hiding.

'Oh, dear Lord,' she whispered, 'please help us?'

Chapter Seventeen

She felt sluggish and had a bit of a tummy ache, but managed to make it through the day. Wearily, she cooked Harry's dinner, bathed him, and tucked him into bed. After she had read him the story of 'Pirate Pete,' she had a warm shower and went to bed. Her tummy was sore and it was hard to get comfortable. 'Maybe I'll feel better in the morning,' she told herself as she drifted off to sleep.

A rowdy rooster woke her early the next morning. Bursting to go to the loo, she turned her bedside light on then felt a wet patch half-way down the bed. 'What the...?' she pushed the bedclothes back and saw a patch of sticky bright-red blood!

Panic welled up and her lip quivered. 'Oh no, what's happening? Dear Lord, not the baby, oh please don't let it be the baby.'

She fell back on the bed and tears spilled down her cheeks. 'I need help, oh please someone help me.'

Never had she felt so alone. 'Betty, I'll phone Betty,' she whimpered. 'She said to call her if I needed help.' Her hand trembled as she nervously scrolled down the list of names on her mobile. She shook so much she nearly dropped the phone, then found the old lady's number and pressed the ring button.

'Hello,' a voice croaked on the other end, 'Who's that?'

'Betty it's me, Kellie, I need h-help. I'm sorry to call this early but I think I'm l-losing the baby.'

'Where are you?'

'In b-bed.'

'Stay there. I'll come over straight away. I've got a key for your back door so I can let myself in.'

The distressed girl put the phone down and tried to keep calm, but fear got the best of her and she sobbed loudly into her pillow.

A short time later, she heard the back door open and close then Betty limped into Kellie's bedroom.

'Oh love, stop crying and tell me what's happened.' The poor girl broke down in a crumpled heap.

'Shhh.' Betty whispered as she held Kellie in her soft comforting arms.

'Yesterday, I w-wasn't feeling well and had a bit of a tummy-ache then when I woke up this morning there's b-blood on the sheets.' The girl's anguish nearly broke the old lady's heart.

'You stay where you are and I'll call Moira, she'll know what to do. This sort of thing happens sometimes and women still manage to carry their baby to full term. You hang in there love. I'll be back in a moment.'

Betty went into the kitchen, found the telephone address book, and made her call.

A sleepy voice answered, 'Moira speaking.'

'It's Betty here – James' neighbour. I'm concerned about Kellie. She hasn't been feeling too good and over-night she's had pain and some blood loss.'

There was a soft whistle on the other end of the phone. 'Holy hell, that's all we need. It's all this other business with James. The poor girl's had too much to cope with.'

'I agree. Tell me how to help her.'

'I'm just thinking. Um…I can't come out this morning, we are two doctors down and Saturday morning surgery is usually pretty hectic. Keep her in bed and I'll speak to Richard Wilkinson. He's Kellie's doctor. Make yourselves a cuppa and I'll get back to you shortly.'

Betty let out a nervous laugh. 'Will do and I'll wait for your call, thanks Moira.'

Moira called Richard straight away and explained Kellie's condition.

'Mmm… tell her to stay in bed. It's probably a result of all the stress she's been under. Are you able to go out there and check a few things for me?'

'I can do, but not until this afternoon.'

'That should be all right. I'll call into the surgery this morning and explain what I want done. If everything's okay, we'll get an ultrasound done next week to be on the safe side. Kellie's a healthy girl, carrying a healthy baby. I feel this is just a hiccup, but if she worsens tell Betty to call an ambulance.'

'Right, I'll phone her back and we'll go from there.'

***

Moira rang and relayed the message. She didn't mention calling an ambulance, as she knew Betty would get back to her if Kellie's condition deteriorated.

'Okay, we'll see you this afternoon.'

Betty put the phone down and breathed a sigh of relief. She was feeling her age. *I'm too old for all of this,* she thought as she limped back to Kellie's bedroom.

By now, the girl's face was a mess, all blotched and swollen. Betty carefully repeated what Moira had said and then gently washed her face and hands. She held the young woman close as once more the tears overflowed. Slowly, ever so slowly she calmed down.

Mid-afternoon, they heard a car pull up the drive. Betty opened the front door and Harry rushed out followed by Charlie. She watched as Don got out and hugged the little boy.

'I tagged along as well, Betty. The lawns can do with a mow, and I'll tidy up the gardens.'

Betty's anxious face relaxed. 'Your smiling faces are a welcome sight.'

Moira hugged the old lady. 'Thanks for all you've done. You're a wonderful neighbour. We're staying here until Monday so I can keep an eye on things.' Kellie wept with relief when she heard them arrive. Now, help was at hand.

Don brought her in some oranges: beautiful big fresh ones. He hugged her affectionately. 'It's time to stop crying, love,' he stated, 'The doctor reckons you and the baby will be okay.' Moira shooed him out so she could tend to the frightened young woman.

'It's all right, darling,' she murmured. 'Richards fairly sure you're just worn out and need a rest. You had shocking morning sickness followed by James' accident, then all this with Serena's death, it's enough to test anyone. We'll check your blood pressure and the baby's heartbeat and see how you're doing.'

Kellie stopped crying and wiped her eyes.

Moira continued, 'I've brought my special medical kit with me. You know love, I had this bag when I first started nursing. It's like me, old as the hills and a bit worn out.'

Kellie giggled, she felt much better now this confident friendly woman was in charge.

As the stethoscope travelled over the baby bulge, a huge smile lit up Moira's face. 'Baby's heartbeat is clear and strong.'

Kellie's face beamed. 'Thank goodness. Wow, I'm so relieved.' This time some happy tears flowed down the young woman's blotchy cheeks.

'Richard wants you to have an ultrasound early next week to check all's well. You'll be able to see for yourself that the baby's fine and be reassured.'

Moira made a few more checks, wrote down a couple of things, and then put her gear back in her bag. 'Great, there are no problems there. I'll run through these checks again later tonight. We're staying the weekend so there's no need to worry about Harry and the dog. Don's got them both outside playing some game. Betty's made a cuppa, so I'll bring yours in, then I'll go and have a chat with her out in the kitchen. What a darling she is. What would we do without her?' Moira patted Kellie's hand and left the room.

***

Kellie lay back in her bed and looked at the thick, green creeper with tiny yellow flowers that covered the wooden side-fence outside her window. She felt something she hadn't felt in a long time – she felt loved. Since her parents were killed, she hadn't really had this warm fuzzy feeling, but with Betty, Moira, and Don all looking after her with such tender loving care, she felt as though a cosy warm blanket had been wrapped around her.

There was a knock on her door and Moira breezed in. 'Here's a nice omelette for you that Betty made.' She waited while Kellie sat up then placed the tray across her knees.

'This looks and smells divine. Thank you both so much.'

'To see an empty plate is all the thanks we need. I'll leave you to it.'

***

Later that evening, Moira ran through the medical checks again. All was well. She sponged Kellie's face and hands, helped her clean her teeth and brush her hair, then kissed her goodnight.

Just as she was hopping into bed, Richard phoned. He sounded worried. 'James has deteriorated. The quicker I get him into grief counselling the better. At the moment, I'm concerned he may turn to self-harm. Just as well he doesn't know about Kellie's problem. How is she?'

'Her colour isn't good, but she's no worse. Her blood pressure's come down a bit and there's no more bleeding or any sign of early labour. The baby's heartbeat's still strong.'

'Good, I think bed-rest for a couple of days, and she should be fine.'

'Thanks, Richard. Will do. Good night.'

She heard a loud sigh at the other end of the telephone. 'Goodnight, Moira.'

***

Sunday dawned bright and clear. Kellie had breakfast in bed then took her time getting up and having a shower. She looked in the mirror and was shocked at the dark circles under her eyes. Once she was dressed, she rested on the sofa in the lounge-room and lay back listening to all the familiar sounds around the house. Harry yelled at something and Charlie barked as Don mowed the lawns. The fresh smell of cut grass wafted in through the open glass doors as Moira came in with coffee and some homemade shortbread for them both.

'Kellie, that friend of yours, Sam, is that her name – the one that lives by herself – well, would she be able to come and stay a couple of days with you when we go home tomorrow?'

'I don't know. I can give her a call and see what she's up to, but don't worry, Moira, I'm so much better. I'll be all right.'

'I'm not really thrilled about you being here by yourself so, just to keep an old lady happy, please call her for me.'

'Okay, where's my mobile?' She looked under the newspaper on the coffee table next to where she was laying, found the phone, and scrolled down to Sam's number.

'Hi Kellie. I was going to give you a call, but you've got in first. How're you doing?'

'I'm all right now, but I had a little scare. I thought I was losing the baby.'

A shocked expletive came over the phone. 'Oh no, is the doc looking after you?'

'No he's in town, but Moira from the surgery's here with her husband. They go home tomorrow after lunch. When are your days off?'

'I've got a shift this afternoon, but then it's my weekend. I don't start back until Thursday morning. Would you like me to come out and stay? I just need to be back here by Wednesday night Kel.'

'That'd be lovely, by then I'll be up and around. Moira worries about me being here by myself with Harry, even though I'm feeling better.'

'You must do what she tells you. I'll jack up someone to feed my cats and be out there by lunch time tomorrow. I'll bring us a couple of hot DVDs, horny ones that'll make you sit up and take notice.'

Kellie laughed. 'You wicked woman; that sounds great. I'll see you then.' Kellie turned off her phone and gave Moira the good news.

***

Don worked out the back and Moira toiled away in the house so that when they left Kellie didn't have too much to do.

Sam came and the two girls had a great time. She walked the dog and prepared their meals. Once the young boy was safely tucked up in his bed at night, they watched Sam's hot sexy movies and laughed their heads off.

'You are so good for me, Sam. Nobody could feel down while you're around.'

'That's what mates are for, my lovely. Now, did I tell you about the new fuchsia pink vibrator I bought online?'

Kellie choked on the potato chip she had in her mouth. 'Oh... Sam, I don't want to know!'

***

Betty called in several times with fresh pies, fruit salads, and other goodies. Gradually the colour came back into Kellie's cheeks.

The surgery phoned to say she had an appointment for an ultrasound Tuesday morning at ten o'clock. Betty looked after Harry and the dog while Sam drove Kellie in. She had to drink a heap of water and hanging on to it was really difficult, but both girls were anxious to see that the baby was safe and well.

The radiologist smeared gel on Kellie's tummy then pressed down on the baby-bump with her electronic wand. On the monitor screen the shape of a foetus appeared.

'There you are. Once more you can see one healthy little baby. I'll just take a few measurements.' While she did that, the two friends watched and listened to the strong foetal heartbeat. It was a beautiful sound.

'You must be someone special. I have to get these results to Dr Wilkinson ASAP.' She wiped the gel off Kellie's tummy and helped her down off the bed.

Kellie smiled. 'Thanks for getting me in so quickly. I've been worried. I had a threatened miscarriage, but now I've seen the baby moving and heard its heartbeat, I feel reassured. Thanks again.'

'My pleasure. We'll get these results off and he'll probably give you a call.'

As the two girls walked back to the car, they let out a loud, 'Whoopee.'

Later, a call from the doctor confirmed that all was well with the baby and its size was quite normal for twenty-four weeks. 'I'd like to see you at the surgery in two weeks' time Kellie, and in the meantime, try to take things easy. No heavy lifting or rushing around and you should be fine. Bye for now.'

The next day the two girls decided to invite Betty to lunch with them at a nice restaurant overlooking the beach at Burleigh Heads. Harry pushed his food off the plate and made a big mess and was really naughty, but the others enjoyed themselves. Betty glowed with pleasure at being included in the outing. On their return, Kellie drove right up to her front door. It was partly open!

'Did you leave your door open, Betty?' Kellie asked in concern.

'N-no, I definitely did not,' Betty stuttered. 'What the... there's a motorbike around the side.' They all looked at one another. Then a tall dirty-looking guy in his forties wandered out of the house.

A big smile lit up Betty's face. 'It's my son, Ross. I haven't seen him for eight years. Oh, Ross!' She fumbled with the door handle impatient to get out. 'Ross,' she called.

He came over to meet her. 'Hi Ma, thought I'd surprise ya. Howya been?'

He hugged her and a couple of tears escaped and ran down the old lady's cheeks. Her love for this long lost son was plain to see and the wrinkles on her worn face creased up as she grinned from ear to ear. The two girls and Harry stepped out of the car.

'Ross, come and meet my friends, they took me out to lunch. I've had a lovely time.' Her face beamed as she turned and introduced him to the young women. 'This is Kellie, she lives just down there.' Betty pointed to James' house, 'and this is Sam, her good friend, and this young man is Harry.'

Kellie felt the hairs on the back of her neck stand up as she shook Ross's outstretched grubby hand.

'I'm pleased to meet you. Have you come to stay?' she greeted him.

'Yer, just for a few days. I haven't seen Ma for a while.' He turned and gave Sam a sleazy grin. 'Sam.' They shook hands then she smartly stepped back.

Betty started to go inside. 'Well, I'm going to put the kettle on, would you girls like to stay for a drink?'

'No thanks, Betty.' Kellie kissed the old lady's cheek. 'We'd better head home and see what Charlie's up to. See you around, Ross.'

Sam put her arms around Betty and hugged her tight. 'I'll come and see you again next time I'm out here. Bye Ross, good to meet you.'

The old lady smiled. 'I had such a nice time. Thank you both for taking me. Bye.'

Kellie backed the car out of the drive way and turned onto the road. Then her mouth dropped open like a fish. 'What a sleaze. I can't believe Betty gave birth to a weirdo like that.'

Sam screwed up her face. 'Some mothers sure do have them. He's an absolute creep! Did you notice the limp handshake? That tells you something. I can't stand dick-heads like him.'

'Neither can I, but with a bit of luck he won't stay long. He's quite pale, maybe he works indoors.'

'Either that or he's just come out of jail. That wouldn't surprise me at all.' They laughed as Kellie parked the car in James' garage.

As the dying sunset spread its orange cloak across the autumn sky, Sam reluctantly left them to return to her home at Broadbeach.

Chapter Eighteen

Kellie became stronger as the days went by and quite enjoyed having only Harry and the dog to care for. Her friends phoned daily to check on her health and were pleased to find there were no more dramas.

Kellie, now six months pregnant could only fit into her maternity clothes. She'd bought several loose tops in bright colours and wore them over patterned leggings. She felt a bit of a clown, but she was warm and comfortable.

They were due for another visit from Harry's case worker. Joy Brennan arrived early Tuesday morning. She was dressed warmly in an old-fashioned grey skirt and jacket with a black woolly scarf. She still reeked of stale smoke.

'Good morning, Kellie. I'm here to check on Harry,' she said, then noticed Kellie's pregnant tummy and gave a rude sniff.

Feeling somewhat offended, Kellie didn't reply, but stood back to let her in and thought, *rude cow*.

Harry hid behind the table when Kellie called him. He didn't like this woman. Charlie made a deep growling noise.

'Well, you can't say he's obedient, can you?'

'Maybe he somehow feels threatened.'

'What do you mean by that remark?'

Remembering the bad report they'd received last time because of the dog, Kellie tried to keep her cool.

In a polite voice, she answered, 'He takes a while to trust people and you're a stranger to him.'

'I visited last month and he kept playing with that dog and just ignored me.'

'If I take Charlie out of the room, Harry will become upset. The dog has played a huge part in his rehabilitation.'

The cranky case worker raised her eye brows. She was not impressed. 'I'd like to use your kitchen table. I need to jot down some details.'

'Sure, come on through.' Kellie led Joy out to the kitchen. It had a fresh clean smell as she had just washed the floor. 'Can I make you tea or a coffee?'

Joy pulled out a chair and sat down. 'No thanks, I won't be here long enough to drink it. Has his eating improved?'

'I think it has, but he's still a small eater and somewhat picky.'

'The night terrors he had, are they still bothering him?'

'He hasn't had one of those for some time and sleeps right through the night.'

'Good, that's something.'

Kellie kept herself busy at the bench getting vegies ready for their dinner. This woman irritated her, but she had to watch her step.

The case worker stood up. 'I want to spend some time with Harry by himself.'

'Sure,' Kellie nodded.

After ten minutes, Joy returned to the kitchen. 'I'm leaving now and my report will be in the mail.' She shoved her paperwork back into her overflowing briefcase. 'Goodbye, I'll see myself out.'

Kellie waited to hear the front door close then rudely mumbled, 'Just push off you stupid old bag and don't bother coming back,' then wacked off a large piece of pumpkin with the carving knife.

***

Kellie had a ten o'clock doctor's appointment the next morning. She wore a long-sleeved bright blue maternity top with white trousers, tied her hair back, and sprayed a little Chloe on her wrists. Her silver flat shoes matched the heap of silver bracelets she slipped over her wrist. Harry got himself ready. He loved dressing up and sat at the kitchen table waiting to have his hair swished back.

They reached the surgery on time and Moira was at reception when they arrived. Harry saw her and quickly pulled away from Kellie's hand to run behind the desk into the older lady's waiting arms.

'Hello, darling boy.' She kissed him on both cheeks and hugged him tight.

'Kellie, it's good to see you love, you look nice. What a lovely top, they didn't make fancy maternity outfits like that when I was pregnant. How are you feeling today?'

'Good, thanks. It's nice to get out even if it is just to visit the doctor,' she said and laughed.

'You're his next patient. I'll look after Harry while you go in if you like.'

'Thanks, that would be great.'

Richard Wilkinson came out and picked up the next file. 'Kellie,' he called, 'Come on through. We're in the end consulting room today.'

She nodded at Moira and followed the doctor down the hallway.

'Take a seat and we'll check your blood pressure first.' With that done, he asked her to hop up onto the examination couch, where he listened to the baby's heartbeat and prodded around her tummy.

'Good, no worries there.' He helped her down then went over to sit at his desk.

'Have a seat.' He picked up a pen and made some notes. 'All seems to be well after your scare. These things happen from time to time but I'd like to see you again in two weeks' time just to be on the safe side.' He put the pen down and spun his chair around to face her.

'Now, I'd like to speak to you about James.' Kellie's heart did a flip as she wondered what was coming next.

'He's made reasonable progress and his leg is almost healed. He manages with a walking stick now and he'll use that for the next couple of months. In two weeks' time, he sees the orthopaedic specialist again for a check-up, but his depression will take some time to come right.'

He rubbed his eyes and suddenly looked very tired. 'I feel he needs to be home with young Harry, to be amongst normal everyday things, and maybe come into work one or two days a week. Being active will keep his mind busy and gradually help drive away the misery overwhelming him.'

Kellie nodded in agreement. 'When do you think he'll be ready to come home?'

'How about you and Harry have some lunch with Moira then follow me around to my place and pick him up.'

'Today!' She nearly had a heart-attack.

'Yes. I knew you had an appointment with me today and told him to get his gear together.' He could see she was shocked. 'Just think how excited Harry will be.'

'It's j-just unexpected that's all.' Kellie stuttered then quickly recovered. 'Harry loves his dad and will be over the moon to have him back home.'

'I wouldn't ask you to do this if I didn't think James was ready, but I'm fairly sure he'll be able to cope. The shock of identifying Serena's emaciated body was too much for him, especially as he was recovering from a serious accident.' Kellie knew he spoke as James' friend not as his doctor.

He continued. 'I'll give you my mobile number and call me if you're worried, but I don't think there will be any problems.'

'Okay, I'll go and find Moira.'

'Tell her to give me a call when you've finished lunch.' Kellie stood up to leave then he held up his hand. 'I forgot to ask if you had any questions.'

She smiled and shook her head. 'No, there's nothing I can think of at the moment. I'll see you after lunch.'

Moira took them to the coffee shop next door. 'Come on Kellie, order something outrageous. Richard's shouting our meal today, so the sky's the limit.' They laughed as they studied the menu.

The food was lovely. Harry had his favourite: a milkshake and a jam-doughnut but nearly brought the place down when he dropped it on the floor. He bawled so loud that the owner rushed over with another doughnut because other diners were getting agitated and giving Kellie nasty looks.

When they'd finished eating, Moira gave Kellie a serious look. 'Are you okay with taking James home today?'

The younger woman nodded. 'I'll be fine. I'm pleased he's improving and Harry will be thrilled to have his dad home, then maybe life will return to normal.'

'What's normal, Kellie?' They both laughed knowing there was no answer to that one.

Moira phoned Richard and he met them at the surgery by the reception desk. Kellie noticed the girls pretending to work at their computers as they gave her the once over, so Moira introduced them all. They were a friendly bunch, prone to gossip and she knew they were wondering what was going on.

Richard jiggled his car keys. 'Where are you parked, Kellie?'

She told him and he went to bring his car around so they could follow him to his home.

Kellie's heart thumped nervously as she drove behind him to an elegant house near the beach. She pulled off the road and waited in the car.

'Oh dear God, please let things work out all right,' she whispered as James came out carrying his sports bag. Harry's lip dropped and he started to cry.

'Shush darling, it's all right, daddy's coming home.'

Richard put James' bag in the boot then the two men shook hands.

James hesitated a moment then looked her way. 'Hello, Kellie.'

'Hi James, it's good to see you.'

He hopped into the back seat next to Harry who was still grizzling. 'Hi mate, have you missed me?' He hugged the small boy, but the bawling continued. They waved to Richard and Kellie drove off. The sky had darkened and she concentrated on negotiating the streets back out to the main road. By then it had started to rain. She glanced in the rear-vision mirror and could see the boy had fallen asleep in his car-seat, his little head resting on James' shoulder; his eyes were shut as well.

She pulled into their driveway as the rain cleared and drove into the garage. Kellie hopped out and left James to bring Harry, who had just woken up. She unlocked the inside door and Charlie bounded out barking loudly, his best mate had come back home. He spun around in circles and rubbed his head against James' leg. Kellie left them to it and got on with her chores.

A short while later there was a knock at the back door. 'Kellie love, are you there?'

'Yes, Betty, come in.' She grinned. Their sweet old neighbour didn't miss a trick. 'James is home,' Kellie whispered, 'He's in the lounge-room with Harry and Charlie.'

'I'm pleased to hear that. I made you a meat pie. There'll be enough for you all.'

'Thanks, James will be tickled pink. I can't imagine the sort of meals he's been having at his mate's place. Go in and see him while I finish off this ironing.'

***

Betty slid open the lounge-room door. 'James, how lovely to have you back home.' Harry ran over and clutched one of her legs and the dog barked madly.

'Hello, Betty,' the doctor got up and hugged the old lady. 'Have a seat and tell me how you've been.'

Bedlam reigned for a few moments as he sat Harry up beside him on the sofa and told Charlie to be quiet. James and Betty chatted for a while, catching up the last few weeks.

'And did Kellie tell you that my son Ross came to stay a few days?'

'No, how nice for you.'

'I hadn't seen the boy for over eight years, he'd changed a lot. The house seemed awfully empty when he left.'

'A great deal can happen in eight years.' He shook his head, mindful of his own situation. 'Excuse me a minute will you, Betty.' James grabbed his walking stick and limped out of the room returning a few minutes later with an envelope. 'This is for you.'

Betty's arthritic fingers were slow to open it. She drew out a card and read the message then looked at the attached voucher. 'Two hundred dollars. James what's all this about?'

'It's a shopping voucher to be spent at Myers. I want you to buy yourself a nice warm cardigan and some slippers. It's a small thank-you for all the help you've given us.'

The old lady shook her head. 'I haven't been to Myers for years. You didn't have to do this. Oh, you wonderful boy, come here.' Betty hugged him and kissed his cheek.

'Kellie will take you shopping as I have one for her as well, but I haven't given it to her yet.'

'Well, thank you very much. I'll get myself home now that rain looks like it might come back. Bye, Harry, come and give me a hug.' He did with a big grin, happy because his dad was home and all was well in his small world.

Later that night, when Harry was tucked up in bed, James called Kellie into the lounge.

'Have a seat.'

Nervously, she sat down opposite him.

'I'd like to thank you for taking care of everything in my absence. Once more, I'm in your debt. Here.' He handed over her envelope and sat back while she opened it. The grandfather clock ticked loudly as he waited for Kellie to pull out the card, read the message, and open the voucher.

'James... one thousand dollars from Myers... goodness me.'

'I know this hasn't been an easy job,' his voice faltered, 'and I'd like you to get a few things for yourself and the baby. One request I'd like to make, when you go to Myers will you please take Betty, I gave her a small voucher to get herself a couple of warm things for winter.'

'Sure, I'd love to take her and we'll have a great old spend-up. She never buys anything for herself. I can't imagine her face when you gave it to her.'

'I think she was embarrassed, however she recovered.' They discussed Harry and his progress and Kellie told him of the case-workers disastrous visit.

'Hmm, we may hear more about that. I don't ever expect you to put up with nonsense from the department and I'll tell them so.'

'Thank you. She is certainly challenging.' Kellie thought he'd finished so she stood up to leave the room.

'When you have time I'd like a coffee. I'll be in the study as I must get back into my work.'

'Sure, and thanks again.' She almost danced out to the kitchen. *Wow, having a voucher was exciting and having a 'one thousand dollar voucher' was even more exciting!*

James returned to the surgery the next morning and worked a half-day. His leg ached and he still limped quite badly, but apparently, in time, that would disappear.

Saturday came, the start of her days off but Kellie stayed close to home all weekend making sure James was able to manage. After lunch, she took her book and a chocolate bar out by the pool. The day was sunny with a slight chill. The gentle breeze carried a hint of perfume from the white blossoms covering the citrus trees. She heard a car door slam.

'James, darling, how are you?' The raucous voice of Ruth Simmonds called out.

Oh no, thought Kellie, *Not her again. She's such a desperate cow.*

Little did Kellie know that inside the lounge room, James was busy defending her.

'Darling, where is your hired help?'

'She has the weekends off.'

'But you haven't been well and she should be here helping out. After all, you provide a roof over her head as well as pay her. Really, it's not good enough.'

'Kellie does an excellent job and accommodation is usually provided for full time housekeeping positions. I have no complaints about her work.'

Ruth realised she was banging her head against a brick wall and changed tactics. 'Well then, let me make you a coffee or something.'

'How about I open a nice bottle of shiraz – that appeals to me more,' James suggested.

'Sounds good. So now, tell me what's been happening. I've rung your mobile a few times, but it went straight to message bank then someone told me you had a bit of a breakdown. Come on, spill the beans.'

James found her perfume quite suffocating and didn't know how to put her off without being rude, so he briefly explained about Serena's death. Ruth came over and sat on the sofa next to him.

She put her arm across his shoulders. 'Oh James, how distressing. If you ever feel the need to talk about this in depth, please call me, I'm a great listener.'

He didn't want to dwell on the past so he quickly changed the subject. They chatted for an hour or so and then Harry and the dog burst into the lounge room.

'Hello, Harry,' Ruth gushed, 'Come and see me.' She held out her arms. The child pulled a rude face then climbed onto his dad's knee and buried his head in James' chest.

'He's just woken up from a nap. He'll come right in a moment.' James could see she was annoyed with his young son.

Ruth felt she couldn't stand too much of this and decided it was time to hit the road.

'Well, I'd better be off. I'm meeting some friends at five o'clock and it's after four now.' She picked up her car keys and handbag. 'Thanks for the wine. I'll be in touch. Bye Harry,' she bent to kiss the little boy's cheek. He quickly turned away then she lifted her head and kissed James.

'Bye, darling,' she purred. 'I'll see myself out. Ring me if I can help. I'm only a phone call away.'

She left but her cloying perfume lingered. James threw open the windows and gulped the fresh air that floated in on the late afternoon breeze.

Chapter Nineteen

Tuesday night after dinner, James came out to the kitchen where Kellie rested up on the window-seat feeling like a bloated whale. She quickly sat up and tried to hide her caramel chocolate bar as he walked in holding some paperwork.

'Don't get up. I received this letter from welfare stating it was okay for Harry to attend the Canungra Kindergarten. Do you remember me getting in touch with them just before my accident?'

'Yes, I do. That's great news. He'll enjoy mixing with kids his own age. When can he start?'

'Anytime now. When I contacted them, they had a vacancy and were happy to hold it until I'd heard from the department. How about you go and chat with them tomorrow and see if he can begin next week. I'll take Monday morning off and go with you to make sure he's quite settled.'

'That's a good idea. If he spoke he could tell us, but as he doesn't, we'll have to watch and make sure he adjusts to his new environment.'

'That's about it. Is there any coffee going?'

'Coming up, it won't take long.'

He nodded and left the room.

***

Monday morning, James took Harry to the kindergarten and Kellie followed in her car. The small boy's face flushed with excitement as he looked around the play equipment and met children his own age. James stayed awhile, showing him how to use the bathroom and where he would eat his morning tea. It was such a fun place. He waved to Harry as he left, but the boy didn't take any notice, he was busy building a fort out of small logs. James looked around for Kellie, gave her a quick wave, and then went out to his car.

Moira spied him entering the surgery. 'How was my favourite boy? Did he like the kindergarten?'

'He didn't even notice when I left to come to work.' James looked peeved. 'I'm quite satisfied with the establishment. The place was clean and well run, so we'll see how he goes.'

'He'll love it and enjoy the other kids' company. Meanwhile back to work. Your first patient's waiting in your consulting room.'

***

Kellie looked at the calendar and noticed another check-up was due. Harry only had kindy three mornings a week so she rang Moira to make an appointment for the following day, as Tuesday was a free day.

'Kellie love, shall I make it for eleven-forty-five? That way we can have lunch together.'

'Sounds good and Harry can have lunch with James. Thanks Moira, see you then.'

The surgery was busy when they arrived and after checking in, they sat in the waiting room. The young guy next to them had a shocking cold and didn't put his hand over his mouth when he coughed. Inwardly, Kellie grimaced. Other patients were giving him filthy looks.

'Kellie,' Dr Wilkinson called as he collected her file from the reception desk. She quickly stood up and followed him, leaving Harry with Moira.

'You're looking well. How far along are you now?' He looked at his notes. 'Mmm, almost twenty-eight weeks. Up on the bed and we'll see what this young nipper's up to. You had that scare, but babies are tough little creatures.'

He listened to the foetal heartbeat and poked around her tummy. 'All good. Does the baby move much?'

Kellie grinned, 'Yes, little butterfly type flutters.'

He laughed. 'You can hop down now and we'll see how your blood pressure is.' She sat quietly while he put the band on her arm and pumped rapidly.

'It's up a bit, but sometimes it's because you've been rushing around. We won't worry about it just now, but I want to see you again in three weeks' time.'

'Okay. Do I need another scan?'

'At this point in time it's not necessary, unless we want to check something. Your baby's a normal size and doing well, so we'll leave it for now. You can always ring me if you have any worries.'

He finished writing and turned in his chair to look at her. 'You're doing a great job out there, Kellie. You've coped with a few hiccups and kept the household running smoothly, so I hear. Good on you.' He stood up and opened the door. 'Take it easy now.'

'Thanks, doctor.'

The next day was kindy again. All was going well until a boisterous boy wanted the same paint brush as Harry. There was a tussle over it and Harry received a nasty bite on his arm. What a commotion. Kellie cuddled him while a staff member bathed the wound and covered it with a Mickey Mouse plaster. He sobbed and became so upset that she took him home. He still sniffed and gulped as they got out of the car and went inside.

Unfortunately, James had come home early to catch up with his paper-work. Harry bellowed the minute he saw his dad and rushed over holding out his arm.

James put his coffee down and gently removed the plaster. 'What the...?'

Kellie nervously explained what happened.

'Bit him, what the hell do you mean some child bit him. Where were you and why weren't you watching him?' He roared angrily.

No person, boss or not, was going to talk to her like that. She stood right up to him and looked him in the eye. 'Do not ever speak to me in that tone again, James. This happened very quickly. The bite is not too bad. He'll get over it.'

'Where were the staff? It's their job to supervise these children.'

'They do a great job there, but these things happen.'

'Not to my son they don't, or they shouldn't, and I pay you to watch him.'

'Please calm down, you're frightening Harry.'

James stomped away to his study and Kellie thought he may have been frothing at the mouth.

After dinner, he came out to the kitchen. 'Kellie, I'll be phoning the kindergarten supervisor in the morning. I want to know how they deal with children that bite. Harry's very distressed and I don't want this happening again.'

Kellie shook her head, *fair dinkum, what a fuss*. 'James, please don't make it a big issue. It will have happened before and it will happen again. Apart from this incident, Harry's really happy there.'

'I know that, but I wish to discuss the problem with them. I'll have a coffee when you have time.' Still angry, he turned to leave the room. Kellie called him back.

'James, did you go for your orthopaedic check-up today?'

'Yes, I did.' He calmed down. 'My leg's healing well and you may not have noticed, but I no longer need a walking stick.' She had noticed, but he still limped badly as he left the room.

Later, as she was getting ready for bed, she heard the explosive roar of a motorbike starting up. *It must be Betty's son, back again*, she thought. For some reason she felt uneasy.

***

Saturday morning, Kellie was making pikelets for morning tea when the front doorbell rang. Ross, Betty's son stood there holding a saucepan.

'Mum said to bring this soup down,' he pushed past her, 'Where's the kitchen?'

Shocked at seeing him, Kellie took a moment to find her tongue. 'Through here.' Reluctantly she led the way. 'You can put the pot down on the stove.' He did and turned around taking a good look at everything.

'Nice digs you've got.'

'I'm only the housekeeper.'

'Who are you?' Neither of them had noticed James come into the room.

Kellie quickly spoke up. 'This is Ross, Betty's son. She sent him down with some soup.'

Ross folded his arms and leaned back against the bench. 'You must be the doctor guy who lives here.'

James looked outraged. 'Yes I am. Thank your mother for the soup.'

'I will.' Ross sent Kellie a sly wink. 'I'd better be off then.'

James stepped forward. 'I'll show you out.' He walked to the front door and held it open.

Ross turned to Kellie. 'I'll see ya again.' He grinned as he sauntered out.

James returned to the kitchen and Kellie noticed his fists were clenched tight as he tried to maintain his composure.

'I don't trust that guy and I don't want him here when I'm not home. Is that clear?'

'I don't like him either. He gives me the creeps, but he's Betty's son.'

James shook his head. 'Remember what I've just told you and for your own safety keep clear of guys like him.'

Kellie went back to making her pikelets and shuddered as she thought of Betty's scary son.

***

Further up the road, Betty struggled to understand Ross. He wanted money. This wasn't the same boy that stayed with her a few weeks ago. She felt uneasy, a bit frightened.

'I don't have funds put aside, son. I used all the money from the Brisbane house to buy this place. I live very frugally on the pension, that's my only income.'

'When's it due?'

'It goes straight into my bank account. It's only enough to keep me.'

'Have you got any stuff worth selling?' He sneered as he looked around the kitchen. Then he spotted the thank-you card James had given her. 'What's this for?'

'James gave it to me for helping out while he was in hospital. He had a nasty accident.'

'What's with this voucher… two hundred dollars… can we cash it in?'

'No, we can't, and I wouldn't even if I could. What do you need money for so desperately? Don't you have any savings?'

He hesitated. 'I lost all I had on a property deal. Since then I haven't been able to get work.'

She didn't believe him. 'What about your motorbike, how did you come by that?'

'I did a deal, okay? But just now I need cash!' he shouted.

'I'll give you twenty dollars. I can't spare anymore. You'll have to go to Centrelink and apply for the dole.'

'Yer, yer, yer. I'll do it, just give me a break.'

She reached for her purse, took out the money, and gave it to him.

'Thanks ma.' He kissed her wrinkled cheek and ran out. The next minute she heard his motorbike start up and take off.

'Now where's he going?' Betty muttered. 'We spoilt him. It's our fault he's turned out like he is.'

***

Harry enjoyed his days at kindergarten; the biting child had found other victims and was now suspended for two weeks while his parents sorted him out. A notice came home informing James of their decision.

'Suspended,' James bellowed, 'I have never heard of a three-year-old child being suspended. What's the world coming too?'

Kellie laughed. 'I have. Where I came from there were very naughty twins at the local play-centre, totally out of control, and they were expelled.'

'What did the parents do about that?'

'Nothing. The dad was a well-known solicitor and the mum a social butterfly. They had seven children, all shockers. People steered clear of them. Usually, the parents went out by themselves and left all the kids with their nanny.'

James shook his head. 'This is all too much. I'm going back to my study.'

***

Mid-week, Betty popped down late in the afternoon with a jar of chocolate chippies. She knew they were James and Harry's favourites.

'Hello Kellie, I thought you might like a few of these to nibble.'

'Thanks, you'll be in the good books. I'm making a cuppa. Would you like one?'

The old lady pulled out a chair by the table and sat down. 'That'd be great love.'

Then they heard the garage door go up.

'Here's James. He's home early today.' Kellie grabbed another mug and made him a coffee.

He came in piggy-backing Harry who had run to meet him. 'Hello ladies. I timed it right didn't I? Nice to see you, Betty. How are you keeping?' He came over and sat at the table then got stuck into her biscuits.

'Mmm. Thanks for these – my favourites.' He handed one to Harry who had scrambled up on his lap. 'Actually, while I have the two of you here, I'm working from home tomorrow so how would you like to go to Pacific Fair and check out Myers? Harry can stay here with me.'

The two women looked at each other and a huge grin appeared on both their faces.

Kellie looked smugly at the old lady. 'Are you okay to go shopping tomorrow, Betty?'

'What time shall I be ready?'

'How about we leave at eight-thirty then we can get an early start.'

'Oh, James,' Betty gushed, 'we will have such a good time. Its years since I did that sort of thing.' She reached over and planted a kiss on his cheek.

***

The next morning, Betty was waiting at her front gate dressed in her 'best frock' when Kellie arrived to pick her up.

'Morning, love.' Betty opened the car-door and slowly got in. 'My legs are a bit stiff this morning and I hardly slept a wink. I'm so excited.' She was clutching an old shopping bag.

Kellie patted her wrinkled hand. 'You look nice today; I don't often see you dressed up. Fasten your safety belt and we'll be on our way.'

They had a good run into Pacific Fair and managed to park close to the entrance doors by the shoe department. Kellie didn't want Betty walking too far in her best shoes. They looked uncomfortable. First, they had morning tea. James had given them two fifty dollar notes to pay for coffee breaks and lunch, saying it was his shout.

Next, they found Betty warm slippers then located the 'frock' department as she called it. Nothing caught her eye there, but she saw a warm cardy and tried it on. It looked awful.

Kellie shook her head. 'No, you need something bright. That's nice, but I think we'll keep looking.' She turned her back to Betty, trying to hide her horror at the ugly woolly garment.

By lunch time, they had found her a nice jumper with a matching scarf and Kellie showed her different ways to jazz up the jersey. In the handbag department, Betty bought a shopping bag she really liked and then they had lunch.

The old lady was pleased to find a table so she could sit down. 'This shopping makes you tired, Kellie, doesn't it?' She bent down and eased off her best shoes. 'That's better. I hope I can get them back on again.'

Kellie laughed. 'You can always put your new slippers on.'

'That'll be the day. A nice cup of tea will do the trick.'

After lunch, Kellie bought maternity bras that cost the earth. 'These are so ugly, why don't they make pretty undies for pregnant women. I like nice knickers and bras, especially when I go to the doctors.'

'Kellie,' Betty sounded quite shocked, but still laughed. 'Don't let James hear you say that.'

By two o'clock, they both felt they'd had enough for one day and headed out to the car.

The older lady lay back in the front seat and sighed. 'I'm so pleased to be off my feet, love, let's go.'

Kellie pushed in a CD and played soft music for the trip home. She felt tired and her feet were killing her.

They pulled into Betty's driveway and Kellie helped carry in her parcels.

'Thanks, love. I've had a great day. It's a long time since I enjoyed myself so much,' Betty said as she hugged her young friend.

'I also had a lovely time, Betty. We'll do this again sometime.'

'Oh dear God, let me get over this one first,' she said and laughed.

James heard Kellie arrive home and came out to help carry in her shopping. 'Did you enjoy your day? By the look of all this, you've done quite well.'

'Yes, thanks, we had a great time. Poor Betty's completely worn out, but she's thrilled with what she bought. She'll tell you all about it when you see her next.' Kellie carried in her parcels and put them on her bed. James followed. She felt a bit self-conscious having him in her bedroom as he put the rest of her shopping on the armchair by the window.

He turned around. 'I'd like you to have a rest now. I'll get the dinner tonight.'

'Oh, okay, what are we having?'

'Spaghetti Bolognese – the old favourite.' He grinned as he left her room. It was a joke. That was the only thing he knew how to cook.

'Wow,' she thought, 'this is a turn-up for the books.'

Chapter Twenty

The weekend came and so did Ross, Betty's son. Saturday morning, he arrived at the Kellie's front door after James and Harry had left to go to Canungra to pick up a few things.

She opened the door not knowing who was there. 'Hello. Oh it you Ross, how are you?' He stepped inside before she could say any more.

'I came down to see if you wanna to go out tonight?'

Trying not to throw up, Kellie replied, 'Thanks for the invite, but I'm a bit of a stay at home, and there's a show on television tonight I especially want to see.'

'Aren't I good enough to go out with? Ya don't have to make excuses.'

'I'm not, that's the truth, take it or leave it.'

'I know about sheilas like you, they say one thing and mean another.'

Quite shaken by his attitude she replied 'Look, you'll have to excuse me. I have work to do and I must get on with it.'

He pursed his lips and without another word stomped out.

Kellie shivered. 'He must have watched James leave,' she whispered as goose pimples spread up her arms.

After lunch, her time off started, so she decided to visit her friends Shirley and Bob Goodwin at Currumbin. She rang and checked to see if they were home.

'Hello Kellie, yes we're here lazing around. Come on over. I'll watch the gate and come out when you arrive to save you from the dogs next door.'

'Thanks for that Bob. I'll see you about two o'clock.'

Dark clouds overhead threatened a downpour and Kellie hoped to arrive at her friend's home before the rain started.

Shirley had coffee ready with hot date scones, a bowl of whipped cream and homemade strawberry jam. Kellie tucked in.

'It's easy to see you're eating for two. Is food rationed out there?' Shirley inquired.

'No, of course not. It's just that these scones are so good and this place has such a tranquil feel about it, I can relax and enjoy them.'

'Well it's lovely to see you, when you've finished eating tell us what's been happening out there. I spoke to Sam and she told me you had a miscarriage scare.' Shirley sat back and folded her arms in a 'hurry up and tell me' position.

After three scones and two cups of coffee, Kellie brought them up to date.

'Wow, I don't like the sound of Betty's son.' Bob felt alarm bells starting up. 'You watch out for him Kellie, it sounds like he's on drugs and they're usually very desperate people.'

'I thought the same. It's Betty I feel sorry for. I wonder what he's like with her. I'll keep my eyes open and see what happens.'

'Keep your doors locked when James is away and be careful.' Shirley had a bad feeling as well. People were inclined to use Kellie as she had such a soft heart. Outside heavy rain had set in and strong wind-gusts pounded against the windows.

Bob looked out the door and scratched his head. 'I don't know about you going home tonight, Kellie, this weather isn't letting up. You shouldn't be driving all the way out there in this rain.' He looked at Shirley. 'Love, I think she should stay here the night … what do you reckon?'

A big grin appeared on her face. 'What a great idea Bob, you can make us a couple of your famous pizzas and we'll get the cards out. Kellie and I were always pretty hot euchre players. We'll teach Bob how to play, then thrash the pants off him.'

Kellie burst out laughing. 'We've certainly had some entertaining nights playing that game. I'd like to stay if that's okay.'

'I'll loan you a nightie and I've got some knickers that are too big for me, you can have them. Help yourself to a new toothbrush and whatever else you need; they're in the bathroom cupboard next to the guest room.'

They had a hilarious evening, Bob was a wiz card player and cheated where possible, totally fooling the girls. Shirley drank too much wine and got the giggles.

By late Sunday afternoon, the rain had cleared and the strong wind gusts had died down to a cool breeze. Kellie hugged her friend's goodbye, thanked them for having her, and set off back to Wonglepong.

***

James stood at the stove cooking boiled eggs and toast. Harry sat at the table playing with his knife and spoon. Charlie ran up to greet her, his tail wagging flat-out. Kellie patted him as she greeted James.

'Hello James,' she said as she went over to give Harry a hug. 'Hi Harry, have you had a good day?'

The small boy nodded, banging his knife on the table.

James turned from his cooking and looked daggers at her. 'You could have let us know you weren't coming home last night, the weather turned bad and I was concerned for your safety.'

She nearly choked on the spot, to think he was concerned about her. 'Sorry about that, my friends didn't like the thought of me driving back here in the rain and invited me to stay.'

'Very sensible, but a short message would have been appreciated.'

'I'm sorry James, next time I'll let you know.' She gave Harry another quick hug and went to her room.

Kellie closed her bedroom door and leaned back against it, flabbergasted. 'What the hell's eating him,' she muttered, 'as though he cares what happens to me. The stupid man.' She grabbed the remote and hopped on the bed flicking through the TV channels. Suddenly, little flutters started up inside her tummy and she tenderly caressed her baby bump sending a message of love to her unborn child.

Wednesday morning, there wasn't any kindy and Kellie felt out of sorts, so she packed a picnic lunch for herself and Harry, some treats for Charlie, and they went to the beach at Burleigh Heads. The sun shone through patchy grey clouds, and a cool wind whipped up rough uneven waves. Harry towed Charlie behind him as he ran up the beach with both arms out-stretched imitating the noisy seagulls that squawked and circled overhead.

Kellie took deep breaths of the bracing sea-air while keeping her eye on the excited young boy and the dog. They ate their picnic lunch, made a few sandcastles, and then headed for home. She had just turned off the Nerang road when there was a crash. A stone from an oncoming truck smashed into her windscreen. Kellie screamed in fright, Harry cried out and Charlie started barking.

Badly shaken, she pulled off the road and took a few deep breaths. 'Oh, dear God, what am I going to do?' There was a small hole in the windscreen with disjointed cracks surrounded by cobweb patterns in the glass. No way could she drive as she couldn't see properly and they were forty-five minutes from home.

'Harry,' she yelled as he was still bellowing, 'stop that noise. Stop it. I can't think.' He lowered the volume, but continued to grizzle. Kellie felt bad for raising her voice.

'Sorry darling, I know you've had a big fright, but we'll be fine.' She turned to the distressed dog. 'Charlie, stop that racket!' He quietened down and Harry's whimper turned into huge sniffs.

Kellie sat there stunned. A few minutes later, she decided she needed some help. 'I'll give your dad a quick call. I'm not sure what to do.' Tears of frustration filled her eyes as she hunted in her handbag for her mobile phone.

Then a car stopped across the road and a woman came over. 'Are you all right?'

Kellie wound down her window. 'Yes, we aren't hurt. We're just recovering from fright. Thanks for stopping.'

'Can I do anything to help?'

'No, I'm just going to call someone to come and help us.'

The lady noticed Kellies red eyes. 'Would you like me to stay with you while you wait?'

'Yes, thank you, I would.' Kellie rummaged in her bag once more and found her phone. 'I'll ring Harry's dad and tell him what's happened.'

The lady stepped back, not wanting to intrude. Kellie found James' name and pushed the ring button. She had never phoned him at work before.

'Kellie, what is it? I'm with a patient.' He sounded extremely annoyed.

'J-James a stone has hit the car-windscreen, it shattered, and I don't know what to do,' she blubbered.

James excused himself and stepped outside his consulting room. 'Is Harry with you and is anyone hurt?'

'Harry and Charlie are in the back seat, nobody's hurt.'

'Good. Now tell me exactly where you are?' He sensed she'd had a big fright.

'We have just turned off the Nerang road heading home.'

'Are you parked off the road and not in the way of other traffic?'

'Yes, I've done that.'

'Stay where you are and I'll be with you in about thirty minutes.' He ended the call, apologised to his patient then carried on with the consultation. Luckily, that was his last appointment of the day and he left the surgery immediately the consult finished.

James found the car easily, parked safely on the grass verge as Kellie had told him. A strange lady hopped out of the front passenger seat as James walked over. Kellie opened her door and stepped out.

'I'm sorry I had to call you James, but I didn't know what else to do.' She turned to the lady who had stopped to help them.

'This is Donna Lambert, a good Samaritan who stopped to check we were all okay and offered to stay with us until you arrived.'

James stepped forward and held out his hand. 'James Harvey. I'm very pleased to meet you Donna. Thank you for coming to their aid.'

'Well, I know I'd be nervous waiting on the side of a busy road and it was a pleasure to meet you all. I'll be off now. Take good care of yourself, Kellie, and good luck with the baby. Maybe I'll see you around.

Goodbye Dr Harvey, it was nice to meet you.' With a wave to Harry, she got in her vehicle and drove off.

James turned to Kellie. She looked cold, but otherwise all right. 'Do you have her address?'

'Yes, Donna is a local hairdresser. She gave me her card.'

'Good, now tell me what happened.'

'A large truck passed us and a stone flew up. It happened in a flash.'

He opened the rear passenger door. 'How are you two rascals?' Harry grinned as he hung on to Charlie's collar. James turned back to Kellie. 'I think we'll put you all in my car and you can drive them home. I'll knock out this windscreen and follow you.'

The setting sun had turned the winter sky a gorgeous shade of pink as Kellie started the car and drove home.

Harry had the grizzles. He was tired and hungry, so she quickly bathed the small boy then cooked him a 'dippy egg' with fingers of toast. He fell asleep at the table just as James arrived home.

'I'll carry him to bed. Could you pull back his sheet?'

When the child was tucked in, they went back to the kitchen.

'You look a tad weary,' James commented kindly, 'so how about we have Chinese take-a-way for dinner?'

Kellie nearly died of shock, she must look pretty bad. 'Sounds good to me, but what about the car?'

'I'll call a local glass company shortly. They'll come out and install a new windscreen. Harry might have to miss kindergarten tomorrow.'

He looked in the local business directory then picked up the phone.

James finished his conversation and turned back to her. 'They'll be out here after lunch tomorrow. Can I get you anything before I go and pick up the food?'

'No thanks. I have a glass of water, that'll do me.'

When he left, she hopped up on the window-seat, and lay back on the cushions, then took her mobile phone out of her pocket and brought up Sam's number.

'Hi Kellie, this is a funny time of the day for you to call me.'

'I wish you could see this, I'm resting up on the window-seat and James has gone to get Chinese take-away.'

'Are you sick or something?'

'No, he thought I looked tired. I had a mishap in the car this afternoon, a stone flew through the windscreen, and he had to come and rescue us.'

'Are you feeling okay?'

'Yes, I'm fine, but it gave me a huge fright. A lovely lady stopped and sat with us until James came from the surgery.'

'Well, that was nice of her and I'm glad the doc's looking after you.'

'I nearly had a fit when he suggested Chinese.'

Her friend laughed. 'Maybe he wants to get his leg over.'

'I don't think so and you're a shocker. Hey Sam, are you doing anything at the weekend?'

'No why, are you coming to visit?'

'I'll let you know. I have to go now James has just arrived back. Bye love.'

Kellie put her phone down and set the table.

The meal was yummy and when she'd cleaned up her plate, Kellie thanked him.

'You're welcome. After such a fright I thought you needed to take it easy.' He pushed his chair back and stood up. 'Now this weekend, do you have any plans?'

'I was going to spend time with Sam. Why what's up?'

'Well, I'd like to take Harry to see his grandparents on Bribie Island and I'd rather not take Charlie with me, Mum's not over fond of pets.'

Kellie hesitated. 'Shall I ask Sam if she would like to come out and stay here with me?'

'She's always welcome. Can you ask her and let me know?'

'Sure.' Kellie picked up her phone and went into her bedroom to call her friend.

'That's a great idea,' Sam exclaimed. 'I might come out early Saturday morning then we can have a slap-up breakfast, how does that sound?'

Kellie smiled. 'Sounds great. Thanks, love. I'll see you then, bye.'

***

The next morning James went to work and sought out Moira. 'I'd like you to organise some flowers to be sent to this lady,' he gave her the card with Donna Lambert's name and address on. 'The message on the card is to read, "Thanks for your help," signed James Harvey, Harry, and Kellie. Thanks Moira, I'll explain later.'

Chapter Twenty-One

Betty sat on the side of her bed, agonising over her son. While dusting her old dressing table she had noticed the lock undone on her antique trinket box.

She lifted the lid. 'Oh no!' It was empty, her mother's fob chain and gold bracelet were missing. Suddenly it hit her. *Ross! Surely, he wouldn't take the only things my mother left me.* Tears rolled down her wrinkly cheeks as she realised he probably had done just that. She stayed there rocking to and fro, brooding over her troubled boy.

Since he'd returned from Sydney, he was a changed person. At thirty-six he should be working – own a home even. Ross hadn't registered with Centrelink and continually demanded money, sometimes taking all her pension.

'What will become of him?' she whispered, remembering the gentle young boy she raised and loved.

Later that day, his motorbike roared up to her front door. 'Are you there, Ma?' he called as he strutted in, a cigarette dangling from the corner of his mouth.

'In the kitchen.'

He waltzed in and hugged her. His clothes were filthy, and he stunk of smoke and stale sweat. 'Any coffee going?'

'You know I don't like you smoking inside.' She shook her head in disgust. He never listened to anything she said. 'I'll put the kettle on.'

He pulled out a chair and sat down.

Betty looked across at him. 'Ross, my mother's jewellery is missing, did you take it?'

His face turned scarlet and he smashed his fist down on the table. 'Straight away you away blame me,' he yelled.

'Well?'

He leaned back in the chair and dragged on his cigarette, the quiet room was loaded with tension. The only sound was the monotonous ticking of the kitchen clock.

The old lady wouldn't give up. 'Where are they Ross? You haven't sold them have you?'

His face took on a menacing expression, but she couldn't stop. 'I can't understand why you'd do such a thing, if you need money why don't you get a job or at least apply to Centrelink for...'

Roughly, he pushed back his chair and stood up, stabbing a finger at her face. 'What would you know about needing money, you stupid old cow. Yes, I took your bloody jewellery. You don't need it. You're stuck out here in this rotten place when you should be in an old people's home. Sell this house, do you hear me, sell the bloody thing. I shouldn't have to wait until you kark it before I get what's mine.'

Stung by his hurtful words she began to cry.

'And you can stop bloody sniveling. I can't stand bawling bloody females.'

'How could you.' Tears flooded her cheeks. Ross' hand snaked out and struck her violently across the face. Betty stumbled and lost her balance then fell heavily to the floor.

'I'm getting out of here,' he yelled, 'but I'll be back and I want this bloody place sold.' He stomped out of the house swearing and cursing.

Betty lay on the floor with tears trickling down the side of her face, her cheek smarting from his cruel blow. She couldn't believe what just happened. For years, she kept those trinkets, hoping one day to pass them on to Ross's wife.

'What am I going to do,' she sobbed, 'he's getting worse.'

She wiped her eyes with the sleeve of her old cardy and tried to get up. 'Ohh.' Her body hurt. Slowly she rolled over, got to her hands and knees, crawled to the table, and used the leg to pull herself up. Then the pain and disappointment became too much for her to bear and she howled out loud.

***

Friday afternoon, James and Harry left to spend the weekend with his parents. The next morning, Kellie made blueberry muffins and had just taken them out of the oven when she heard Sam's car come up the drive. Charlie barked letting her know someone was there. Kellie flicked the switch on the kettle and hurried out to greet her friend.

'Sam, it's so good to see you.'

'Hi, girlfriend.' Sam hugged her fondly. 'That baby bump's starting to grow and you have great boobs. Just look at them.'

'Yep, for the first time in my life I have great boobs,' declared Kellie. She showed her friend inside to the guest room.

'Pop your things in here and we'll have our breakfast.'

'Thanks.' Sam looked around the beautifully decorated bedroom. The drapes and carpet were a soft green and the bedcover and cushions a dusky pink and beige. A chair upholstered in the same pink had a fluffy beige throw folded over one arm. 'Last time I stayed in this room, I never wanted to go home.'

Kellie laughed. 'James told me in that 'poofy' voice of his, that you are "most welcome out here at any time", so when you need a break just book in.'

They had a great day and just before it got dark, they took Charlie for a walk.

Kellie hooked on his lead. 'Come on, Sam, we'll pop in and say hello to Betty.'

A few minutes later, she knocked on her neighbour's front door. There was no reply. They walked around the back. The old lady came towards them wearing an ancient floppy hat and carrying a rickety basket with a few vegies inside.

'Hi Betty,' the young pregnant women called out, 'I've brought Sam to see you. James has taken Harry to see his parents.'

Sam hugged Betty and kissed her cheek. She felt the older woman cringe slightly. 'Lovely to see you again, just look at your fantastic vegies. I don't know how you do it.'

'They keep me going.' The old lady bent down and patted Charlie. 'How are you mate?' The dog's tail wagged crazily. He thrived on attention.

Kellie waited; usually Betty invited them in for a few moments, but not this time.

'Oh well, we'd better get back and organise some dinner.' Kellie stepped forward and kissed her friend. She felt Betty pull back. 'Bye love,' the younger woman said, 'we'll pop in again shortly. Take care.'

Their goodbyes said they started to walk home. When they were well down the road, Kellie turned to Sam.

'Something's not right. I can't put my finger on it, but she's not her usual self.'

'I thought the same thing. I felt her cringe when I kissed her cheek. What's that all about?'

'The same thing happened when I hugged her. She pulled away. Sam what the hell's going on?' They discussed Betty all the way home, trying to fathom out what was wrong.

'I'll talk to James about this when he comes home and see what he thinks.'

The weekend flew. All too soon, it was Sunday afternoon and time for Sam to head home. Kellie waved and Charlie barked as Sam left. *She is such a terrific girlfriend, one in a million,* Kellie thought.

It was nearly seven o'clock when James and Harry arrived home. Charlie ran around in circles. He was so pleased to see them. The young boy was grumpy and tired. Kellie made him some toast and vegemite and after a quick wash, she popped him into bed and read him his favourite pirate story.

James unpacked his bag then came out to the kitchen. 'How did your weekend with Sam go?'

'Great, she loves it out here. How were your parents?'

'Looking old. It's a while since I'd seen them. I think we wore them out. They aren't used to small children. They're so old fashioned. It's like going back in time.'

'You're lucky to still have them.'

'I know. Could you make me something light, a sandwich or something and a coffee? I'll eat mine in the study. I have a heap of paperwork to get through before I leave in the morning.'

'Sure, I'm making one for myself so it's no bother.'

A while later she knocked on his door. There was a scraping sound as James stood up and came over to let her in.

'Thanks. These toasted sandwiches smell good.'

'They're savoury mince. Yesterday, I made pies for lunch and this was left over.' He took the tray from her and put it down on his desk.

Kellie lingered by the door. 'Can you spare a minute?' James sat down and started eating. The hot sandwich burnt his mouth and he quickly put it back on the plate.

'Fire away Kellie, what's up?'

'Well, Sam and I walked Charlie yesterday afternoon and thought we'd drop in to see Betty. She was down in the back garden getting vegies for her dinner. I called out and she came to meet us, but usually she invites us in and that never happened. When I hugged her, she sort of cringed and stepped back. The same thing happened when Sam kissed her cheek. I think she's somehow hurt. I couldn't see much of her face as it was getting dark and her old hat was pulled right down on one side. I'm quite worried about her.'

'I think you might have reason to worry. Has Ross been there?'

'He comes and goes. She doesn't tell me, but I hear his motorbike.'

James sipped his coffee. 'Leave it with me. I'll find an excuse to call in and check her out.'

'Thanks, that's a good idea. I'll leave you in peace to finish your sandwiches.'

'I don't trust that guy,' James said as he shook his head. 'He has a chip on his shoulder and at a guess I'd say he has a very short fuse.'

He was late getting away from work the next afternoon and Kellie was bathing Harry when he arrived home.

He put his head around the bathroom door. 'I'll take Charlie for a quick walk before dinner.' Harry roared like a bull, he wanted to go with his dad, but Kellie knew what James had in mind.

He knocked loudly on the old lady's front door. 'Are you there, Betty? She took a while to answer his knock but he wasn't going anywhere until he'd seen that she was all right.

'James, how nice to see you. Come in. Is everything okay?'

'Yes, thank you,' he said as he followed her into the kitchen. It was an old farmhouse type kitchen, with faded paintwork and an ancient coal range. It smelt of herbs and some sort of sweet-smelling spice. 'I came to tell you that I took young Harry up to see my mum and dad. We stayed the weekend with them.'

Betty plugged in the kettle. 'Have a seat. Kellie told me you were at Bribie Island visiting them. How were they?'

'Jolly good for their age. They found Harry a bit of a handful, but enjoyed seeing him.'

He pulled out two chairs then sat down, leaning an elbow on the table. In the centre was a huge bunch of gorgeous flowers.

'These are lovely. Is it your birthday?'

'No, Ross gave them to me. He knows how much I like carnations and they're beauties.'

They chatted a while over a pot of tea then James got to his feet. 'Well I won't hold you up as it's nearly dinner-time. Harry's in the bath, hopping mad as he missed out on a walk, but he was tired and a bit cranky.'

Betty took their empty cups back to the sink and James had a quick look around. Over on the sideboard several fifty dollar notes stuck out from under a picture frame. Where on earth would she get that amount of money from? Something smelt fishy.

'What's for dinner tonight, Betty' he asked casually. 'Usually you have something cooking away.'

'I'm just having scrambled eggs tonight with some toast.'

'That sounds good. I leave you to get on with it.' He kissed her gently on the cheek. 'Bye, I'll pop in again soon.'

'Bye bye James, and thanks for coming.' She turned away, trying to hide the tell-tale tears filling her eyes.

He did notice them and anger built up inside him against the person who had physically hurt this dear old lady.

Over dinner, he told Kellie about the flowers and the money.

'Where on earth would she get all that from?' she asked.

'I think Ross must have given it to her. She said he gave her the flowers, but why?'

'Because he's sorry, but what's he sorry about?'

'Your guess is as good as mine. I think he has hit her. We can't prove anything, but we'll keep an eye on the situation. I detest violence of any sort and violence against a defenseless old woman is unforgivable.'

Chapter Twenty-Two

The next day Kellie had a check-up with Dr Wilkinson at eleven-thirty. Moira gave her a late morning appointment again so they could have lunch together.

Dressed in white pants and a loose blue top with matching blue shoes, Kellie arrived at the surgery ten minutes early, accompanied by Harry. He wore a pair of trendy new jeans with a bright red shirt, his hair was slicked up, and he looked pretty cool.

The waiting room was full of people. Two of them looked as though they should be home in bed, a child coughed continually and a poor old guy sitting opposite Kellie had a bad twitch, his head flicked sideways every few seconds. She didn't like these sort of places and always felt she was about to catch some dreaded disease just from being there.

'Kellie' Dr Wilkinson called a few moments later as he picked up her file. Harry stayed with Moira as she followed the doctor to his consulting room.

He held the door open, 'Come on through, Kellie. You look well.'

'I feel great and the baby's fairly active, so hopefully all's well.'

'That's what I like to hear. Hop up on the bed and we'll have a listen.' He pressed around her tummy and checked the baby's heartbeat.

'Good, your baby's starting to put on weight.' He looked at her notes. 'Hmm, I see you are almost seven months. Now let's check your blood pressure.'

He took that then wrote something down. 'A little high, Kellie. I want you to rest whenever you can. Maybe you've been rushing around a bit much. Apart from that, you're doing well. I'll see you again in four weeks' time.'

'Thanks doctor, bye for now.'

He smiled as he held open the door and thought, *What a lovely young woman. I wonder what happened to the baby's dad. No one seems to know anything about him. Oh well, it's none of my business.*

Out at reception, Moira had organised the staff so she could have lunch with Kellie. Harry had gone off with James. He'd told Moira they'd be back by one o'clock.

'Come on Kellie… we're out of here.' They didn't go far, just to the coffee shop next door. The owner greeted them like long lost friends.

'How nice to see you again. Take a seat and I'll be right there.'

They chose a corner table and caught up on all the latest gossip. Kellie told her about Betty. Moira went white, she had heard of such things before and a chill shot up the back of her neck. She felt Kellie was in as much danger as Betty. *I'll be having a word with James about this,* she thought.

James walked in with Harry saying he had a patient waiting and Moira needed to get back to work. Both women got up to leave.

'I'll keep in touch, Moira.' Kellie hugged the older lady. 'It was lovely to see you and catch up on all the goss. Say hi to Don.'

'Take care of yourself, love. Bye, Harry.' More hugs, and the small boy giggled as he was smothered in Moira's kisses. Waving and smiling, they went their separate ways.

Later in the afternoon, Kellie went to check the mailbox and found a handful of mail for James. One had the Social Services logo in one corner. *I wonder what they want now,* she thought.

When James came home later in the day, Kellie made him a coffee and handed him his mail. He said thanks and took his drink and the post to his study. During dinner, he didn't have much to say. He didn't even ask her how her check-up went.

Oh, well, thought Kellie, *he's obviously got something on his mind.*

***

The next couple of days passed uneventfully, except for the cards she received in the mail. Saturday the twenty-fourth was her birthday. She would turn twenty-nine. Her friends couldn't join her this weekend. They all had other things happening, but the following weekend, Sam had organised a birthday dinner with a few special people.

Saturday morning the local florist delivered a lovely arrangement of mixed roses. Kellie looked at the attached card. "Happy Birthday, girlfriend, heaps of love from Shirley, Sam, and Mary". Luckily, the florist came when James had taken Harry into Canungra. He didn't know it was her birthday and she didn't tell him. Quickly, she pulled off the card and put it in her room, then stood the flower arrangement on the buffet where it looked great and smelt lovely.

The two guys returned with dog food and a few other things, then Harry noticed the flowers and pointed them out to his dad.

'Wow, what lovely roses, Kellie. Are they from a secret-admirer?' James queried.

'No, they're from some friends of mine.' *Not that it's any of your business,* she thought. No more was said, and after lunch when her time off started, Kellie drove into Nerang. She looked around and picked out some new movies then sat in a coffee shop feeling incredibly lonely. Her thoughts turned to her mum and dad. She missed them so much her insides ached and her eyes watered.

She took her time driving back home, it was cold, and the sky was dark with heavy rain clouds.

Back in her bedroom, she turned on the heater then chose a movie to watch while she had a rest. To help keep her misery at a manageable level, she opened a bag of chocolate honeycomb squares.

There was a great deal of noise coming from the kitchen as James organised dinner for himself and Harry. She could smell something burning. *I wonder what's happening out there* she thought, then went back to her movie. *It's not my worry. I just hope he cleans up when he's finished.*

Later, she made herself cheese on toast and carried it outside to the table on the covered verandah. Next to where she was sitting, large pots of flowering gardenias filled the night air with their delicate sweet perfume and the feeling of deep sadness came over her again.

'It's my birthday and look at me,' she whimpered. 'Seven months pregnant, no husband, nothing at all to show that I've been on this earth for twenty-nine years.' A few tears spilled over onto her cheeks as she gave into her misery. 'I own nothing. I'm not trained to do anything, and here I am bringing a child into this world. What would my parents think of what I've done with my life?' More tears followed. A mental picture of her mum and dad came before her and she was overwhelmed by grief and home-sickness. The huge gap they left in her life was more than she could presently cope with. Kellie dropped her head down onto her hands and cried as though her heart was breaking.

She didn't hear the screen door open as James and the dog came outside.

The doctor wondered where the mournful sound was coming from and then he saw Kellie. He went over and gently put a hand on her shoulder. 'What on earth is the matter?'

'G-go away.'

'No, I won't go away. Please tell me what's wrong. Are you feeling unwell?'

Kellie gulped and sniffed. 'No,' she shook her head, 'I haven't got any tissues.'

'Where are they? I'll get them for you?'

'By my b-bed.'

James opened Kellie's bedroom door and saw the tissues on her bedside table. As he grabbed the box, his attention was drawn to the table on the other side of her bed where three birthday cards stood. Suddenly it came to him, 'It's her birthday!'

He went back out to the verandah. 'Kellie, is today your birthday?'

She nodded and pulled a handful of tissues from the box to wipe her face.

'Why didn't you tell us? We could have organised something special.'

Kellie shook her head. 'No, it's n-not that important.'

'Where are those girlfriends of yours?'

'They all h-had something else on. We are meeting next Saturday night for a birthday dinner.'

'Come inside where it's warmer and I'll make some hot chocolate, come on.' She stood up knowing she must look an absolute mess.

'You go and freshen up while I make the drinks.'

Kellie went into her bathroom and looked in the mirror. Her mascara was smudged, her eyes were swollen, and her cheeks were red and blotchy. Feeling terribly embarrassed, she washed her face and brushed her hair. Bracing herself, she walked into the kitchen where James had steaming mugs of hot chocolate waiting on the table.

'Come and sit down.' He pulled out a chair for her. 'Now tell me, what's so terrible that you would sit in the cold by yourself and be so upset on your birthday.'

Kellie had to swallow a couple of times before she could reply. The kitchen still smelt of whatever he had burnt at dinner time. Charlie rubbed his head against her leg in an attempt to comfort her. Dogs always knew when you were unhappy.

'I f-felt homesick and I miss my mum and d-dad very much. They wouldn't be happy with the situation I've got myself into...' Tears threatened again but she swallowed and tried hard not to let them escape and make a right fool of herself.

'How do you feel about your situation?'

By now, her nose was running and she had to grab more tissues. 'I feel as though I'm doing nothing with my life and I'm giving birth to a child that I'm not sure I can support and give the sort of life all kids deserve.'

'Was there something you would like to be doing?'

She took a sip of her drink. 'Yes, I would really like to work with special needs children.'

'You can still do that. Why don't you inquire at the local university and do the course from home. I'd be happy for you to study in your spare time. And now Harry goes to kindy, you'd have more opportunity to do so.'

'I'll have the baby to look after on top of what I do now.'

'Give it some thought. You'll find time and you'd be very good with those children.' They chatted as they finished their drinks then James picked up the empty mugs and carried them to the sink.

'Do you feel better now?'

Kellie blushed. 'Yes, thank you. I'm sorry to burden you with all that.' The grandfather clock struck ten and the noise echoed around the quiet kitchen. He noticed her blush and thought what a kind sensitive young woman she was. Since losing her parents, life obviously had not been easy.

'You aren't a burden Kellie. You've been a great help out here and I understand how much you miss your mum and dad. They must have been wonderful people.'

She nodded and stood up. 'Yes, they w-were.' She swallowed again. 'Goodnight James, thank you for listening and for the hot chocolate.'

He grinned. 'I hope it helped. Goodnight.' As he rinsed the mugs, he was deep in thought. He had problems of his own.

Sunday morning, Kellie woke early and saw shafts of daylight peeping through a gap in the curtains. She wasn't in the mood to lay in bed so she dressed and headed for the beach at Burleigh Heads to go for an early morning walk.

***

The countryside was just waking up as she drove through the deserted roads. Bright golden rays indicated that the sun was about to burst over the horizon and flocks of brightly coloured birds ducked and dived through the clear blue sky.

After parking her car, she tightened the laces on her sneakers then made her way down to the beach. Many people had the same idea as she did – some jogged, fishermen stood in the water holding tight to long bent rods and kids and dogs ran free. Surfers struggled to find a decent wave and a few brave souls were enjoying a swim.

'Rather them than me,' she muttered. Walking past beach-side restaurants, Kellie watched families arriving to have breakfast and felt envious that she didn't have a family to be part of. She walked on looking for comfort and peace as she breathed in the salty sea air.

A couple of hours later she returned home to an empty garage. There was a note on the kitchen bench. "Kellie, have your best outfit on by twelve o'clock. We have a surprise outing. James and Harry."

What's all that about, she thought? *Oh well, I'll be ready.*

She came out of her bedroom ten minutes early to see James brushing Harry's hair as the child sat quietly by the kitchen table. Both were dressed in their good clothes. Harry's face lit up with a huge smile.

James looked Kellie up and down. She wore a turquoise, long sleeved maternity top over black trousers, and had tied her hair back with a turquoise scarf. A bunch of silver bracelets on one wrist matched the fancy silver hoops hanging from her ears.

'You look very nice,' he said, 'I'll just take Charlie out to the toilet and then we'll be off.' Harry couldn't wait, he ran out to the station wagon. Kellie followed to help him do up the strap on his car-seat.

James came around and held open the front passenger door. 'Hop in.'

She did and felt self-conscious about being in such close proximity to him. He put on a disc, *The Wiggles singing travelling songs,* and Harry clapped his hands along with the music. He had been doing a bit of that since he started kindergarten.

Kellie didn't know where they were going and James didn't tell her. Forty minutes later, they pulled up outside one of the beachside restaurants she had walked past earlier in the day.

She looked at James with a grin. 'Here… we are lunching here?'

'Yes, is that all right with you?'

Smiling, she nodded and unclipped her seat belt. James helped Harry get down from the car and held his hand as they crossed the busy road. Kellie grabbed Harry's other hand and felt a warm fuzzy feeling as though she too had a family.

Wonderful food smells greeted them as they entered a plant filled foyer. James gave his name and they followed a smartly dressed waiter to a table by the window where Moira and Don sat waiting.

'Happy birthday, Kellie,' Moira called and came over to give her a big hug.

Don stood up and kissed her cheek. 'Happy birthday, love. Isn't this a great place for a birthday lunch? I love looking out over the beach.'

Kellie beamed. 'How nice to see you both. This is such a surprise. James didn't tell me where we were going and this place looks fabulous.'

They all sat down and James ordered drinks. 'This is my shout today folks, so enjoy yourselves and order whatever you like.'

Kellie felt very special. They were enjoying a second cup of coffee after their meal when a voice interrupted.

'James, how lovely to see you,' drawled Ruth Simonds as she kissed his cheek. Kellie couldn't believe her eyes, the cow from the hospital. Fancy her turning up here of all places and on the same day.

'Hello, Ruth.' James stood up and smiled. 'How are you?'

'I'm great. Just had lunch with some friends. The food's great here isn't it?'

'Very nice. You know Kellie and Harry and this is Moira and her husband Don, they're good friends of mine.'

'Hello,' she looked down her nose at them all. 'We have met before James, at your home after your accident. Oh well, I'd better get back to my table.' She kissed James again then purred, 'I'll give you a call sometime.'

'Sure, nice to see you.'

With a wave, Ruth left and returned to her table. Moira caught Kellie's eye and gave her a wink.

'Well,' James announced, 'If you've all finished I think we'll head off home. Thank you both for joining us. I'm sure you've helped make Kellie's birthday quite special.'

'Thanks, James for asking us. Kellie, love, we hope you've enjoyed yourself.'

There were hugs all round before they left the restaurant and headed to their cars.

When they arrived home, Kellie thanked James for her birthday treat.

'It was my pleasure, Kellie,' his poofy tone of voice indicated that things were back to normal. She went to her room and closed the door then picked up her mobile phone and rang Sam for a girly-chat.

After a short rest, she decided to visit Betty. Outside, dark clouds were gathering and a strong wind had risen.

The old lady was pottering around in her garden.

'Hi neighbour, how are you doing?'

Betty looked up and when she saw who it was a huge smile lit up her wrinkled face.

'Hello Kellie, how nice to see you. I'm nearly finished here, have you got time for a cuppa?'

'I'm hanging out for one. Shall I go and put the kettle on?'

'Good idea. I'll be right there.'

Kellie let herself into the kitchen. A fruit slice sat cooling on a wire rack and her mouth watered at the thought of wolfing down a piece or two. She filled the kettle, and plugged it in, just as Betty came through the screen door. She put a few vegies down on the bench.

'You get the cups out and cut us a piece of slice while I go and give my hands a scrub.'

They chatted away while enjoying their afternoon tea. The roar of a motorbike interrupted their conversation.

'It sounds like R-ross,' Betty stammered, 'I wonder what he wants this time.'

Alarm bells sounded in Kellie's head. *What's going on here,* she wondered *why's Betty so agitated?*

'You there, Ma?'

'I'm in the kitchen.' Betty stood up and gripped the side of the table as Ross charged into the room.

He yanked open the drawer where his mother kept her wallet. 'I need money.'

Betty's face reddened. 'I'm sorry son. I haven't got any cash at the moment.'

'What do ya mean no cash? You get the bloody pension, where is it?' He looked in her empty wallet then threw it across the room. 'Ya frigging useless old cow,' he yelled, 'I need money, I need it now!'

Outraged he swung around to Kellie. 'What about you?'

She had just noticed the word 'Revenge' tattooed on his neck, between that and his shouting she was almost speechless with fear. 'I c-can't help you.'

'Useless bloody shelias,' Ross ranted, 'Only good for one thing and you've had plenty of that haven't you, living with the doc,' angrily he stabbed a finger right at her belly. 'Telling us you're the housekeeper when he's screwing the bloody pants off ya.'

'Stop it, Ross,' his mother cried, 'I won't have you speaking to Kellie like that.'

'I'll say what the hell I like. She wouldn't come out with me. No, I wasn't good enough was I?' Bang! He thumped the table with his fist as he eyeballed Kellie. 'But you let that friggin quack in your knickers fast enough. Bloody whore!'

Kellie was so frightened she started to shake. 'You've g-got it all wrong.'

Betty stepped forward to shield her pregnant young friend. 'Ross please leave. I want you to go now.'

'Shut it you stupid old woman. Shut your fuckin mouth or I'll shut it for you.'

Crash! Over went a chair and he violently struck the wall beside his mum's head leaving an unsightly hole in the plaster board. 'Hurry up and die you old hag then I'll get what's mine.' As he spoke, he gave his mother a look of pure evil then spat in her face. 'You get plenty of money from the government, but you won't give me a bloody cent will you, and I'm your only child. You old bitch.' He kicked her chair then stomped out and slammed the front door.

The ancient alarm clock on the kitchen windowsill ticked loudly in the silent room as Betty wept into her crumpled apron. Kellie, still reeling from Ross's outburst, had to clutch the table for support as she got up and put her arms around the traumatised old lady.

'Hush,' Kellie murmured. 'It's all right now, he's gone. Sit down and I'll make us another cuppa.'

'I'm s-sorry, love, for the things he said,' she sobbed, 'He's not a bad boy it's just that his f-father spoilt him. He gave into him all the time and now he's angry because he can't get work.'

'What did he do before he came here?'

'I don't know. He hasn't told me. He gets angry when I ask him anything about the last few years.'

'Never mind. Drink up your tea and remember we are just down the road. If ever you need help or even if you're just frightened, ring us and we'll come over.'

'I'll be all right. I'm just being silly.'

'No, you're not. Now let's have another piece of your fruit slice before I go home.'

Chapter Twenty-Three

James wasn't his usual self. Something was bothering him. Each night he came home from work, walked the dog, and then shut himself away in the study. During dinner, he hardly said a word. He bathed Harry then went back to his office and stayed there. Kellie didn't know what was bugging him, but he obviously had something on his mind.

Tuesday morning, when she took Harry to kindy, his little mate Isaac and his mum Helen came over and she handed them an envelope. Isaac was jumping up and down with excitement.

'This is an invitation for Harry. I wondered if he would like to come to Isaac's birthday party. Only four other children are coming. It's at our home this Friday afternoon.'

'Thank you very much. Can I get back to you?' Kellie wasn't telling her she would have to check with James.

'Sure, our phone number and address is on the invite. We live the other side of the Canungra hospital.'

'Thanks, I'll be in touch.' Kellie smiled at the friendly young mum and then followed Harry as the boys ran outside to play with their friends.

When James came home, she made him a coffee and told him of the invitation. He looked at the card.

'Mmm yes, he might enjoy a birthday party. Can you get a gift for the child? A nice book, perhaps?'

'Sure, that would be a good present. Harry will have a great time as he knows all the other kids.'

James put the invite down, 'I'll be in the study.' He picked up his coffee and left.

What on earths the matter with him, Kellie thought, *something's really got up his nose.*

James certainly had something on his mind. Wednesday morning at the surgery, he sought Moira out. 'Can you meet me for lunch today? There's something I need to run past you.'

Moira looked at him. 'Judging by the bags under your eyes, it must be something important.'

'You could say that. How about I meet you next door about twelve-thirty?'

She had sandwiches in her bag, but he looked a mess, something was obviously wrong.

'Okay,' she replied then returned to her work.

***

She hurried into the coffee shop. She'd been held up and was five minutes late. James waved out from a corner table.

'Have you ordered?'

'Yes,' he replied, 'I asked for two lots of Turkish bread with melted cheese and steaming hot coffees. Is that all right?' She nodded in agreement. The tables around them were empty and a lovely cheesy-garlic smell wafted over from the kitchen.

'Well, what's up?' she asked as she plonked herself down.

James reached inside his suit jacket, produced an envelope, and pulled out a letter.

'This is from Child Services, telling me that they want a meeting with Ms. Kellie Lund, the housekeeper-carer of Harry Harvey.'

Moira looked vague. 'Why do they want to meet with her?'

James frowned. 'They say that the last time a case-worker visited the home of Harry Harvey she noted the housekeeper-carer of the boy was obviously pregnant. They request a meeting with her regarding her plans when the child is born and how this will affect his future.' Scowling, he laid the letter down as their lunch arrived.

He managed to eat and explain at the same time. 'The case-worker who comes out to our house isn't the easiest person to get on with. She rubs Kellie up the wrong way every time. Last time she rudely stared at Kellie's stomach and you know how she wears those tight maternity tops, well...'

'James,' Moira interrupted him, 'that's the fashion now. There's nothing wrong with what she wears.'

'I know that, but the case-worker came out of the ark. Kellie was pregnant before she came to me and now Child Services wants to have this meeting with her. They'll be asking all sorts of questions. I can read between the lines, they want to know if I'm the father of her baby.'

'Oh James, that's going a bit far.'

'No, it's not. This letter requests a separate meeting with me after they have spoken to the housekeeper-carer. I have a bad feeling about this. I haven't been able to sleep properly worrying about it.'

'I don't see that they can do anything.'

'Only take Harry away if he isn't being looked after in a safe and healthy environment.'

'They won't do that James. You're getting carried away.'

He went over to the counter and ordered another coffee then returned and sat down. 'I can only see one solution to all of this,' he told her.

'What... throw that stupid letter away?'

'Moira,' he looked nervous and suddenly sat up very straight in his chair. 'I'm seriously considering asking Kellie to marry me.'

'You're w-what!' Moira cried then choked on a mouthful of coffee. After coughing and spluttering a couple of times she got her breath back. 'Are you serious?'

'Very, I've given the idea a great deal of thought. It will get the department off my back, Harry gets a suitable stepmother, and Kellie is guaranteed security for herself and the child.'

'James! You don't get married just for security – what about love?' You have to live with each other for the rest of your lives. Marriage is hard enough when you love each other. I can't believe you're saying all this. You're usually so sensible.'

'Sensible won't get Harry a mother and I've had enough of love to know it only brings pain and heartache. This marriage will be in name only – a business arrangement.'

'Oh dear God, James, what makes you think Kellie will agree to marry you on those terms. She'll probably pack up and run. I know I would.' Moira dropped her head onto her hands. 'I feel a headache coming on and its time I went back to work.' She pushed her coffee away and stood up shaking her head. 'I can't go along with you on this one, James. And I don't think marriage is the answer to your problems.'

James continued to sit there long after she had left. *What on earth am I going to do?*

A loud crash from the kitchen brought him back to earth and he rushed through the swing doors.

'Anyone hurt?' He called out as he poked his head around the corner.

The harassed owner came over. 'It's okay doc, just a few broken dishes that needed replacing any way.'

'All right, thanks for the lunch. I'll get back to the surgery.' Grim-faced he made his way back to work.

***

Betty was pruning roses, and it was almost time to call it a day, when she heard a distant rumble. She thought it was thunder but then decided to walk around the side of the house to investigate. The noise became louder and to her horror, she saw a group of leather-clad bike riders' rumble up the driveway towards her. They stopped and she stood there petrified. The front rider removed his helmet then got off his bike and walked over to where she stood.

'Where is he?'

'Who w-were you looking for?'

'That scum, Ross, He's here isn't he?'

Betty shook so much she had trouble getting her words out. This rude person smelt terrible and she was very frightened.

He took a step closer. 'Where is he, bitch. You betta tell me?'

'I d-don't know where he is. He comes and goes. He h-hasn't been here all week.'

'You'd betta not be stuffing us around. You wouldn't like how we deal with fuckin, dumb bitches like you.'

Betty felt warm liquid running down the inside of her legs and started to cry. 'I- I truly don't know where he is or when he'll be-b-back.'

A loud voice called out. 'Leave the stupid, dumb bitch alone, she knows fuck all.' He started his bike and revved it up.

The guy confronting Betty snorted and kicked a stone in her direction. 'When you see him bitch, tell him Pusface wants his fuckin money. He's got to the end of the month.' Then he ran his finger across his throat indicating what would happen if Ross didn't pay up.

He strutted over to his bike, flung his helmet on, and roared off, followed by his mates.

Betty sank to the ground sobbing, she had never been so afraid in all her whole life. 'Ross, Ross,' she cried, 'what on earth have you done?'

She got up and went inside, locked the doors and pulled down the blinds. *How much does he owe?* She wondered. She didn't have to wait very long to find out.

Later that night, she had just put her nightie and dressing gown on when she heard his bike rumble up the drive. Still shaking from her earlier encounter, she didn't know how she would cope with a visit from her troubled son.

He banged on the front door. 'Ma, open this bloody door.'

Betty turned the key in the deadlock and he pushed the door open, looking more rugged and unwashed than ever.

'You took your bloody time. What where you doing, knitting?' he jeered.

Betty walked through to the kitchen and sank down on a chair by the table, trying to find the words to ask about the money he owed. She had to know. 'Who's Pusface?'

Ross started to fidget and looked uneasy. 'What the fuck do you know about him?'

In a shaking voice, she replied. 'A g-group of bikie-guys came here today,' she said then started to cry. 'It w-was awful Ross, I was so frightened. That guy said you owed him money. How much m-money do you owe?'

He banged his fist on the table and Betty jumped in fright. 'They had no bloody right coming here. The mongrels must have had me followed. You can't trust that fuckin Pusface. What did you tell those bastards?'

'Nothing, I said I didn't know where you were.' She reached in her dressing gown pocket for her hankie to dry her eyes. 'What's going on, tell me how much you owe and what's it for?'

'Ten bloody grand,' he spat out, 'Now you fuckin know, what are ya going to do about it?'

Betty dropped her head in her hands. 'You owe that man ten thousand dollars. What on earth for?'

Ross jumped up and belted her across the face, knocking her off the chair 'That's none of your bloody business. I owe it okay,' he yelled. 'What else did the fuckin mongrel say?'

'Oh-h Ross!' She landed with a jolt on her behind and leaned back against the chair, covering her sore face with both hands. 'Y-you only have until the end of the month,' she whimpered, 'and t-then he indicated they would cut your t-throat.' She struggled with those words.

'You have to fuckin help me – sell something. You're my bloody mother – it's your job to help me.'

'I d-don't have any money Ross and you've taken all my jewellery.'

Angrily, he picked up a chair and threw it at her, missing her head by a whisker.

Betty put her arms up to protect herself. 'Stop it Ross, oh p-please stop.'

Plasterboard cracked and splintered as he punched the wall leaving another hole. Then the front door slammed and she heard his motorbike roar off into the night.

Later, much later she managed to get herself off the floor. Clutching the walls, she made it to her room and fell on the bed. Her head and back hurt, but worse than that was the pain of her breaking heart.

***

Kellie had no idea what had happened up the road. After lunch, James called to say he would be late home, so when Harry woke from his nap they went to Nerang shopping for a book to give Isaac for his birthday.

First, they visited the local library. They did this once a week. She always let Harry choose two or three books and then she would find a special pirate story to read to him while they were there. He loved sitting at one of the little tables with his chin propped up on his hands as he listened.

After they left the library, they found the ice-cream shop, bought yummy, strawberry ice-cream sundaes, and sat outside to enjoy them. In the local bookshop, Kellie came across a beautifully illustrated book of Australian bush poems for children, ideal for Isaac's birthday gift. She let Harry help choose a birthday card then they headed back to the car.

Dusk was approaching as she drove home. The sky was streaked with red and gold – such a spectacular time of the day. A group of leather-clad bikies rode towards her and the thought crossed her mind, *I wonder where they've been,* as they roared past. She often noticed huge groups of them gathered outside the Canungra hotel when she drove Harry home from kindergarten.

Chapter Twenty-Four

Friday arrived and they went to Isaac's party. Harry clung to Kellie's hand as some of the adults were strangers to him, but he knew all the children there.

'This is the first birthday party he's ever been to,' Kellie explained to a lady watching Harry as he nervously clutched his gift, not yet ready to give it to the birthday boy.

'That's unusual in this day and age,' she remarked unkindly and walked away. Kellie felt out of place, as she didn't know any of the mothers well enough to go and chat with them. A few kept glancing at her tummy. She could almost read their minds as they turned away.

Isaac's mum came over. 'Hi, Kellie. Harry, we are so pleased you could come to the party.' She noticed how tightly he clutched his gift so she held her hand out to the small boy. 'Come with me and we'll find Isaac, then you can give him your present.' Harry went with her, handed over the parcel to the birthday boy, and then raced back to Kellie.

An older lady noticed her being ignored by the other mums so she came over and sat in the next chair. 'Hello, I'm Isaac's grandmother. Is that shy boy your son?'

'No, he's not. Harry hasn't been to a party before.'

'Kids don't judge like adults do, give him ten minutes and he'll be racing around like all these other rascals.'

Her presence helped Kellie relax and feel part of the celebrations. Harry joined in the games, ate plenty of sticky party food, and then spilled red cordial down his good clothes. Kellie didn't care – she just wanted the child to enjoy himself. He did. He joined the other kids as they played games and had races. He even won a prize and gave it to Kellie to hold.

A little later, while she was in the loo, she overheard two women chatting in the bathroom next door.

'Doesn't she live with that doctor just out of town?'

A different voice replied. 'I heard she's his housekeeper.' Kellie heard them snigger.'

The first voice added, 'Housekeeper's right. He obviously has fringe benefits.' They giggled and Kellie's face burnt with embarrassment, as she stayed hidden in the toilet.

The other voice replied, 'Do you think the baby's his?'

'Could be, you know as much as I do. Poor little Harry, I hear he doesn't even talk. With his dad being a doctor you'd think they'd be on to that, wouldn't you?'

'I think she looks a bit uppity. Living as she does, I don't think she's got much to be uppity about, that's for sure.'

'I agree. Women like her should stick to their own sort. Let's go and check on our boys, at least they come from respectable homes.'

Kellie heard the bathroom door open then close and she leaned against the toilet door unable to move. 'Is that what people really think?' she whispered and took a deep breath. 'I don't know if I can face the people out there. Oh dear God, I can't believe this is happening.'

Slowly, she came out of hiding, washed her hands, and splashed cold water on her smarting cheeks. Fighting back tears, she took another deep breath, straightened her shoulders, and went to find Harry.

He threw a terrible wobbly when she said they were going home. He was overtired and not at all ready to leave the party. Kellie was beyond caring who saw her and carried him yelling and screaming to the car.

When James arrived home, he noticed she had been crying, but said nothing. Harry didn't eat any dinner and his eyelids kept closing.

'I think it's early to bed for you, young man.' James lifted the tired boy from his chair. When the boy had settled, he went back to the kitchen and interrupted Kellie who was nosily cleaning out the pot cupboard.

'If you're making coffee, I'll have one, and bring yours in the lounge-room. I'd like a word with you.'

Kellie sniffed. Burning tears threatened to spill over once more. 'Sure, give me a few minutes. *What's all this about*,' she wondered and shut the cupboard door with a bang. *'I've had enough for one day.'*

James stood up as she carried the two hot mugs into the room.

He rescued his from her shaking hands. 'Have a seat.' She sat across from him and glanced at the news on TV for a few minutes. When the weather came on James picked up the remote and turned the volume down.

'Kellie, tell me what happened today that upset you so badly? Are you not feeling well?'

Trying not to blubber in front of him and make a complete fool of herself, she focused on a moth flying round and round the centre light.

James waited. He wanted to help. 'I know you're worried about your future, is that what's upsetting you?'

The grandfather clock ticked loudly in the pregnant silence. A whole minute passed. Suddenly it all became too much for Kellie and she covered her face with both hands and the floodgates opened. James grabbed a nearby box of tissues and handed her a fistful.

'Come over here and sit by me, I need to know what's wrong.'

She gulped and dabbed at her eyes then moved to the couch. Taking her time, she swallowed then repeated what she overheard the two women say at the party.

'Good grief, what a couple of nasty small-minded people – that's terrible!' He put his arm across her shaking shoulders. 'I'm sorry you had to listen to such rubbish Kellie, but please stop crying, you'll do yourself harm.'

It took a while for her to calm down. In her misery, she had leaned into his shoulder. It felt warm and sort of safe.

He slowly pulled away and stood up. 'I think a light sedative and a good night's sleep is what you need now and we'll talk tomorrow.'

Kellie hiccupped and lay back against the cushions, embarrassed at her lack of control.

He returned with a tablet and a glass of water. 'Take this, it's very mild and won't harm the baby, then I want you to hop into bed.'

Weary and confused, she swallowed the pill, then heaved herself up and went to her room.

James poured a large brandy and sat down, deep in thought. He couldn't believe the nastiness of those women. 'I wish I'd been close by, I would have given them an earful they wouldn't forget in a hurry,' he mumbled, 'Admittedly, the fact poor Kellie is pregnant with raging hormones doesn't help, but those women were simply malicious.'

He waited awhile then tiptoed into her room to that check she was all right. A curtain fluttered at an open side window and her room smelt of some perfumed soap she'd used in the shower. Kellie lay on her side fast asleep with one hand tucked under her cheek clutching a crumpled tissue.

James stood there a moment then quietly left the room. Back in the lounge, the grandfather clock struck eleven as he poured another drink and sat staring into space.

***

The next morning being Saturday, Kellie was off to stay with Sam once lunch was over. Mid-morning James came into the kitchen where she was busy ironing

'Care for a coffee?' he asked.

'Thanks, I could do with one.'

He made the hot drinks then carried them over to the table. 'Come and sit down for a minute.'

She hooked the iron on the safety stand and did as he asked.

After seeing Kellie seated, the doctor sat down and folded his arms, then nervously cleared his throat. 'I've given a great deal of thought to what happened yesterday at the party as I have much the same problem with child services. They're hinting I'm the father of your child and are questioning whether this is the right environment for Harry to reside in.'

Ham and pea soup bubbled away gently on the stove top. Feeling something unpleasant was about to unfold, Kellie went over and gave it a stir. 'What do you mean? I don't get where this is leading.'

'Um,' he hesitated. 'I'm not really sure where to start.' She sat back down and he continued. 'I have a proposition to put to you that will benefit us both. Please don't make your decision hastily as there is a great deal at stake.'

The young woman felt like a mouse caught in a trap. *What's going on here?* She pondered as she picked up weird vibes.

James sipped his coffee, his hand shook slightly as he put the mug back down on the table. 'How would you feel ... if we were to get married?'

Kellie had just taken a sip of her coffee. She coughed and sputtered then choked. James jumped up and patted her back until her breathing returned to normal.

'I'm sorry, I didn't realise my proposal would give you such a shock.'

Kellie still couldn't speak her throat was dry and sore, causing her eyes to run.

'I'll fetch some water.' He quickly filled a glass and brought it over.

'Oh my God.' Kellie put her hands over her eyes trying to shut out this moment in time.

'Here have a few sips, it will help.' James held the glass up to her lips.

She caught a whiff of his after shave as she gingerly sipped the water. A fresh cologne fragrance that sent her already racing heart into overdrive. *Why*, she thought, *why does he affect me like this?*

'I've had enough, thanks,' she whispered and pushed his hand away.

He returned to his chair, the air electric with unspoken thoughts. In the next room, the grandfather clock struck the half-hour and James waited for its melodious chimes to settle.

'Do you think you could give my proposal some consideration?' He asked, feeling somewhat mortified by her reaction. 'I'm willing to bring your child up as my own and I know you are particularly fond of Harry.'

Kellie looked down and brushed a couple of dog hairs off her tights thinking, *Is this for real, or am I dreaming?*

He took another sip of his coffee. 'I forgot to mention, this would be a marriage in name only. Our sleeping arrangements would stay the same as they are now.'

Bloody hell, thought Kellie, *What makes him think I'd even contemplate hopping in bed with him?* She didn't say a word.

'Let me point out,' he continued in his poofy voice, 'that I would expect you to act in a way that didn't bring shame or embarrassment to me or my name.'

Completely lost for words, Kellie jumped up and stalked into the dining room. James waited a few moments then followed.

The tense atmosphere stressed her out. 'I don't k-know what to say,' she stuttered and pulled out a chair then sat down dropping her head onto to hands.

'Please don't say anything at the moment. I realise this has come as a shock, but will you at least think about it?' She nodded.

'Thank you.' He walked away. The child inside her tummy did a flip and Kellie felt a little foot kick against her ribs, as though it knew something with far-reaching consequences had just taken place.

She heard James call Harry and the dog then his station wagon backed out of the garage. She went and lay on her bed, staring at the ceiling, her mind blank. She took several deep breaths then picked up her mobile and called Sam.

'Hi Kellie what's up, are you still coming in for the weekend?'

'You will never believe what's just happened.'

'What do you mean?'

'You had better sit down. This can't wait until this afternoon. I can hardly believe what has just taken place.'

'Oh my God, Kellie, if you don't bloody hurry up and tell me what this is about I'm coming out there to shake it out of you.'

'James asked me to marry him.'

'He what?' screamed Sam.

'You heard me. He said he's willing to bring up my child as his own and I'll be Harry's stepmother. It's a business arrangement and I'll be financially secure.'

'Oh my Lord, what did you say?'

'Nothing, I choked.'

'Good grief, has the man lost it or what?'

'He was serious; he said not to answer just now but to give it a great deal of thought.'

'Oh Kellie, don't make any hasty decisions. Get in here as soon as you can and we'll discuss it, but oh dear, I'm almost speechless – which is bloody unusual as you well know.'

'Sam, oh Sam, what am I going to do? Maybe he's having male menopause or something. Men,' she sighed, 'they're so difficult to understand.'

'And even harder to live with,' Sam added. 'I don't know what to say. We'll chat more when you get here, meanwhile don't worry. I'm sure you'll manage in the future, with or without a bloody man.'

'Thanks, girlfriend. I'll see you this afternoon, okay?'

'I'll be waiting, drive carefully.' Kellie finished the call and packed her bag, ready to get away when she'd served and cleaned up from lunch.

***

Kellie struck trouble on the road as she drove into Broadbeach, a three car pile-up caused massive delays. In her frustrated state, she struggled to cope. The baby didn't help – it twisted and kicked nonstop. There wasn't much room between Kellie's tummy and the steering wheel and she felt irritable and uncomfortable. The afternoon was almost over by the time she reached at Sam's unit.

Her friend breathed a sigh of relief when Kellie arrived as she had become anxious. 'What took you so long? Come in and I'll put the kettle on.'

'I've had the most awful trip and I'm badly in need of a drink!'

'You're in one piece love, that's the main thing.' Then Sam gave her friend the once over. 'Wow! Just look at you girlfriend, you've popped out since I saw you last and your boobs are enormous.'

'Yep,' sighed the frazzled pregnant girl. 'These are the best boobs I'm ever likely to have, there's even a few stretch marks appearing. I'm not really happy about that.'

'Have you dropped yet, or whatever it is that pregnant bellies do?'

'No, I haven't 'dropped' as you call it,' Kellie informed her friend. 'That happens towards the end, or I think it does.'

They drank the teapot dry and cleaned up a plate of yummy pikelets topped with jam and cream.

'Now,' Sam became all serious, 'let's stop avoiding the subject of James' proposal, and tell me how it came about.'

'I'm not avoiding it. I keep hoping a solution will suddenly come to me.'

'Well, I'm not in favour of this 'marriage' at all.'

'I know, but there are some aspects of his proposition that appeal to me.'

'Like what?'

'Well, being financially secure. That is huge in my mind, having a child to consider probably makes security the most important part of the whole thing.'

'Oh, I can see that you have almost made up your mind.'

'Not yet, but as things are now, I'm quite happy out there. James keeps his distance and he's assured me it will stay that way, and I do love young Harry, he's a super kid.'

'How do you know the doc will keep his side of the bargain? Will he always stay in his own bedroom? How about when his testosterone flows and he needs a bit, what makes you think he won't be a'knockin at your bedroom door.'

'You're awful, Sam,' Kellie giggled. 'He can always go and get "a bit" somewhere else.'

'Men will be men Kellie. I know. They turn when you least expect it. After a few drinks, any agreements you may have made in the past will go right out the window.'

'Well, I'll just have to trust him. He's never tried anything with me in the few months I've been there.'

'No, because for most of that time his leg has been in plaster.'

They collapsed laughing and Kellie had to rush to the toilet, almost wetting her knickers as she ran.

Sam waited for her to come back. 'I want you to do something for me,' she asked suddenly becoming quite serious.

'Yes, what?'

'In the morning I have to go to work for a couple of hours and while I'm away I want you to take yourself down to the beach wearing a sunhat and sunscreen. Take a note-pad with you and write down a list of reasons "for" and "against" this decision. Two columns; think carefully about this, and with a clear mind, do as I ask.'

'M-mm I don't know about the sunhat, they don't do much for me, but okay I'll give it a go.'

'Good. Now go and tidy yourself up, we're off to the movies. George Clooney's in the one we are going to see and he's orgasmic material to say the very least.' Kellie giggled all the way to her bedroom.

***

The next morning, Kellie did as Sam suggested. Wearing a ridiculous sun hat and a light-weight jacket over her maternity dress, she felt a real idiot as she made her way down to the beach, clutching a folded beach chair under one arm. There were only a few people about as it was quite cool and the white-capped waves looked wild and dangerous. The salty tang of the sea air wafted up Kellie's nose and hungry seagulls fought over food scraps carelessly dropped on the sand.

She found a sheltered spot, opened her chair, and sat down. Near the water's edge, a man let his dog poo on the wet sand then walked away from the mess.

'Oy,' Kellie shouted, but if he heard, he chose not to listen. 'It's people like you who spoil the beach for others.' She yelled louder, but he walked faster. 'Lazy creep,' she muttered.

Settling back on her seat she reached into her coat pocket for her pen and pad. Nothing came to mind. Two more guys walked past with dogs one had a go at the other and there was a lot of shouting and swearing before one guy pulled his dog away. Then a group of jet-ski riders appeared and did acrobatics through the waves, like annoying mosquitoes, they were very distracting.

'How am I supposed to give serious thought to James' proposal when so much is going on down here?' she muttered in disgust and shoved the pad and pen back in her pocket. Then to top it off, it started to drizzle.

Heaving her heavy bulk out of the beach chair, she trudged back to Sam's unit and flopped on the couch. 'Well that was a flaming waste of time,' she grumbled.

***

When Sam came home she found Kellie fast asleep on the sofa in the lounge-room with her mouth wide open snoring loudly.

'Oh, Kellie, love,' Sam whispered softly, 'what's to become of you. Don't let people take advantage of your generous nature.' Quietly she left the room.

Kellie woke a while later and called out to her host, 'Why didn't you wake me?'

'Because pregnant ladies like you need their sleep. I kept my eye on you to make sure no flies went down your cake-hole.'

'Oh no, did I really sleep with my mouth open?' Embarrassed, Kellie hid her face in her hands.

'Yep, but don't worry about it, we have more pressing issues to discuss. Now let me see the list you made.'

'Oh, the list…'

'What? Did you make the bloody thing or not?'

'Well, it's like this…'

'You didn't do it!'

'No, I couldn't.' Kellie gave a big sigh. 'There were so many distractions that I didn't get a chance and then it started to spit and I had to rush back.'

Sam shook her head. 'What are we going to do with you? Well, when you get home, find a quiet spot and please, do this, not just for me, but also for yourself.'

Kellie looked her friend straight in the eye. 'Sam, if I do marry James my child gets a name, an education, and if anything should happen to me I know he'll look after the child.' She stopped for a breath. 'Mothers sometimes kark it in childbirth you know. At least this way I know it will have a home.'

Sam noticed a tear trickle down Kellie's cheek and realised how important this was to her friend. She did have a point. 'I understand where you're coming from, I just hope he doesn't break your heart the same way Barry did.'

'How can he?' Kellie replied. 'I have no feelings for him and he doesn't feel anything for me. This will be totally a marriage of convenience.'

'I have heard of them, usually amongst middle eastern people, not sane Aussies.'

Kellie looked around for something to throw at her. 'I'm a Kiwi remember.'

Sam pretended to duck for cover. 'I'm not sure what *they* get up to. Sorry, but I couldn't help that one.'

'Some friend you are.'

The cuckoo clock on the dining room wall struck twelve, mid-day.

'Look sharp, Kellie, it's time to put your best big dress on…'

'Oh, you're such a bugger of a girlfriend, you can't help yourself. Wait until it's your turn and then I'm going to give you heaps.'

'Before I was so rudely interrupted, I was saying that we are off to have lunch and it's my shout.'

'Oh lovely, give me ten minutes and I'll look a new woman.'

'I hope so.'

Kellie threw the hated sun-hat at her and waddled out of the room laughing.

Later in the afternoon, she drove back to Wonglepong. In the distance, the sun's brilliant rays burst through horizontal wisps of red and orange clouds, signalling the day's end.

She breathed a huge sigh of relief; her decision had been made, for better or for worse. *I will agree to James' proposal for the sake of my unborn child. I can't think of any other way to guarantee a roof over our heads.* A lonely tear escaped down her cheek. *I wish my mum and dad were here. I need them so badly.*

She pulled off the road and stopped the car. All the pent up emotions of the last few days took their toll and she burst into tears. The baby, as though sensing her despair, moved and kicked. Somehow, she pulled herself together, cleaned up her face and carried on.

Chapter Twenty-Five

James and Harry were out when Kellie arrived home. She couldn't settle, so decided to walk up to visit Betty.

'Yo hoo,' she called through the screen on the front door. No reply. 'That's strange.'

She tried again. 'Are you there Betty, its Kellie?' Still no reply. She walked around the side of the house and peered through the kitchen window. Her elderly friend was sitting at the table staring into space.

'Betty, let me in.'

Slowly the old lady got up and limped to the front door to unlock the fly-screen. Kellie pushed the door open and Betty turned back towards the kitchen.

'Are you okay? What's wrong?'

The elderly woman turned; her face was black and blue, her eyes bloodshot and swollen – one was almost closed.

'Oh my God,' cried Kellie, 'Did Ross do this?'

Betty sat back down and covered her face with both hands.

'Do you need me to fetch James to check those injuries?'

'No, no, please don't do that.' Tears ran out between her fingers and streamed down her withered cheeks. Kellie gathered the poor woman in her arms and held her as she sobbed. Then she put a bunch of tissues in the old lady's hand and went over to the sink to switch on the kettle.

'A nice hot cuppa, Betty, that's what we need. It fixes almost anything.'

The young woman placed the steaming cups of tea on the table then sat down and looked around. In the corner of the kitchen, lay a broken chair, and there was another gaping hole in the wall by the table.

'What went on here?'

Betty bowed her head.

'Please tell me. I can't help you if I don't know what happened.'

'He desperately needed money. Some rough men on motorbikes came here yesterday. I could tell they were a bad lot – they frightened the daylights out of me. He owes them money. They've threatened to kill him if he doesn't pay up.'

'Oh dear God, what's he been up to?'

'I don't know, but Ross was desperate.'

'You can't go on like this. Maybe we should get the police…?'

'No, no we mustn't do that, it will make things worse. I'll be okay. Please don't say anything to James – I want you to promise me.'

'Oh Betty, you need help with this.'

'No, please, I'll work something out. Now you'd better be off before it's too dark to see your way down the road.'

Kellie put her arms gently around the old lady. 'Bye love, please be careful and ring us if you need help.'

'I will and thank you Kellie, you're like the daughter I wished for but never had.'

***

Life went on as usual for the next few days and James didn't mention their conversation, she started to wonder if she had imaged it all.

The weekend came and went, still nothing. She didn't go away, but spent some time with Betty. The swelling in her face had gone down, but multi-coloured bruises remained. Kellie took her to the beach at Coolangatta, where they paddled in cool salty water then ate ice-creams sitting at a picnic table, watching people go by.

Monday night after dinner, James came out to the kitchen as she wiped down the benches. The room still had a fishy smell from the flounder she had cooked for their meal.

'Could you spare a moment, Kellie?'

'Sure.'

He pulled out a chair and indicated for her to sit down then he did the same. 'Have I given you enough time to consider my proposition?'

She covered her face with her hands then after a few moments removed them and looked at him. 'Yes, yes you have.'

'What did you decide?'

'This has been very difficult.'

'I realise that as there's a great deal at stake.'

Kellie blushed. It was awkward having this chat. 'My answer is yes, I will marry you.' There it was out – she almost felt some relief. 'When I looked at the whole picture, the future of my child being foremost in my mind, I knew what my answer would be.'

'Thank you.' He sighed and some of his frown lines lifted. 'We will all benefit from your decision.'

Nervously, she nodded and her unborn child did a near summersault.

James continued. 'Do you mind if we get married in a registry office?'

She hesitated. 'No, that's okay.' And thought sadly, *my parents would be disgusted at the thought.*

'Today I checked with them as to how we go about this. We need to lodge a document stating our intention to marry then give them one month's notice of the wedding date.' James walked over to a calendar hanging next to the fridge. 'Today's the ninth of August so one month would take us to…,' he tapped his pen on the wall, 'How about the eleventh of September, that's a Saturday.'

'Phew, that's close to my due date but,' Kellie shrugged her shoulders, 'what the heck, let's make it Saturday the eleventh.'

'Good, I would rather we were married before the baby was born.'

She nodded in agreement.

'Well, we need witnesses. I'd like to ask Moira and Don. I'll leave it to you to choose two other people.'

'Okay and I'd like to invite a few friends, four or five maybe.'

'That's fine. Now, we need the Notice of Intended Marriage form. I think we should go tomorrow, fill in the form, and lodge it while we're there. Is that all right with you?' She nodded again and he continued. 'Harry can come with us. It won't hurt him to miss kindy. I'll call them in the morning.'

'Do we need an appointment?'

'No, not for this, but we do need to go back there for an interview and take all the necessary documents, original birth certificates etc, and you'll need your passport. I have my paperwork in the study safe.'

'I have both of those.'

'Good. I'd like to get away in the morning about nine.'

'Nine's fine with me.'

'Well, I'll say goodnight.'

'Goodnight, and James, I won't be changing my mind.'

A slight smile curved his lips as he nodded and left the room.

***

Sleep was impossible for Kellie. She tossed and turned. The baby seemed to be doing cartwheels. She decided her wedding guests would be Sam, Shirley and Bob, and Mary. Mary's drunken bum of a husband wouldn't come, but Kellie would still invite them both.

Oh and what will I wear? This thought nearly blew her away. *I'll probably have to wear a tent dress and look like a big fat whale.* The thought of saying 'I do' in a tent frock was too much and once more tears welled up and overflowed. She cried tears for her parents who wouldn't be there, tears of pity for herself for getting in such a mess, and tears for Barry who she had loved. But he used her, took away her innocence, and left her with his child.

At one o'clock, she felt so depressed she decided to get up and make a hot drink. Misery filled her heart as she leaned over the bench waiting for the kettle to boil. She didn't hear James come into the kitchen. She sniffed loudly. As she reached over to grab a handful of tissues from the box on the bench, she saw him.

'Oh James...'

'Kellie what on earth...?'

He walked over and grabbed the tissues as once more tears spilled down her cheeks.

Gently he wiped her eyes. 'Hush, it will be all right.'

'I'm sorry. It all got t-too much for me,' she stammered and covered her eyes with her hands.

'I know how you feel. This is a very stressful time and we're making a decision that will affect the rest of our lives.'

'I'm trying to be s-sensible, but doubts kept creeping up on me. I tried to sleep, but things were going around in my mind.'

He took hold of her hands, his thumbs gently rubbing her wrists. 'Kellie look at me.' She lifted her eyes and met his gaze. 'Have I ever given you a reason not to trust me?'

She shook her head.

He continued. 'Well then, as I told you nothing's going to change, but it will be a fresh start for all of us.'

Kellie gulped and Charlie came in to see what was going on. He wagged his tail as he rubbed his cold nose against her leg and licked her ankle. 'I know,' she hiccupped 'and I do trust you James it's just...'

'Look, you are almost ready to give birth to your first child. It's a very emotional time, and I understand that. Then, I go and drop this bombshell.' He cleared his throat then continued. 'Believe me you are coping very well.' He looked right into her eyes as he spoke and Kellie felt herself warming to this kind but blunt man.

'How about you go and hop into bed. I'll make some hot chocolate and bring it in. Give me five minutes.'

She nodded and the grandfather clock in the lounge struck two as Kellie waddled back to bed. He was true to his word, and five minutes later, she heard a soft knock on her door.

'Come in.'

He walked in with a steaming hot mug and placed it down on a coaster on her bed-side table. 'Here you are. This is hot so be careful.'

'Thank you.' She looked up at him. He looked tired. 'I'm sorry to have kept you up so long.'

'I wasn't asleep either.' He grinned. 'I'll see you in the morning.' He turned and quietly left the room.

***

Going to the Registry office with James and Harry was no big deal. They went in separate cars, as James needed to be at the surgery by eleven o'clock. Kellie felt a bit overwhelmed to be walking in with him, but he held Harry's hand and was very polite to her. She wore her three-quarter length red coat over black maternity trousers and black boots. A white roll-neck skivvy, topped off with her favourite long black scarf (it hung down over her huge tummy) completed the look. They collected and filled in the form, lodged it, then made the booking for their ceremony and the required interview in two weeks' time.

'Is there anywhere you'd like to go before you head back?' James asked.

'We might go to Pacific Fair and find something trendy for Harry to wear to the wedding.'

'Would you like to come with me to the jewellers and choose your wedding ring?'

Kellie stopped in her tracks. She hadn't given any thought to a ring. 'Oh, okay. Where shall I meet you?' The jeweller he suggested was at Broadbeach.

They met outside the shop and for a few moments, she gazed at the beautiful window display. 'Come inside,' James said 'I know the chap who owns this place and I called him. He's waiting for us.'

A middle aged man in a dark suit with a shaved head came over and shook hands with James. 'Great to see you, my friend. And this is the lovely lady you told me about. Good morning, Kellie,' he reached over to shake her hand. 'I'm David Campbell. I'm very pleased to meet you. Let me offer my sincere congratulations to you both.' Kellie blushed and adjusted her scarf.

David let himself in behind the counter. 'I've put out a selection of gold wedding bands for you to see.'

Kellie's eyes nearly popped out of her head, the rings were so gorgeous. Most of them had small diamonds forming delicate patterns edged in gold. She tried a few on and there was one she particularly liked, it had small round diamonds going all the way round the ring with a gold band top and bottom. This was her ring. Harry started to grizzle and James lifted him up.

'Would you like to see a different style?' David asked Kellie.

'No thank you. I like this one, it's beautiful.'

'Good, that is a very nice setting. What do you think, James?'

'I had my eye on that one as well. I think Kellie has made a good choice.'

'I don't need to see anymore, thank you.' She smiled at the jeweller.

He promised to have it ready for James to collect the following week, as it was too big for her finger. They thanked him and left. Outside the shop, Kellie looked up at James expecting him to say something meaningful or...'

'Oh well, now that's out of the way, I'll go in to work.' He patted Harry's head and nodded at Kellie. 'I'll see you both later,' then he walked off.

I must be going soft in the head expecting anything to change, she thought, then pulled herself together, grabbed Harry's hand and walked to the car.

***

The next few days passed in a blur. While she felt anxious about the marriage part, there was also a settled feeling. She didn't have to worry anymore that she might do something silly and lose her job. She was safe and this was going to be a real home for her and the baby, security and a roof over their heads. All these thoughts turned over in her mind.

Her biggest worry now was what she would wear for the wedding. She phoned her friends to invite them to the ceremony. It was to be held at eleven o'clock on the eleventh of September. James suggested they all go to the Sheraton Mirage for a reception afterwards.

Sam laughed. 'I wouldn't miss this for quids,' making it sound like a three-ringed circus. Her friend Mary, the one with the loser husband, couldn't stop crying when Kellie told her.

'Are you sure about this Kellie? It's a big step and married life isn't easy you know.'

'It's not a love match Mary, we get on okay, and I desperately need a home for the baby. I'm sure things will work out okay.'

They chattered a while longer and Mary calmed down. 'I'll be there for you love, but Todd won't come, weddings aren't his thing. I'll see if I can get a lift with Sam.' She sniffed and said goodbye. Kellie knew she was thinking about her own marriage, it was a disaster and she didn't want her friend going down that same road.

She rang Shirley and Bob.

'Did I hear you properly? You're going to marry that doctor? Are you feeling all right?'

'Shirley, this isn't a love match. I need a proper home and he needs a mother for Harry. Child Welfare is convinced he's the father of my baby and in their eyes, we're carrying on an unhealthy relationship in front of a child under their care.'

'You're what? I've never heard such crap in all my born days. Are you for real on this?'

'I certainly am. That's what prompted James to ask me, that and knowing how desperate I am to get a roof over my head before the baby arrives.'

'Well I never, bloody hell.'

'I know it's a bit of a shock.'

'A shock is putting it mildly, I damn near passed out. Oh well, we'll come and support you love, you know that and I hope all goes well.'

'Thanks Shirley, I knew I could count on you and Bob.'

'Yer, I just hope he doesn't have a flaming heart-attack when I tell him. He's very fond of you Kellie.'

'He's a darling – give him my love.'

'I will. I hope I've got something suitable to wear to such an auspicious occasion.'

'What about me! I may have to go to the camping shop and hire a tent!'

'I forgot about that. Good luck with finding a wedding gown,' she laughed.

'Don't be horrible. You're as bad as Sam.'

'You are not the first person to get married with a large bump under your dress and you certainly won't be the last, so don't worry about it.'

'I'll find something. I must go now.'

'Okay love. Now you take good care of yourself and if James doesn't look after you, Bob will have his guts for garters. You tell him that.'

'Oh my God, here we go, bye love.'

She turned off her mobile phone and sat down. Betty was the only other person she hadn't invited, so she called Harry and they clipped Charlie's lead on and walked up the road. Overhead, the sun was close to setting and the horizon glowed with streaks of fiery colours.

Betty noticed them coming as she struggled to mow her front lawn with an ancient push-mower. 'You two are out visiting late today.'

'I know, but I have something to tell you. Can we go inside for a few minutes?'

'Sure, I'll just take these old gumboots off. They're nearly falling to pieces.'

Kellie and Harry removed their shoes and went inside, leaving Charlie to chase lizards, which was his favourite occupation.

'Now what's so important that you walked up here when it's nearly dark?'

'Well, I think you had better sit down.' Betty lowered herself onto a chair by the table; the bruises on her face had started to fade, but still looked nasty. 'James asked me to marry him and I've agreed.'

'You did! Oh my God,' she gasped. 'You've almost taken my breath away, but good on you. A roof over your head and someone to bring in a wage is very important when you have a child to consider. No matter what others might say, love doesn't pay the bills. You can work on the other parts of marriage as you go. I know James well and he'll look after you and the baby.'

'Yes, I'm sure he will.'

'Harry will love having you for a mum and it'll do him good to have the company of a baby brother or sister.'

'I think so and it's a good feeling to know I can't be sacked.' Kellie laughed.

'It certainly is, now you'd better get off home. Thanks for coming to tell me your news.'

'Not just to tell you but to invite you to the wedding. It's at the registry office in Southport, then lunch at the Sheraton Mirage. We'll give you a lift. Harry's coming as well, and we both have a couple of friends we'd like to be there.'

'Oh Kellie love, how nice.' The old lady hugged her. 'Harry, my boy,' he got a hug as well. 'You are getting a wonderful mother,' then she turned back to Kellie. 'I have a good feeling about all this.'

'It's no love match. You know that.'

'Love grows. It creeps up on you when you least expect it.'

Kellie smiled. 'Don't hold your breath. Come on Harry give Betty another hug then we'll head off home, it's nearly dinnertime.'

'Bye love, take care. See you Harry.'

That night Kellie was ironing and watching a movie when James came looking for her. He could smell the instant starch she sprayed on the clothes. She was such a fussy ironer, too fussy in his opinion. 'Kellie, when's your next doctor's appointment?'

'Tomorrow, why do you ask?'

'Well, since I'm going to be the father of your child, I'm interested.'

'Oh, okay.'

'Would you like me to come in with you?'

Bloody hell, she thought, *this is getting a bit much. I don't really want him seeing me with my knickers down.* She kept ironing to cover her embarrassment. 'No, I'll be fine thanks, but if you want to look after Harry I'd appreciate that.'

He looked a bit taken back. 'What times your appointment?'

'Eleven-thirty, does that suit you?'

'Get Moira to buzz me when you arrive. It's time to put that ironing board away for tonight, your ankles are swollen.'

'I only have a couple more things to do then I'll hit the hay. I am a bit tired.'

'I'll see you tomorrow when you get to the surgery, goodnight.' Kellie finished off then went to bed. She was tired, very tired.

Chapter Twenty-Six

In the morning, finding something to wear was a real challenge. Not much fitted. The choice was very limited. She decided on the black maternity trousers that stretched over her bump, topped with an emerald green shirt and her long black vest. Then she found a black and white scarf to loop under the shirt-collar and hang down over her enormous belly. She checked the outfit in the mirror and shook her head. 'I'm going to burn these bloody clothes when this baby arrives. I'm so sick of looking fat.'

Harry was dressed and ready, so they set off. She had trouble fitting behind the steering wheel. 'Good grief, I think I must be having an elephant!'

They arrived at the surgery ten minutes early. Kellie always felt the staff were staring at her and thought, *I wonder if they know we're getting married, I bet they do.*

'Hello, Kellie,' Moira came around the desk and gave her a hug. 'It's lovely to see you. Harry come here and give me a big kiss.' People in the waiting room stared as she hugged the small boy.

'Is James busy?' Kellie asked.

'He's with his last patient for the morning. Have a seat. Dr Wilkinson won't be long.'

A few minutes later, a lady came out to the reception desk followed by James. He caught Kellie's eye and gave her a brief nod then winked at Harry. With that, the child ran over to his dad who scooped him up and carried him out the back.

'Kellie,' Dr Wilkinson called.

She heaved herself up and followed him down to his consulting room.

'I hear congratulations are in order.' He grinned, 'I'm very pleased. Now pop up on the bed and we'll check this baby out.'

He listened then poked around her tummy. 'Hmm, you still have a few weeks to go yet, but all seems well. I hope you're resting.'

'Yes, thanks doctor. The baby's very active. That's a good sign isn't it?'

'It certainly is.'

He completed his examination then sat down at his desk. 'Your blood pressure's still up, so try to get more rest. Now, I plan on being at the delivery; where did you book in?'

'At the Tweed hospital.'

'Great, that's a good choice. All seems well with the baby, so I'll see you in two weeks' time.' He stood up and walked over to open the door. 'Bye for now.'

Harry and his dad were waiting by the reception desk. 'Would you like to have lunch next door?' James asked.

Kellie nearly died of fright. He'd never asked her before, but she supposed it was all different now.

She nodded. 'Yes, I would, thank you.'

'Moira's coming with us … it's her lunch break.'

Kellie smiled at the older lady. 'That's nice. Has Harry been all right?'

James answered. 'He wet his pants, but I found another pair in the car so all's well.'

They walked down to the coffee shop and the two ladies found a table while James ordered for them all.

Moira sat down and smiled at the young woman. 'You're looking well, Kellie. You've filled out quite a bit since I saw you last.'

'Yes, I'm totally over this big belly so I hope the baby comes early.'

'Well, they tend to come just when they're ready, that is something I do know.' 'Kellie,' Moira hesitated, 'the girls at the surgery would like to give you a baby shower and we thought our house would be good as we have a large deck out the back. What do you think?'

Kellie's eyes watered. 'Moira, that is so lovely. I can't believe they would want to do that for me.' She searched for tissues buried deep in her handbag and was still sniffing when James pulled out a chair and sat down.

'What's going on? Kellie, what's the matter?'

Moira patted his arm. 'It's all right James, they're happy tears. We're organising a baby shower for Kellie at my place.'

'Who's we?'

'The girls at the surgery and me.'

'Oh dear God, if they're involved you can count me out.'

'It's a girl thing, no men allowed. I'll even be kicking Don out for the afternoon.'

Moira looked at Kellie who by now had herself under control. 'How about this Saturday Kellie, does that suit you?'

'Yes, that's fine. Please thank the girls for me.' She reached over and hugged the older lady.

'Also,' Moira started…

'Don't tell me there's more,' James muttered with a pained expression.

'Zip it James. Kellie I want you to invite your girlfriends, Sam, Shirley and anyone else you would like to be there.'

'Thanks, I will. I'd also like to bring Betty, our neighbour. She's been wonderful to me and would enjoy seeing you again.'

'Okay. I'll leave all that up to you, so that's this Saturday at one-thirty. James, move your elbows. Here's our meal.'

As she drove home with Harry fast asleep in his car-seat, she couldn't believe the kindness of other people. 'I'm so lucky to have such wonderful friends. I wish my mum could see all this and be at the baby shower.' Tears once more filled her eyes and she had to pull over to the side of the road. She grabbed some tissues from the glove-box and had a good cry then blew her nose. 'I wish I didn't bawl all the time,' she complained, 'I don't know what's got into me.' Five minutes later, more composed, she drove on.

When they arrived home, Harry had the grizzles. She lifted him out of his car seat and put him on the ground where he threw loud wobbly. Kellie tried to pick him up, but he went all limp and screamed. Fed up with his nonsense, she left him where he was. She made a coffee then carried it out to the table on the back verandah. Five minutes later, he rushed past followed by the dog, laughing as he climbed up to the tree-house Don had built for him the previous week. He liked to sit up there with some old binoculars and watch the birds.

'I'm so pleased with his progress,' she whispered. He could pick out characters and numbers when she read to him and complete puzzles a five-year-old would normally struggle with. He laughed and yelled when he played outside with Charlie and often came to Kellie with his arms outstretched wanting a hug. She always stopped whatever she was doing, hugged the small boy and told him how much she loved him, indicating right up to the sky and they would both giggle.

Sometimes he came inside holding out one finger, indicating he wanted her to follow him. Usually he wanted to show her something, a stick insect or butterfly. She felt he was close to speaking, but nothing had happened so far.

She also showed him how to call his dad by pressing one on the speed-dial at the base of the telephone and his eyes would light up when James answered and then he'd pass the receiver to Kellie. They only did that before the surgery opened when Kellie knew James wasn't with a patient.

When Harry heard his dad's car come home, he would stop whatever he was doing and madly jump up and down accompanied by Charlie who barked and spun around in circles. It was hilarious watching them. The door through to the garage was kept locked so he didn't run in front of the car. She dearly loved this small boy and felt blessed at being given the chance to be a real mother to him.

Saturday came and so did the rain. In between showers, she managed to pick up Betty whose face beamed with happiness at being invited to the baby shower.

'I haven't had this much excitement in years, Kellie love. How wonderful of them to include me.'

'I'm sure you'll enjoy meeting my friends, you already know Moira and Sam. Hang on to your seat and we'll be there in no time at all.' Betty laughed and tightened her seat-belt.

They found Moira's home after a few wrong turns. Kellie couldn't miss the 'party-house' with bunches of coloured balloons tied to the letterbox and along the front fence.

'Congratulations, Kellie,' yelled the happy group gathered on the terrace when they arrived.

'Come on in,' shouted familiar voices. Feeling a little embarrassed at first, she didn't take long to settle down and enjoy herself. She chatted to the girls from James's work, and wondered how much they knew about her. They were a great bunch and dead set on enjoying themselves. The champagne flowed and the noise level grew.

Then it was time to open her gifts, and Kellie was amazed at how generous they all were. There was so much food, 'Enough for half the street,' someone commented.

Betty knocked back quite a few drinks and looked to be having a right old time. The afternoon was fun and Kellie was pleased that James wasn't there to hear the jokes and stories the reception girls told, as he would have had a seizure or a heart attack!

Night was setting in when they left. The time had just flown. Betty chatted and giggled all of the way home. 'They gave you some lovely gifts this afternoon Kellie, you'll have the best dressed baby in Wonglepong.' She kept coming up with all sorts of funny expressions.

At least she's keeping me awake, thought Kellie. It had been a long exciting day.

Chapter Twenty-Seven

The following week they were due for another visit from Harry's case worker, Joy Brennan. A letter arrived advising them she would call Tuesday the 17th August at approximately 10am. Kellie braced herself and made sure the maternity outfit she wore that particular day looked prim and proper. Bang on ten o'clock the door-bell rang.

Kellie put a smile on her face as she answered the door and hoped the grumpy lady was in a good mood. 'Good morning, Joy.'

'Good morning, where's the boy?' The smell of cigarette smoke remained as she passed Kellie and marched into the lounge-room. Harry sat on the floor doing his favourite word puzzle.

'Hello, Harry,' the case-worker called. The child looked up then continued with what he was doing.

'Hmm,' she brought a clip-board out of her bag with forms attached to it then glanced at Kellie, her eyes lingering on the pregnant woman's tummy. 'Can we go somewhere to talk?'

'Sure.' Kellie led the older woman through to the kitchen and pulled out a chair. 'Please have a seat.'

Joy put her bag down and placed her paperwork on the table. 'I presume he still isn't speaking?'

'No, sometimes I think he's close, but no, nothing so far.'

'Hmm, I wonder if he shouldn't have some professional help with that.'

'I understood they left that decision to James, Dr Harvey, to make at his discretion.'

'I know that, but he obviously isn't getting any results. There doesn't seem to be much improvement.'

'These are still early days – you know that,' replied Kellie brassed off with this frustrated middle-aged spinster who always made her feel as though she didn't know what she was talking about. 'That's not true. There is a huge improvement in Harry. He's a different little boy. He mightn't speak, but he sleeps all night and isn't plagued by the night-terrors that made him scream in his sleep. He doesn't wet the bed and the teachers at his kindy tell me he mixes well with other kids and does all the normal things kids do.' Kellie was sick of this old tart. 'They also told me he's a well-adjusted little boy, who in their opinion will speak when he's ready.'

'Well, you're a bit full of yourself for just being the housekeeper around here.'

What a bitch Kellie thought, *I'll fix her.*

'I may be the housekeeper, but I'm also Dr Harvey's fiancée, and by the time you make your next visit here I'll be Harry's stepmother.'

If Joy Brennan hadn't been sitting down, she would have fallen on the floor.

'Hmmp,' she coughed and looked in her bag for something, keeping her hands busy while she thought up a suitable answer. 'Has Dr Harvey let the department know?'

'I'm not sure, but I'll check with him.' Kellie sat down, scared that her blood-pressure had gone through the roof. *Put that in your pipe and smoke it you old cow*, she thought and waited for the next comment.

The somewhat shocked case-worker picked up her clip-board and bag. 'I'll go in the next room and observe him for a few minutes.'

'Sure,' Kellie stood up and folded her arms while she waited for the obnoxious woman to leave the kitchen then she put the kettle on muttering to herself. 'Dear God, I need a strong drink after that outburst, but I'll settle for a coffee.'

Joy Brennan returned to the kitchen. 'I'll leave you now and be back in one month. Dr Harvey will be contacted by the department. I don't see there's any real problem here.'

'Thank you. I'll see you out.'

'I can see myself out, thank you,' and in a huff she left, but the stink of stale smoke remained.

Later, when Kellie relayed the conversation to James he grinned. 'You certainly gave her the message. I'm sure in future, she'll be extremely careful of how she speaks to you. We'll wait and see what the department has to say. I'll send them a short email letting them know we're to be married.' He smiled as he left the room.

***

Kellie was still worried about what she could wear for her wedding and called Sam.

'Hi Kel, how's it going out there in the sticks? Have you got the pre-wedding nerves yet?'

'No, I haven't. I've called you for some help.'

'Sure, what's up?'

'I need something nice to get married in.'

'Okay. How about we go up to Brissy and have a look, we're sure to find something there.'

'It will need to be large.'

'My dear friend, you are not the only person to get married in your condition. I've told you this before, now for heaven's sake get over it.'

'Okay, when shall we go?'

'Can't do anything until Thursday, how does that grab you?'

'Thursday's great. I'll speak to James about minding Harry. He might be able to take time off. I don't really want to take him with me.'

'Good idea, shopping's no good with kids. How about I pick you up about nine o'clock, so we can get an early start.'

'I'll be ready. Thanks Sam, it's very nice of you to do this for me.'

'My pleasure love, see you then, bye.'

'Bye Sam, thanks again.'

'Wow,' murmured Kellie, 'things are actually starting to happen.'

She let James finish his dinner before she broached the subject.

'Not Thursday as I have a full day, but how about I call Don and ask if I could drop Harry at their place before I go into work and collect him when I finish.' He pulled his mobile phone out of his pocket. 'I'll give them a call,' he scrolled through his contacts as he walked out the back door. A few minutes later, he came back inside, grinning. 'All organised. Moira said Don would be over-joyed to have Harry for the day, he's looking forward to it.'

Kellie smiled. 'Thanks, James.'

***

Sam arrived early Thursday morning and the two girls headed for the city. 'Well, I never thought we'd be shopping for a pregnant wedding dress love, did you?' They both cracked up.

'I certainly never thought I would be,' replied Kellie. 'However, here we are and it's starting to get exciting.'

'That's the girl; make the most of it. Oh and I forgot to ask, do I need a bridesmaid's dress?'

Kellie nearly choked. 'No you fool, we're at a registry office, remember?'

'I know. I thought I'd get you going.'

Kellie shook her head, she was so lucky to have such a wonderful friend.

They looked around and were not impressed with any of the maternity shops they saw. After lunch, when Kellie's feet were swollen and sore, they got lucky. Rounding a busy corner of the Brisbane Mall Sam spotted a sign.

PROUD and **PREGNANT.** *Casual and Formal Maternity Clothes and Exquisite Lingerie for Fashion-Conscious Mothers To Be.*

A swinging sign showed a colourful picture of a stork holding a smiling baby slung in a nappy hanging from its mouth.

'Look, Kellie,' Sam pointed across the street, 'that shop could be just what we're looking for.'

'I like its name, although with the size of my belly who could be fashion-conscious.'

'Shut up and keep walking, Kel.' She grabbed her friends arm. 'Come on moaning minnie, move it.'

The shop window had striking outfits displayed. One mannequin had a flowing turquoise kaftan over black leggings. It looked stunning.

'Oh, I like that, Sam.'

'Yes, it's lovely, but not for a wedding.'

'I know that, but I still like it.' The door dinged as they went inside. The shop smelt of some nice fragrance wafting away from an oil burner.

A trendy-dressed woman approached them. 'Good afternoon, ladies, if you need any assistance please let me know.'

'Thanks, we'll do that,' replied Sam.

'We'll find two or three outfits and take them to the fitting-room, ah Kel?'

'Mm, here's one to start with,' Kellie held up a cream slinky number.

The sales lady came over holding a peach-coloured dress. 'I don't know if you are interested, but I've just unpacked this and with your colouring it would look lovely.' Kellie took the frock and held it against her. The colour was gorgeous.

'That's beautiful, Kel,' commented Sam, 'really nice.'

The sales lady continued. 'There's a matching lace coat in a slightly deeper shade. I'll go and fetch it, one moment.'

Sam came over. 'You have to try that one on, girlfriend.' Off they went to the fitting room. The dress was made of peach-coloured satin, in a wrap-a-round style and it had a belt of the same fabric going around the back where it had hooks placed every few centimetres to cope with an expanding tummy. Kellie undressed and carefully stepped into it as Sam held it then did up the hooks.

They looked in the mirror and a huge smile lit up Kellie's tired face. 'This is it Sam. I love it.'

'You'll love it even more with this lace coat,' the assistant said as she held it up. They all smiled. It was beautiful. Kellie slipped the coat over the dress then stood back to admire it.

'Oh, that's smashing,' commented Sam. 'Not too fussy, but nice and dressy. You know what, I remember Princess Mary wearing a similar outfit when she was having her twins. It was on the cover of one of the magazines. It hid the fact that she was so big.'

Kellie made a friendly swipe at her. 'This outfit makes me feel good. I'll need something like this to get me through the day.'

'We haven't asked the price yet.' Sam turned to the lady.

The sales assistant looked at the tags. 'It's expensive, but I can take ten percent off.'

'Ten percent off what?' queried Sam.

'Five hundred and forty-nine dollars.'

Kellie and Sam covered their mouths in horror!

'Oh my God,' blurted Kellie.

'Bloody hell, excuse my French, but that's quite dear,' Sam stated.

The lady read the shock on their faces. 'I'll leave you to think about it. Oh, by the way, I have pewter shoes and a matching clutch bag that would look nice with this outfit.'

Sam still in shock slowly replied, 'Thanks.'

Kellie was in a daze. 'What will I do? That's an awful lot of money.'

'I know kid, but I think it's worth it. You look a million dollars and I can tell you're happy with it.'

'How much is it with the discount off?'

Sam did the sum in her head, 'Four ninety-five.'

Tired and footsore, Kellie rubbed her eyes. 'What shall I do Sam?'

'Take it. This is your wedding dress for heaven's sake.'

'I know, but I'll never wear it again.'

'Who cares, sell it on eBay after the wedding.'

That did it. They cracked up laughing and Kellie was terrified she would wet her knickers. 'Stop it Sam, don't make me laugh, my bladder can't cope with it.'

The sales lady returned. 'How's it going in here?'

'I'm going to take the dress and the coat thank you,' Kellie replied.

Sam piped up, 'Quick, wrap it up before she changes her mind – you know what pregnant women are like.'

The sales lady smiled. 'Would you like me to show you the shoes?'

'Go on Kel, no harm in looking,' Sam whispered. Kellie nodded and the lady fetched the box.

'Are you about a size seven?'

'Yes, I am that's a good guess.' She gazed at the shoes. 'Oh, they're lovely.'

'Sit down and try them on,' Sam said reaching for Kellie's handbag. She steered the bride-to-be towards a padded seat.

The shoes fitted perfectly and the heels were a medium height, not too high. Kellie thought that was important, because if she was nervous on the day, she might take a tumble. She walked across to a nearby mirror holding the clutch purse. 'What do you think Sam, will they do?'

'Take them and then you've got the whole outfit. You look great Kel. James will think he's getting a fashion model.'

Kellie burst out laughing, 'Yep, a fat one at that.'

The sales lady pretended not to know what they were talking about and carefully placed the tissue wrapped dress and coat in two separate bags and the shoes and clutch purse in another.

'Thank you, ladies. That will be seven hundred and fifty dollars.'

'What,' shrieked Sam, 'I thought we were getting a discount?'

'You have. I've given you a very good discount. The shoes were three hundred and seventy dollars and the purse eighty, so let's make it an even seven hundred, that's the best I can do.'

Kellie reached into her handbag for her wallet. 'Here's my visa. I'm too tired to care about money. Do you have a loo I can use?'

The assistant smiled. 'Follow me.'

On her way back from the bathroom, Kellie passed a display of thick fluffy dressing gowns. One caught her eye and she lifted it off its hanger.

'What are you doing?' called Sam.

'I'd like to get a dressing gown like this for Betty. You should see the tattered old one she gets around in, it's a shocker.'

Sam came over and felt the fabric. 'Oh it's lovely. I can see Betty in that. Which colour do you think she'd like?'

'This lilac one, it's soft and cuddly just like her.' Kellie carried it over to the sales lady and got her visa card out again. They thanked the woman and left the shop, both weighed down with shopping bags.

Dusk was approaching as they turned into James's driveway. Kellie unlocked the side-door and Sam carried in their precious purchases and put them on her friend's bed. The house appeared to be empty.

'I don't know where James and Harry could be; would you like to stay for dinner Sam?'

'Thanks love, but I'll get on home. I'll give you a call tomorrow.' She hugged Kellie.

'Thanks Sam. I owe you big time for your help today, now drive safely, bye.'

Kellie hung the new clothes in her wardrobe and shortly afterwards heard James' car come down the drive.

She walked out to meet them. 'I wondered where you all were.' Charlie jumped out of the station wagon and bounded up to her.

'We went to get Chinese for dinner,' James called out. 'I thought you'd be too tired to cook.' He put the steaming bags of food down. 'You grab some plates and we'll dish this lot up while it's hot.'

'Mmm, smells good. Harry did you have a good time with Don?' She bent down and hugged the small boy. He nodded with a huge grin.

'Well,' James uttered. 'Don's been quietly doing up an old pedal car for his nibs here. Harry loved it. He even ate his lunch sitting at the wheel! It's not ready to bring home yet, but it won't be long.'

'Wow,' Kellie looked at the excited boy. 'You are so lucky. I can't wait to see it.'

The young boy's face said it all.

'Did you find a suitable outfit?' James asked.

'I sure did and paid through the nose for it, but I was too tired to care, so I can cross that off my "to do" list.'

The doctor grinned as he piled the hot food on their plates.

'Oh, and I bought Betty a lovely warm dressing gown. I wanted to give her something nice for all the help she gives us.'

'That was a good idea, that old one of hers is disgraceful,' James commented. 'How about we put a Myer voucher in the pocket, then she can get herself some new clothes. She always looks like she's dressed from the rag-bag.'

'Don't be horrible, James, not everyone is as well off as you. She gives most of her money to that useless son of hers.'

'More fool her.' He finished his meal and sat back patting his stomach. 'Now tomorrow's Friday and I'm only working a half-day. I'll be home at lunch time. Would you like to go and spend a couple of nights with your friends?'

It took a moment for his words to sink in. 'Y-yes, thank you, I'd like to do that.'

He stood up and started to clear the table. 'I'll finish here and bath Harry. You go and have your shower or whatever you'd like to do, you look tired, and your ankles are badly swollen.'

That's a back-handed compliment if ever I heard one, Kellie thought. 'Thanks,' she replied, 'I am a bit bushed.'

She went to her bedroom and shut the door then picked up her mobile phone and called Shirley.

'Hi Kellie, it's lovely to hear from you. How's it going out there?'

'Hi Shirls, I wondered if you're home this weekend?'

'We sure are. Would you like to come and stay?' her friend asked hopefully.

'Is it all right if I come tomorrow afternoon and stay until Sunday?'

'That would be great. Just wait until I tell Bob, he'll be tickled pink. I won't chat now, but give me a call as you come down the road, and he'll come out to make sure the neighbours' dogs keep away so you can come in – bloody mongrels.'

Kellie laughed, 'I'll do that. They terrify me. See you tomorrow, bye.'

Feeling tired but content, she showered then lay on her bed with some chocolate that she'd been waiting for an excuse to eat, and watched a movie on television.

Chapter Twenty-Eight

The next afternoon, Kellie packed a few things and headed to the coast. She stopped at a French bakery not far from Bob and Shirley's home and bought crusty rolls and Danish pastries then called them on her mobile. Bob answered.

'Hi, Kellie here. I'm about ten minutes away.'

'Okay, I'm on my way up the drive with a big stick.'

Kellie laughed. Sure enough, as she pulled up there were those blasted dogs snarling through the corner of their fence.

'Get away, you flaming mongrels,' Bob waved his stick at them and they snarled baring their teeth at him.

'How your neighbours get away with keeping those dogs in a built up area is beyond me,' shouted Kellie.

'The council doesn't seem worried, but I must add we don't get any break-ins around here.'

'No self-respecting burglar would attempt to go near those rotten dogs.'

'Don't worry, love, I'm here with my big stick to protect you.'

'Yer, I almost need protecting from you, you old womaniser.'

Bob laughed. 'I'm harmless these days, Kel, especially since I had the big snip.'

'Oh, you're a shocker. Where's my friend, Shirley?'

'Waiting inside, so waddle on down she's already made the tea.'

Kellie carried in her rolls and pastries. 'You ho,' she called.

'Oh, Kellie love, how nice to see you. Blimey, are you sure you're not having twins?'

'I certainly hope not, because if I am I'm giving one to you.'

'I bet you wouldn't, but I know what you mean. That baby seems low. Did the doctor say if you've dropped?'

'You're as bad as Sam and no he didn't mention it. Come on; pour the tea and let's get stuck in to these goodies.' Kellie sat back and relaxed. Their old home with its water-features, plants, and cushion filled sofas was cosy and very relaxing.

They had a great afternoon followed by a scrumptious dinner of lasagne and spring vegies. Then later, the cards came out and they spent the evening playing poker and reminiscing. The next morning Shirley quizzed her about the wedding.

'We wondered if you would like to come and spend a couple of days here with us before the wedding, then we could help you get dressed and so on.'

'Thanks for the offer, but I have young Harry to see to and James will be at work.'

'Bring him with you. Bob's great with kids. He asked me if you would like him to give you away. I don't know what they do at a registry office, but it would be nice if you could go in on his arm.'

'What a lovely idea. Yes, let's do it. I'd be honoured to have Bob give me away.'

'Would Sam like to come as well? Tell her she's very welcome.'

'That's a good suggestion. She'll make sure I look bridal, or as bridal as this fat tummy will let me be.'

Shirley cracked up. 'Let's give her a call.' They did and she came around and spent the rest of the day giving Kellie heaps about her wedding night.

'What wedding night. Even if he did want to sleep with me, there's no room in my bed, that's for sure. No, the deal is he stays in his room and I in mine.'

'Hmm.' Sam looked her right in the eye. 'He will be entitled to his conjugals.'

'Sam, you read too many crazy novels and watch too many weird TV programmes. I think it's time for another cuppa. Shirley, what do you think?' Anything to get Sam off her flaming bandwagon.

'How about we go to that new bistro at the Oasis later on and check it out,' Shirley suggested. 'I've heard great comments about their food.'

Bob had dinner by himself that night as the three girls went out on the town.

***

Late Sunday afternoon, Kellie drove home. Dusk was approaching and the sky had wisps of fiery cotton-wool like clouds streaked across the pale-blue horizon.

No one was around when the tired young mother-to-be went inside so she decided to have a long hot bath. She poured herself a glass of lime juice and fetched her book then carefully lowered her bulging frame into the perfumed bubbles. She relaxed in the scented water, sipped her drink, and enjoyed her read. As the bath cooled, she manoeuvred her foot to turn the hot tap on and off, keeping the temperature comfortable. 'This is the life.' She sighed blissfully.

A while later, she heard James and Harry arrive home and Charlie barking impatiently for his dinner.

'Oh well,' she muttered, 'I'd better get out of this tub and put some clothes on.'

She held both sides of the bath while she tried to raise her swollen body, but couldn't find the strength to lift it up. 'Oh no.' She had another go, that was no good either. The frothy water was too deep. Awkwardly, she rolled over onto her hands and knees and tried to reach the plug, but couldn't get close enough. Her big fat belly was in the way. Then, she slipped.

Bubbles stung her eyes and bath water filled her mouth. 'Bloody hell.' Kellie coughed and choked, and almost caused a tidal wave. She took a few moments to recover then clumsily manoeuvred her bulky frame over onto her back and tried again. Her body was so cumbersome; it was hopeless.

By now, tears of frustration trickled down her cheeks. 'Why the hell did I get in here,' she whimpered as she lay in the water, miserably contemplating her plight. After so much activity the bubbles had increased and the bath was about to overflow.

'There's nothing else for it,' she wailed, 'I'll have to get some help.'

Could she stand the embarrassment of having James come to help her, but what was the alternative? Because of her huge tummy, Kellie could only see her private parts by looking in the mirror and she was bloody sure she didn't want James Harvey seeing them, doctor or no doctor.

'Oh, what am I going to do?' she blubbered. There was no other way. She would have to call him.

Kellie prepared herself by covering her girlie bits with the facecloth and crossing her arms over her monstrous boobs.

'James,' she yelled at the top of her voice. There was no reply. 'He must have the flaming television going and can't hear me,' she grumbled. Three times, she called out and he didn't answer.

By now, she was crying hysterically. 'Oh, someone please help me.' The bath had cooled so using her toe she ran more hot water and that made things worse as the bath deepened.

'James, help me!' she screamed in desperation.

Then she heard a knock on her bedroom door. 'Kellie, are you all right?'

'No, I'm stuck in the bath.' Oh how she hated this.

'Good Lord,' she heard him mutter.

Another knock. This time on her ensuite door. 'Do you need help?'

She scowled. 'I c-can't get out.'

He slid the door across and saw her predicament. 'Good grief, the bath's almost overflowing.'

She went hot and cold with embarrassment. 'I know that. I h-had to keep adding hot water as I was getting c-cold,' she bawled. He could see the distressed state she had got herself into.

'Shhh, stop crying.' He grabbed a bath towel off the heated-handrail and threw it over his shoulder. 'Now try and sit up so I can reach under your arms.'

She did so and he knelt down and put his hands under her armpits. She moved her arms and knew her massive boobs would be in his full view and her humiliation increased.

He took a deep breath and after a couple of attempts had her standing upright. James grabbed the warm towel, wrapped it around her bubble covered body, and helped her step out of the tub.

'You'll be all right now, so stop crying.' He pulled her pink shaking body close to his chest. 'Oh Kellie, in your condition its best to use the shower.'

'I k-know that, but I felt like a bath,' she blubbered.

He let her go and leaned over to pull out the plug. 'Will you be all right if I leave you now?'

She clutched the warm towel tightly to her chest. 'Yes, thank you. And James…' she called as he turned to leave, 'if you ever tell anyone about this, anyone at all, I won't be responsible for my actions.'

A slight grin appeared on his normally sombre face as he nodded and left the bathroom.

Kellie dried herself and put on her huge tent-like nightie and dressing gown then lay on her bed. 'Oh dear god, how awful was that. I don't know how I'm going to ever face him again.'

She didn't have to wait long. The next minute there was a soft tap on her bedroom door.

'Can I come in?'

Oh not again, has he come to rub it in? she wondered. 'Yes,' she called out and pulled herself up.

The door opened and in came James, Harry, and the dog.

'We brought you some spaghetti bolognaise. It's nice and hot.' He carried a tray over to her bed and put it across her lap. Harry climbed up next to her and Charlie took a great leap and only just missed the tray.

James shook his head. 'Get off there you two. You'll spill the food.' He pushed the dog off the bed and lifted Harry down. 'I'll take this pair of rascals out and leave you to eat in peace.'

'Thank you. This smells good.' She met his eyes and saw a touch of humour in them. 'Thanks for before,' she murmured then quickly turned her attention back to the food as the trio left the room.

Chapter Twenty-Nine

Tuesday morning they had a nine thirty appointment for their pre-wedding interview at the registry office. They took separate cars again as James had a busy schedule at work. Harry went with them and quickly became bored. Climbing over a chair he accidentally kicked a glass stand, sending a large pot-plant flying, spreading dirt everywhere.

James apologised. 'I'm sorry, if you get a broom, I'll clean up the mess.'

'Don't worry, I call one of the cleaners,' said the gentleman conducting the interview. He asked a few questions and outlined the wedding ceremony. 'Do you have two witnesses?' he asked.

James nodded. 'Yes, we do.'

'Good. On the day, be here fifteen minutes before the service. Please don't be late as we have several weddings that particular day.'

They were both embarrassed to leave such a mess in his office and James looked cranky as they left. 'I'll see you two later,' he muttered. He walked to his car, hopped in and drove off.

Oh well, thought Kellie as she strapped Harry into his car-seat, *Kids will be kids and have accidents, it's no big deal.*

The rain that had been threatening all morning suddenly pelted down so she headed for a shopping centre where they could have morning tea.

'Come on, Harry let's go and have a big nosh-up.' The young boy grinned, he didn't know what she meant, but he could smell food. By the time they arrived home, the rain had stopped so she phoned Betty up the road.

'Hi, it's me Kellie.'

'How are you love?'

'Good, are you doing anything at the moment?'

'No why?'

'How would you like to come down for a cuppa and see what I'm wearing to the wedding?'

'Give me five minutes to change my old cardy and I'll be there.'

Kellie struggled into the dress then added the coat and looked in her mirror. She smiled at her reflection, happy with her extravagant choice, then stepped into her shoes and picked up the matching purse.

True to her word, the old lady was there five minutes later. 'Oh Kellie, you look lovely,' she commented. 'That style hides your tummy and it's very classy if I may say so.'

Kellie grinned. 'This should look classy, it cost me a fortune.'

'Yes, but its lovely material and such a pretty colour. You could get it altered after the baby comes, it would be worth doing.'

'I hadn't thought of that, what a good idea.'

The old lady's face beamed with pleasure at being able to help.

'Excuse me a moment,' Kellie said and left the kitchen. She waddled into her bedroom and grabbed the shopping bag containing the dressing gown. Back in the kitchen, she handed the gift to the old lady and dropped a kiss on her wrinkled cheek. 'This is for all the times you've helped me.'

'What the...' stuttered her neighbour as she opened the bag and removed the large tissue wrapped parcel.

Her eyes nearly popped out of her head when she saw what it was. 'Oh Kellie love, what a beautiful dressing gown and my favourite colour.' She stood up and tried it on. 'Look at that, just the right size.' She hugged the pregnant girl. 'You couldn't have given me anything nicer.' She slipped her hands in the pockets. 'And what's this?' She pulled out the Myer voucher James wanted her to have. 'Another Myer's voucher – one hundred dollars. Oh dear me, what a day I'm having. Here let me sit down.' She sat back at the table. 'You know Kellie, I've never really had much to spend on myself, there were always others that needed things, but look at me now!'

'That was James's idea, the voucher is from him.'

'I'll have to thank him. Oh how lovely.' She took off the dressing gown and put in back in the shopping bag. 'Where's that cuppa love, I think I need it.' Betty huffed and puffed as she flopped back in the chair, a dazzling beam of happiness spread over her timeworn face.

After dinner, Kellie asked James about his parents. 'Are you inviting them to the wedding?'

'I did, but they can't make it. My dad has prostate cancer and is having chemotherapy. In between treatments, he's so ill he has to rest. At the moment my mother can't leave him.'

'I understand, the poor man.'

'I told her we would visit them in a couple of months when he's up to seeing people.'

'We'll have the baby with us then.'

'That's all right. I told Mum we're expecting a child.'

'Does she know this is not your child?'

'No, I'll tell her at some later date, but they will love the child, you wait and see. They only have two other grandchildren, my sister Sarah and her partner live in South Africa and my parents have never seen their six-year old twin girls.'

'Oh, what a shame.'

'They lead busy lives. Sarah's a nurse and Michael, her partner, works at a gold mine in administration.'

'I feel sorry for your parents, but I've heard Bribie Island's a lovely place to live.'

'It's nice, but there's not much to do. It suits my parents as they like a quiet life-style. They've made good friends there and they play bowls and cards down at the local club. It's very social.' He called Charlie. 'We're off for a walk now, how about you hop up on that window-seat and have a rest.'

Kellie grabbed a chocolate bar, turned on the television then did as he prescribed.

Friday morning she had an eleven-thirty appointment with her doctor.

James phoned before she left. 'I'll mind Harry while you're in seeing Richard, tell Moira to buzz me when you arrive.'

'Okay, I'll do that.'

It was getting harder and harder to fit into decent maternity clothes. They all seemed to be stretched to their limit. She pulled out the black maternity pants again, and her long green shirt then tied her hair back and wound the black scarf around her neck so that it hung down over her massive bulge.

Moira saw them walk into the surgery and came around the reception desk to greet them both. 'Kellie, you look a picture of health and Harry my boy you grow taller every time I see you.'

Harry rewarded her with his most charming grin and she hugged him tight.

'Take a seat you two, Dr Wilkinson won't be long, and I'll let James know you're here.'

Kellie didn't like waiting rooms and looked around for a seat well away from the other patients who sniffed and coughed as they fingered the magazines.

'Kellie,' Dr Wilkinson called, 'Hello there, young Harry, I think your dad's looking for you.'

The young boy took off towards the back of the surgery just as James came out to get him.

'Whoa there, you young rascal.' He called as he picked up his son and disappeared into the kitchen.

'Come this way, Kellie.' Richard called and she followed him into his consulting room.

'How have you been?'

'A bit tired, but otherwise I feel fine.'

'Well, hop up onto the couch and we'll see how this baby's doing.'

He listened to the foetal heartbeat, gently prodded around, then helped her down.

'Hm-m, all's well, but your blood-pressures creeping up. I want you to rest as much as you can. Delegate some of that housework. Maybe you could ask James to do the vacuuming.' They both laughed. 'I'll see you again,' he looked at his calendar, 'Friday, the third of September. Not long to go then until the wedding.'

Suddenly he turned serious. 'James is a great bloke you know,' he met her gaze as he spoke. 'If he says he'll look after you and the baby, take it from me he will really look after you.' He smiled kindly.

'I know what you mean and I'm sure that's exactly what he will do.' She stood up and smiled. 'Thanks for your help and…' momentarily, she was lost for words, 'Oh well, thanks for everything.'

He knew what she meant and shook her hand as he said goodbye.

***

James took them to lunch and invited Moira, who always kept Kellie up to date with the latest surgery gossip.

'You know Sandra, the young red head that works with me, well would you believe her boyfriend's behind bars and each weekend she goes off to visit him. I don't know what he's in there for, I daren't ask. He could be an axe murderer for all I know.' They cracked up laughing, although James' laugh sounded tinny, and he didn't look happy about it. All too soon, it was time for him and Moira to get back to work.

Kellie drove home with Harry fast asleep in his car-seat. Just as she slowed down to turn into their driveway there was a sound like thunder. She pulled into the garage, unbuckled her seat-belt, and looked to see where the noise came from. 'Oh no' she whispered in horror as a group of leather-clad motorbike riders thundered past the end of the driveway.

They were slowing down and she realised where they were heading. 'Oh my God, Betty!'

Quickly she woke Harry and lifted him out of the car then hurried inside. She was terribly worried about her old friend up the road. After a few minutes, the noise started up again and then the sound gradually disappeared. She grabbed Charlie's leash, he carried on like a dog from some circus because he'd been shut inside for the last few hours. 'Come on Harry, we need to go and check on Betty, quickly now.'

***

Betty had been sweeping the steps out the front of her house when suddenly, she heard a distant rumble and started to shake. It was the bikie mob again. 'Oh please, dear God, let them pass on by,' she whispered. The noise was slowing. 'Oh no…' They turned into her driveway.

She stood rooted to the spot as they rode in and stopped. One rider got off, kicked the stand to hold up his bike then removed his helmet and came towards her with a baseball bat.

'Where's the mangy little grub?' he snarled.

'H-he's not here,' panic caused her to stutter.

'You'd better tell me where he fuckin well is, bitch-face or I'll rearrange your ugly old dial.'

Once more, her bladder let her down and she felt a warm trickle running along the inside of her leg. 'I h-haven't seen him this past w-week.'

He came towards her brandishing the bat. Betty clutched her broom, paralysed with fear.

'Do I need to loosen your fuckin tongue, you dried up old hag?'

She shook her head, tears of sheer terror coursed down her crinkly cheeks. 'I d-don't know,' she wept, 'w-where he is.'

The angry mobster stopped and wacked the bat into his opposite hand then laughed as he noticed the puddle at her feet. 'Tell him we want the dough, you old piss pot. He's dead meat, you hear me, mother of scum, dead as a doornail.' His mates revved their machines as he turned and sauntered back to his bike. With a look of pure venom directed at the terrified old woman, he flung his helmet on and kick-started his motorbike then they all thundered off.

Betty slowly sank down onto the wet wooden steps as they turned out of the drive and with an almighty roar headed back the way they had come.

***

She was still there when Kellie and Harry arrived a few minutes later. 'Betty, are you all right? I saw them go past on their way here. Oh, you poor love.' She reached down and put her arms around the old lady's shoulders.

'I wet myself, Kellie,' she cried, 'they frightened me so much I w-wet myself.'

Kellie sank down beside her. 'Harry, you take Charlie and go and look at the goldfish, there's a good boy.' They ran off.

She turned back to her old friend. 'Let me help you up.' With her arm around Betty's back, somehow, between them, the old lady managed to get to her feet. Somewhat shaken and embarrassed she made her way inside.

Kellie followed close behind. 'I'll put the kettle on while you go to the bathroom.'

Betty returned a few minutes later. 'I didn't think they would ever come back.' She pulled out a chair and wearily sat down at the table. 'I really didn't,' she mumbled and dropped her head down onto her folded arms.

Kellie gave her a few moments. 'Were they after Ross again?'

The older woman nodded.

'Did they hurt you?'

Betty shook her head. 'No, but he said they're going to kill him. I'm scared this time they really mean to do it,' she whimpered as she dabbed her eyes with her apron.

'I don't know what to say. We should call the police.'

'No, we mustn't do that. Just leave it. Please, just let it be.'

Kellie put the two mugs of tea on the table. 'Oh Betty, you can't go on like this.'

'I know I have to think of something – maybe mortgage the house…'

'Let's sleep on it for now,' Kellie advised, 'drink up your tea its getting cold.'

Kellie stayed a while longer, then called Harry and Charlie, and they set off home. She was worried sick about the old lady and told James what happened when he came in.

'We should tell the police.'

'I know, but she begged me not to.'

'This has the potential to turn very ugly. The next time there's an incident at Betty's I'm calling them no matter what she says.' He left the room shaking his head.

***

Kellie stayed home over the weekend. She rested by the pool on a sun lounger, ate chocolates, and read magazines. Spring had arrived early, with warm sunny days, and bulbs of all descriptions popped through the ground – daffodils and freesias bloomed and fruit trees that had been in bud were now in full-flower. Large trees that lost their leaves before winter now sprouted fresh new ones and noisy Lorikeets chatted non-stop as they went about their daily business.

Kellie ate too much chocolate and ended up feeling ill. The baby kicked and jumped, and seemed to do summersaults. 'Probably protesting over its mother's diet,' she mumbled.

Betty came down and brought them some yummy ginger biscuits and a banana cake. James made a pot of tea and they all sat out on the verandah watching Harry and Charlie roll around the soft green lawn. Betty looked pale but seemed all right.

'She holds it all inside,' Kellie told James later. 'Fancy someone as lovely as her having such a rotten son, it's hard to believe.'

***

The following Friday she saw Dr Wilkinson again. 'Your blood-pressure is still a worry. Are you resting like I advised you to?'

'Yes,' she answered and thought to herself, *If only he knew how worried I am about Betty, he would understand. Her troubles are enough to send my blood-pressure through the roof.*

'Well, the next time I see you will be at the wedding. I hope all goes well, Kellie and remember, call me if you have any worries. Now I'll see you again...' he looked at the calendar; 'we'll make it in one and a half weeks, Wednesday the fifteenth.'

***

James thought it was a great idea for Kellie and Harry to stay two days with Shirley and Bob prior to the wedding. It gave them both a short time apart. He took a couple of days off and dealt with a pile of paperwork and Child Services. They had to be notified each time Harry's circumstances changed. He took Charlie on long walks trying to adjust to the idea of being married again.

The first time had been wonderful until Serena became pregnant and put him through sheer hell. Kellie was already pregnant, her moods swung to and fro, but she was never nasty or mean. Even though he wasn't the father of her child it didn't bother him, he felt as though he was, in a protective sort of way, and looked forward to the baby's arrival.

The more he walked and chewed things over the better he felt. Charlie helped, you could talk to the dog and he never answered back just gave unconditional love.

He collected Kellie's wedding ring from the jewellers and bought her a stunning gold and diamond watch as a special gift, to celebrate their marriage.

I'll give it to her when we get home after the wedding, he thought as he put the beautifully wrapped box away

Chapter Thirty

Kellie covered her dress for the wedding and hung it on a hook in the car making sure James couldn't see it as he waved them goodbye. Harry jiggled with excitement in his car seat, clutching his old teddy and two new books his dad had bought him. He had a new suitcase with Thomas the Tank Engine on it, and his good clothes for the wedding were neatly packed inside.

'We are going to stay with Aunty Shirley and Uncle Bob. They live by the beach. You're going to have such a good time,' Kellie told him. James waved goodbye and her stomach did a flip as she realised the next time she came back to Wonglepong she would be his wife.

She took a deep breath, checked on Harry in the rear-vision mirror and then drove off, heading for Currumbin.

Bob had told her to call five minutes before they arrived and he'd go out and open the gate so Kellie could drive right up to the house. They didn't want the scary dogs frightening Harry.

As they pulled up, Shirley and Sam came rushing out to meet them. 'Here comes the bride,' they sang in unison then Sam continued, 'fair, fat, and wide.'

Kellie patted her tummy. 'Fat and wide's right.'

'Hi Kellie, darling,' called Shirley as she opened Harry's door and undid his seat-belt.

'Hello, Harry.' She helped him out of the car with his teddy and books then reached for his little suitcase.

Nervously, he looked around. He smiled when he saw Sam, who grinned at him.

'Hi Harry, what have you got there?' She knelt down and he showed her his new books, but kept hold of the teddy. 'Would you like Aunty Sam to read you one of these books afterwards?' He nodded and held out the one on native birds.

She opened it and looked at the pictures. 'I like wild birds as well. Remember how we watched them in your garden at home.' The young boy nodded. 'Come on, we'll go inside. There are lots of nice things to see in this house, they even have water-falls.' Harry eyes opened wider as he took Sam's out-stretched hand.

Shirley gave Kellie a welcoming hug. 'Come inside, love. Here, I'll carry 'the dress' and your bag. You look tired. The tea's ready I made it when you phoned a few minutes ago.'

They made a real fuss of her and Harry. After a light meal and a bath, Sam read the young boy his bird story and he soon fell asleep. Shirley left a soft night-light going in case he woke during the night.

Bob made an extra special dinner and bought a bottle of Moet to celebrate, 'this auspicious occasion', as he called it. 'I even bought a bottle of non-alcoholic wine for you Kellie with...' the telephone rang and he stopped and answered it.

'Kellie, its James, for you.' He handed her the receiver.

'Hi James, is everything okay?'

'All's well. I called to see how you both were. Did Harry settle down all right?'

'He's fast asleep. He had a very exciting afternoon. Bob took him down to the beach and he collected more shells to bring home.'

There was a moan on the other end of the phone. 'What about you – you're not too tired?'

'I'm fine. Bob bought me a bottle of non-alcoholic wine and cooked a fabulous feast. I'm being very spoilt.'

'Good. Oh well, take care, goodnight.' He finished the call without giving her a chance to wish him goodnight, but she thought it was nice of him to call.

Sam piped up, 'Wow, is the doc checking up on you Kel?'

'He wanted to know if Harry settled okay.'

Bob looked up from his meal. 'He's probably lonely in that big house and it would be very quiet without the two of you there.'

'Thanks Bob, are you saying I'm noisy?' Kellie teased.

'Not at all, I admire the guy for what he's doing, and I wish you both all the best.' He raised his champagne glass. 'Let's drink a toast to Kellie and James.'

The other two did the same. 'To you both.'

'Yer,' spouted Sam, 'May all your problems be little ones, like in nappies.'

'Oh,' cried Kellie, 'You're hopeless,' and shook her head.

Sam went home and returned the next day. She painted Kellie's fingernails and her toenails then made sure 'the dress' was ready to wear.

'He's not likely to be seeing my toes you silly goose,' muttered Kellie.

'Silly goose yourself, all this titivation will help you feel more confident and you'll be beautiful as well.'

It went on and on and Kellie appreciated all the trouble they went to. They made her feel quite special.

Harry enjoyed his stay, he potted around outside with Bob who gave him small jobs to do, and Shirley made a big fuss of him. The young boy thrived on all the attention. He ate his meals and did small things for himself that he never did at home.

'He's a great kid, Kellie, and it's a shame he doesn't speak,' Bob said. 'Once I thought he was close to saying something as he showed me a blue tongue lizard, but no luck there.'

'He is a lovely boy,' she replied. 'Especially when you think of all he's been through in his young life.'

***

Saturday morning dawned overcast and humid. Kellie woke to find Shirley standing by the side of her bed holding a tray.

'Hi love, it's traditional for brides to have breakfast in bed the morning of their wedding, so here it is.'

Kellie sat up and leaned against her pillows, then pushed her bedclothes back. 'Hold it a minute, Shirls, I need to go to the loo first.'

Back in bed, savoury smells wafted up as a daintily presented tray was placed across her lap. A plate held strips of hot crispy bacon, two small sausages, half a tomato, and one egg sitting on a piece of toast. Next to it was a small pot of tea with a dainty milk jug and matching cup and saucer. A small rose and a pretty serviette were placed on one side.

'Oh Shirley, what a great looking brekky. Thank you so much, I can't wait to get stuck into all this.'

'Eat up and enjoy. I'll take care of Harry. He's sitting at the table eating Weet-bix and toast with Bob.'

Sam arrived soon after breakfast and started on Kellie's hair.

Shirley came into the bedroom amongst all the chaos. 'Hand me Harry's clothes and I'll get him ready for you. By the way, Mary rang and she can't make it to the wedding, she's got the vomiting and diarrhoea bug. That useless husband of hers went down with it and now he's given it to her.'

'Oh poor Mary, what bad luck. I'll give her a call tomorrow to see how she is. Here's Harry's gear. Thanks Shirls.'

Sam helped Kellie get dressed. It was a real challenge. Getting the maternity pantyhose on was a struggle. They appeared to be too small.

'These flaming things are the wrong size, Sam,' yelled Kellie in frustration.

'They're meant to stretch love, just keep pulling. They are designed for big bellies like yours. Here let me get a good grip.' She yanked and pulled until she had them up and over her friends bulging tummy.'

'Whew,' they gasped then sat back and giggled.

The wedding dress was next. It was another struggle and when they eventually pulled it into place, it was too tight. Kellie's waist had expanded so much since they bought it that the belt at the back had to be adjusted. Next came the coat. They looked in the mirror.

'Wow!' Sam murmured, 'you look absolutely stunning.' Then she produced a small box. Nestling inside was a tiny spray of miniature white orchids.

'Oh Sam, they're so beautiful?'

'All brides need flowers of some kind and I thought these would look nice on your lace coat.' She pinned them just above Kellie's left boob then stood back. 'Yep, lovely. Now you look like a real bride, girlfriend.'

Kellie looked in the mirror. Sam had made a lovely job of her hair, at home, she usually tied it up in a pony-tail, but now it hung loose in a shining mass down to her shoulders. She stepped into her high-heeled shoes then picked up the matching clutch bag and again checked in the mirror. Was this really her, she found it hard to believe she could look this good.

'That dress is worth every cent you paid for it Kel. You look a million dollars. Come on, we'll go and show you off.'

Trying not to waddle, Kellie followed her friend out to the lounge-room where the others waited.

'Oh, Bob, just look at her,' cried Shirley. Then Harry ran over and clutched her legs just like he did at home.

'Come here, Harry' Bob called, scared the child might somehow mark the special outfit. Then he coughed, as he tried to keep a tight rein his emotions. 'Kellie, y-you look absolutely fabulous.'

Shirley wiped her eyes. 'I'm sorry, but beautiful things make me cry and you look truly lovely, my friend.' She gave the bride a gentle hug.

Bob produced a silver tray containing four small glasses. 'Now let's have a toast to a very special bride. May you find happiness, Kellie, the sort you so richly deserve.'

They all sipped their drinks. 'Here, here,' her friends called in unison.

'How are the butterflies, Kel?' Sam whispered.

Kellie gave her a watery smile, 'Don't ask.'

Bob realized the bride-to be was struggling with her nerves and couldn't take much more. 'How about I drive Kellie and Harry to the registry office in her car and you two,' he looked at Sam and Shirley, 'follow us. We'll all meet there.'

'Sounds a good plan to me. Grab your clutch-bag, love,' Sam said to Kellie as she helped everyone get organised.

'Come with me young fella,' Bob called to Harry, 'and I'll help you get in your car seat.'

As they left, Shirley crossed her fingers. Sam did the same. Kellie wondered what the hell she was doing and Bob whistled as he drove, trying to keep the bride's spirits up. Harry sat in his car-seat clapping away to Bob's happy tunes.

***

Out at Wonglepong, James had been for an early morning run, trying to settle his jittery nerves. He showered then sat out on the back verandah with his coffee, contemplating the life-changing commitment he was about to make. He had sworn never to trust a female ever again and now he was letting this young pregnant woman be part of his private life! 'Oh dear God.' He sighed. 'What have I got myself into?'

He couldn't eat any breakfast and wondered how Kellie was coping. This was also a huge step for her.

He got up and walked around the garden. Down by the back fence, lorikeets danced on the branches of native grevillea trees and roses in a nearby plot gently scented the early morning air. He took several deep breaths, and slowly, very slowly, he calmed down and felt ready to face the challenges that lay ahead.

He'd asked Betty, their elderly neighbour to be ready by nine-thirty so they had plenty of time to get to the registry office.

She was ready and waiting, dressed in her best clothes as she called them. 'Oh James,' she gabbled 'I didn't sleep a wink last night. I was so excited about today.'

'Hop in, Betty, you look very nice.' He lied. She wore a mottled blue coat with a yellow scarf and dark blue shoes. James thought she looked like a scary canary!

'Thank you James, I haven't had this good coat of mine out for years. You look very smart.' They both smiled then chatted about the weather.

They reached the Southport Registry office a little early. There was no sign of Kellie, but Moira and Don were there, as well as his colleague and best mate Dr Richard Wilkinson.

'Hi James,' Moira hugged him, 'and nice to see you again, Betty.' They chatted together. A few minutes later, Kellie's car arrived, followed by Sam's.

Bob quickly hopped out and went round to open Kellie's door, then unclipped Harry from his car-seat, and lifted him down. The young child saw his dad and ran over.

'Who's this good-looking boy,' exclaimed James as he lifted him up. Harry beamed with delight. James looked over and saw Kellie. He thought she looked quite charming, but somewhat nervous.

He walked over. 'You look very nice,' he said quietly. Her heart pounded and she nodded her thanks. She couldn't speak, her emotions were threatening to rise up and spill over.

James introduced himself to Bob and shook his hand then the older man took Kellie's arm.

'Shall we go in?'

She nodded and they walked into the building. James and their small group of friends followed behind. The room they were shown into was very plain. It had half a dozen wooden chairs and a small desk. The air was musty and cold.

Bob passed Kellie's hand to James in front of the man waiting to conduct the simple ceremony. There was a heart stopping moment for Kellie when James reached for her hand and put the wedding ring on her finger. His hands felt warm and strong. *Much like him,* she thought.

Next, they signed the register. Moira and Don signed as witnesses.

The registrar declared them man and wife then presented them with their marriage certificate. He wished them all the best and shook their hands.

James held Kellie's arm as they walked outside. Their friends congratulated them, and then they all headed to the Sheraton Mirage, where they were booked in for the wedding luncheon.

'I'd like you and Harry to ride with me, then Bob can take Shirley in your car, and Sam can take Betty.' Kellie nodded, it looked better if they travelled together.

As they headed towards the hotel for their meal, Kellie felt overwhelmed with the enormity of what she'd just done. James didn't say anything and Harry grizzled, he was hungry and needed to go to the toilet.

There was a reserved sign on their table as well as three floral arrangements. Kellie thought her new husband had done really well, then later found out that Sam had organised the flowers. James sat Harry between them, which suited her fine, as she didn't want James' thigh rubbing against hers. With a fake smile, she played her part and tried to enjoy herself.

She was up at the buffet getting desert when Moira whispered in her ear. 'Are you okay, love?' Kellie nodded.

Moira continued, 'You look smashing. I even saw James gazing at you before, and he had a funny look on his face, almost a doting husband sort of look.'

'I think you've had too much to drink, Moira.'

'No, I know what I saw. He probably couldn't stop staring at you because you look so gorgeous.' They both laughed to pass off the embarrassing moment.

The variety of food was amazing and their friends made the next couple of hours a fun time. Moira's Don had a bit much to drink and his jokes were to getting naughty so Richard Wilkinson quickly decided to propose a toast to the Bride and Groom.

Their friends all drank to their health and happiness, Kellie's smile wobbled as James replied, thanking them all for coming, and their good wishes. Harry was in his element. He sat on different people's knees and smiled for Sam as she took happy snaps. A short while later he accidently spilled chocolate ice-cream down the front of his good clothes. A kindly waiter produced a damp cloth, and Kellie cleaned him up the best she could. Then James said it was time for them to leave.

'I'll take Harry home, and leave you to give Betty a lift – is that all right with you?' he asked.

Kellie nodded. 'That's fine, but I need to go to Bob and Shirley's place first to pick up our gear. We won't be far behind you.'

Bob drove Betty and Kellie back to his place and Sam took his wife as she'd left stuff there as well.

Sam couldn't wait to comment. 'How do you think Kellie handled it all?'

Shirley took a deep breath then answered. 'On the outside she looked great, but underneath it all, I felt her anxiety and hesitation. Still, she knows what she's letting herself in for. I like James, but he's such a stuffed shirt, not at all her type.'

'I agree. He always seems so up himself. Still we'll just have to wait and see how it all unfolds, the poor cow. I certainly wouldn't want a cold fish like him in my bed.'

'She said he won't be in her bed. They are keeping separate rooms.'

'Yer until his hormones get the best of him, like any other randy male.'

Shirley giggled, 'Oh you're awful Sam, no wonder you're not married.'

'Na, I'd rather have no one than have what she's got.'

'The only difference is that she's got a child to consider and they both need a roof over their heads.'

'I know that, but at what cost? I stay on the pill all the time just in case I get lucky.'

Shirley nearly choked. 'Oh my God, Sam, I've got sore ribs from laughing, but seriously we need to keep in touch and make sure she's okay.'

'I'll do that all right, if he doesn't step up to the mark, he'll have me to answer to. I've decked a fella before now and he came off second best, let me tell you.'

Shirley held on to her ribs. 'What on earth did he do to warrant that?'

'He screwed the pants off me, then I found the mongrel had concealed a camera in the light fitting. Dumb bastard, I kicked him a beauty in the crown jewels and he gasped like it was his dying breath. He left town soon after that as I let it be known what he'd been up to.'

'Oh, Sam,' Shirley nearly went to pieces. 'Remind me never to cross you.'

They arrived at Shirley's house just behind the others. Bob was wheeling Kellie's suitcase out to her car and under one arm, he clutched a large beautifully wrapped present.

'Oh, what have you lot been up to?' exclaimed Kellie.

'Don't open it until you get home,' Shirley said as she hugged her.

The weary looking bride gave them a lop-sided grin, her lips wobbled. 'I don't know what I'd do without you wonderful people.' She fought back tears as she spoke. 'Betty and I'll be off now. Thanks again for all you've done.' They wiped their eyes and waved until Kellie had turned out of driveway and headed down the street.

'Good luck, darling,' murmured Shirley.

'Here, here,' joined in the other two.

'She'll need it,' Sam whispered.

***

Betty had knocked back a few whiskies at the wedding and on the way home, she was in fine form. 'I had a great time today, Kellie love, that Sam had me in stitches. Did you hear her tell the one about the old prossie? That nearly blew my socks off,' she roared with laughter. 'Not that I've got any socks on,' she giggled. 'I'm glad I'm going home with you and not James as I might need to stop for a pee, it was the fruit salad I had, too much juice in I for me, far too much juice.'

Kellie laughed, 'I think it might have been the whisky, Betty.'

'Oh yer, and what about that Don, he knows a few good jokes doesn't he. He told a couple that nearly made my hair curl, dirty old bugger.' She chuckled away laughing at herself.

Kellie listened to this all the way home and twice had to stop on the side of the road for Betty to pee. The second time the old lady fell over with her undies down around her knees and Kellie had to help her up. It was a relief to deliver the tipsy old woman safely to her door.

Chapter Thirty-One

James and Harry had changed their clothes and were ready to take Charlie for a walk when Kellie arrived home. She felt strange walking into the kitchen where they were and babbled to hide her nervousness.

'What a character Betty is, she drank far too much whisky and giggled all the way home. I think she'll have a whacking great headache in the morning.'

'I'm glad she enjoyed herself, she gets very few pleasures,' James commented.

He went to leave then turned back. 'Don't worry about dinner, I've ordered something in.'

She looked up at him. 'Oh, that's nice,' and wondered what he'd organised. 'By the way, there's a wedding gift in the back of the car to bring in, when you've got a spare moment.'

He grinned. 'There are two more in the lounge-room. We'll open them later.'

'Okay, I'm going to have a rest now.'

He nodded, Harry waved, and they left with Charlie.

***

Kellie undressed and lay on her bed totally exhausted, physically as well as mentally. She briefly closed her eyes and when she woke up it was dark outside the window. She felt like staying where she was, but thought she had better make an effort since James had ordered a meal.

After a warm shower, she put on her large tent-like flannelette nightie and cosy dressing gown. It wasn't a good look, but what the heck, it maybe her wedding night, but the marriage wasn't a love-match, so this look would do.

She walked into the dining room and felt somewhat embarrassed. James had the dining table set nicely with a candle in the middle and a single orange rose out of the garden in a drinking glass.

He stood there looking awkward. 'I couldn't find a small vase.'

'We don't have one. That looks okay.'

He pulled out a chair. 'Here have a seat.' She sat down and he brought over the wedding gifts they had been given. 'Do you want to open them or shall I?'

'You can. We'll watch.'

From Shirley, Bob, and Sam, there was a superb beach seascape. It was beautifully framed and she instantly loved it.

James looked at the painting. 'That's fabulous and will look great in the lounge-room above the china-cabinet. What do you think?' He gave her the wedding card to read. The words were very moving. Kellie couldn't speak for fear of losing control.

The next one he unwrapped was from his work, a cutlery set housed in a dark wooden stand and there was a beautiful card signed by all the staff at his surgery.

James shook his head. 'This is superb quality. They have been extremely generous.'

'They must think a lot of you to give us such a gift.'

He nodded and picked up the last package. 'This one is from Betty.' He carefully opened the gift box. Inside, wrapped in masses of white tissue, was a fragile crystal vase. 'This is exquisite,' he murmured and gently handed it to Kellie, then he opened the attached card and read it out loud.

'"To Kellie and James, all the best, much love from Betty". Underneath she's written, "This vase belonged to my grandmother. She left it to my mother and I'm giving it to you. Treasure it as I have done. My love to you both". What a nice gift.' He looked at Kellie, she sniffed and pulled out a tissue as tears welled up and spilled down her cheeks.

'W-what a lovely thing to do, giving us something that is so precious to her.'

'I agree,' and with that he put another small gift in front of her. 'This one is for you.'

Oh my God, she thought, *what's this all about?* Nervously, she undid the elegantly wrapped present.

She found a red-velvet jewellers box. Not daring to look at James, she lifted the lid. Inside nestled a beautiful gold and diamond watch, in a very delicate setting. 'Oh James, this is gorgeous.'

'I wanted to get you something special as today you did me a great honour. I know our marriage is a bit different, but to me it's worth celebrating.' He looked slightly embarrassed as he spoke.

Kellie struggled to find a suitable reply. 'T-thank you, thank you very much. This is the most beautiful watch I have ever seen. I will treasure such a gift, thank you James.'

Then they heard a vehicle come up the driveway.

'That's our dinner arriving.' He said. The dog barked madly and Harry jumped up and down with excitement as James answered the door. Kellie stayed where she was, nearly freaked out by what had just taken place.

She looked at the watch again. 'I can't believe he did this. Wow!' Lifting it out of its box, she decided to put it on, turning her arm this way and that. She loved it. It looked terrific on her wrist. 'Just wait until I show this to Sam, boy will she be envious.'

James came in and carefully put a platter of steaming Italian food in the centre of the table. 'Here, you help yourself and I'll put some on a plate for Harry.'

They soon cleaned up the platter and it was followed by her favourite desert, tiramisu.

Kellie was tired, but very grateful. 'Thank you for going to all this trouble James. I enjoyed every mouthful.'

'I didn't do much just made the phone call, but I'm pleased you liked my selection.'

He still has a pompous manner about him, she thought, *even when he's being nice.*

'Harry and I will tidy up, you have a rest. This has been a huge day for all of us, but more so for you.'

Blimey, thought Kellie, *I am on a fuss.* She went into the lounge-room and turned on the television, then lay on the sofa, fiddling with the remote.

Sleep overtook her and she woke to find James gently shaking her arm. 'Kellie, wake up.'

She woke with a start and couldn't believe she'd nodded off. 'I hope I wasn't snoring with my mouth wide open?'

'No you weren't, but I think you should hop into bed. I'll bring you in a hot chocolate drink if you like.'

'That would be nice, thanks.' She hugged Harry. 'Night, night, love, you've been a good boy today, and I was very proud of you.' He snuggled into her neck and gave her a sloppy kiss on the cheek.

Kellie lay back on her bed propped up with pillows and waited for her bridegroom to bring in her drink. *Crikey,* she thought with a grin, *some brides would be getting Moet champagne and a night of steamy passion, but I'll happily settle for a mug of hot chocolate.*

She was fast asleep when he came in with her drink so he switched off her light then tiptoed out of the room leaving the door slightly ajar. He went back to the lounge-room and poured himself a glass of red wine. 'To my wedding day,' he toasted.

The next couple of days passed quietly. Kellie didn't feel all that great so she took it easy, resting whenever possible. She read books and had lengthy gossip sessions with her girlfriends on her mobile. Sam couldn't believe James had given her such a magnificent gift and suggested he'd given it to her hoping to get his conjugal rights! They both cracked up laughing knowing that wasn't going to happen.

By Tuesday, she had perked up and after collecting Harry from kindy, they had some lunch and she decided to write out her wedding thank you cards while the young boy had his afternoon nap.

Chapter Thirty-Two

Further up the road, Betty had just finished her lunch when she heard the deep rumble of a motorbike. 'Oh dear God, what does he want this time?' She cringed with fear. Ross hadn't been around lately. She hoped he'd found a job.

The front door crashed back against the wall as he stormed in. 'I need money, where's your wallet?' He couldn't remember which drawer it was in and yanked them open one by one. Some came right out and he threw them across the room. 'Didn't you fuckin hear me, I need money now!' As he pulled out her tea-towel drawer, he saw what he wanted. 'Ha ha your wallet, is there any bloody thing in there?'

Terrified, Betty cowered beside her kitchen bench.

Ross ripped it open. 'Twenty dollars, is that all, where the fuck's the rest?'

She shook so much she couldn't speak.

He grabbed the front of her old cardy and jerked her towards him. 'I fuckin well know you've got money somewhere, find it bitch.'

'T-that's all I have,' she stammered.

'You stupid ugly old mole...' he yelled and belted her across the cheek.

'Oh don't...' she cried and covered her face with her hands.

He spat at her. 'I fuckin hate you, old woman, do you hear me, I hate you!' Then he delivered a mighty backhander to the side of her head, knocking her off balance and over she went. She fell heavily, landing on one of the drawers he'd thrown on the floor.

She felt a bone snap in her arm and screamed in pain. 'Ohhh, p-please Ross, no more.'

He booted the leg nearest him, again and again. 'Shut the fuck up you old hag, if you won't give me money, I'll call on the doc's whore down the road, I'm sure she has cash to spare.'

'No, Ross,' Betty whimpered, 'no...'

He grabbed the twenty dollar note then stormed out the front door, leaving his mother in a twisted groaning heap on the cold kitchen floor. Convulsive sobs racked her body and there was pain, so much pain.

She tried to move. 'Ohhh,' she whimpered and then her world went black.

***

Kellie was still writing out thank you cards on the kitchen table when she heard Ross's motorbike come up the drive.

'Oh no,' she whispered, 'what's he doing here!' Her heart raced and she started to tremble. There was a loud crash as he booted open the front door. Kellie felt a warm trickle run down her leg.

He charged into the kitchen. 'Where do you keep it, bitch?'

She couldn't get any words out.

'Money!' He screamed. 'Where do you fuckin keep it?'

Terrified she stood there as a puddle formed around her feet.

'You filthy bitch. If you won't find it I will.' He upended drawers and threw things around while yelling filthy insults at her.

Her thoughts went to Harry, cuddled up asleep with the dog in the bedroom across from the kitchen. 'Please, dear Lord,' she silently prayed, 'keep them safe.'

Ross found the housekeeping tin above the fridge and shook it violently. 'Ah ha, what have we got in here?' He shoved the week's housekeeping money in his pocket then noticed her watch; the one James had given her as a wedding gift. 'A nice little piece that is. Give it here!'

'No, please don't take...'

'Can't you hear me bitch, I said give it here!' He pulled her arm and roughly yanked off the watch.

'Oh please Ross, just take it, and leave us alone.' Protectively she placed her hands over her large tummy.

He sneered. 'That's right, having the doc's bastard aren't you bitch. I'll give you "please Ross", he mimicked and struck her hard across the face.

'She gasped. 'Ohh!' He hit her again then grabbed her left arm twisting it around and up behind her back.

'You're hurting me,' she shrieked, 'stop, please stop!'

'He keeps drugs here doesn't he, where are they?'

'He doesn't...'

'Where are they?' He pushed her arm higher.

'Ahhh, stop, stop! There aren't any here,' she cried.

Driven by jealousy and drug-fuelled anger, he let go of her arm and wildly lashed out catching Kellie across the forehead. She saw bright lights and stars as she reeled backwards, catching her head on the corner of the buffet before she fell and lay unconscious on the floor.

Ross gazed down at her in disgust. 'Stupid bloody bitch you can't even stand on your own two fuckin feet.' Then the sparkle of her wedding ring caught his eye and he grabbed her limp hand and brutally tugged the diamond band off her finger. 'Wake up you fuckin whore. You're pissing me off, wake up…' He kicked her in the stomach, but she didn't move. 'Well stay down there then and here's one for your fuckin brat,' and he booted her again.

He dropped the ring in his pocket and looked around. Satisfied with his lucrative haul he smiled and decided to leave. Heading for the front door, he passed James' bedroom and went in. He smirked. On the bedside table lay two expensive men's watches. 'Oh my, these will bring in a few readies,' he muttered then went into James' ensuite where he nicked some tablets from the bathroom cabinet.

Feeling quite chuffed with himself, he whistled as he high-tailed it out the front door and leapt on his Harley and sped away.

***

Harry had been woken from his sleep by screams, loud voices and crashing sounds. The noise and yelling got worse, he was really frightened so he hid under the bed and put his fingers in his ears. Then he clutched the dog, and they both kept very still.

Then it became quiet, all the noise stopped. He waited a few minutes then ventured out of his room. At the door he listened again, it was still quiet, so he tip-toed to the kitchen. Kellie lay on the floor, he could see some blood by the side of her head and down by her knees. He tapped lightly on her arm, usually she woke up when he did that, but this time she stayed asleep. The young boy knew something was seriously wrong and he needed to get help. *Dad*, he thought, *Dad*, and reached for the telephone. Kellie had taught him which button to press and his dad would answer. He pressed it and waited.

***

James' phone rang in the middle of a consultation. 'Excuse me,' he said to his elderly patient and answered the call. 'James Harvey speaking.' There was no sound at the other end. 'Hello. Who's calling?' Still no answer. He stood up and left the room. He could hear someone sniffing and then he heard a dog bark, *Charlie!* Something made him say, 'Harry, Harry is that you?' No answer. 'Harry, give the phone to Kellie.'

'Dad... dad!'

'Harry, give the phone to Kellie, there's a good boy.' Fear started to build in his stomach.

'Sleep, sleep,' the child repeated.

'Harry! I'll come straight home, you stay there with Charlie.' *Oh dear God, what was going on!* He went into an empty treatment room and called the police station at Canungra, it was located about ten kilometres from his home, and he quickly explained the situation.

'We'll send someone out there straight away. Where can we contact you?'

He gave them his mobile number then went back to his patient, apologized, and wrote out the scripts he required.

'I'll see you again in a month's time,' he told him.

Immediately, he called reception and asked Moira to come to his room while he grabbed his medical bag and mobile ready to leave.

She knocked briefly. 'What's up, James?' He told her, she gasped and placed a hand over her heart, such was her sense of panic.

James continued. 'Ask Dr Wilks to see the patient I have waiting and I think there are two more later this afternoon. Can you ring them and ask if they could reschedule their appointments?' He took a deep breath and tried to keep calm. 'I don't know why, but I have a bad feeling about this.'

Moira nodded. 'You get on home. Drive carefully and keep in touch. Off you go.'

As he left, she quietly prayed.

***

The local police sergeant pulled into James' driveway and got out of the car. As he walked up the front steps, he could see the door had been kicked open. 'Police,' he called and drew his baton. 'Police,' he called again as he cautiously made his way through the house. Just inside the kitchen, a young lad crouched in a corner with both arms around a small dog. The boy let out a soft whimper and tucked his head into the dog's neck.

'It's okay mate, I'm a police officer, and I've come to help.' He patted the hand of the small frightened boy and scratched the dog's ears then looked further into the room. A young woman who looked to be heavily pregnant lay on the floor, gasping and holding her stomach. Blood was caked on the side of her head and there was more blood and water forming a small puddle under her legs.

'It's all right, Miss, I'm a police officer. I'm just going call an ambulance.' He went outside and called back to the station, then trying to appear calm, he knelt down by the injured woman and quietly told her help was on the way.

'Kellie is it?' She blinked. 'Your husband's on his way home. We'll get you to a hospital and someone will stay with the boy until he gets here.'

Kellie had regained consciousness just as the police sergeant arrived. Her head hurt – it hurt something awful and the pain in her tummy was unbearable. 'Ohhh,' she tried to move.

'Lay still Kellie, you might do more damage.' He noticed a tea towel on the bench and he wet it under the tap then gently wiped her face, not going near the injured side of her head. He'd been called out on many occasions that had been upsetting, but to see a young expectant mother with such injuries choked him up. He had a wife and two young kids at home. Nausea rose in his throat.

In the distance, the wail of an emergency siren could be heard and he breathed a sigh of relief.

The paramedics quickly took in the scene, one worked on Kellie, while the other brought in a stretcher then radioed for the rescue helicopter.

More police arrived and a young policewoman chatted quietly to Harry. After a few minutes, she lifted him to his feet and along with the bewildered dog, they went out the back and sat on the verandah in the warm afternoon sun.

Charlie bounded out for a quick pee then sat back beside Harry. The small boy looked a mess, his runny nose had mixed with tears, and his pants were wet. She kept talking to him as she patted the dog, trying to comfort and soothe the distressed child as they waited for his dad to get home.

Before long she heard the throbbing sound of the helicopter, it was going to land in the local sports field just a short distance away.

The police sergeant came out. 'The paramedics have just left to meet up with the chopper. I've been in touch with her husband, Dr Harvey, and he's about five minutes away.' He looked at Harry and patted the arm clutching the dog. 'Your dad will be here soon mate.' He looked around the backyard and noticed the tree house. 'Is that your cubby up there?' Even though his little face was awash with tears, Harry nodded. Charlie started to bark and pull away. 'That must be dad arriving now.'

Harry jumped up and took off. James met him coming in from the garage and swung the young boy up in his arms then walked over to sit on the window seat. Nothing was said.

James rocked to and fro with the boy on his lap. Harry's thin arms clung tightly around his dad's neck and the dog had his head against the doctor's leg. The police officers left the room for a few minutes so James and Harry could have some private time together.

James lifted his head and looked at the mess, and then noticed the blood and water on the floor. His stomach heaved and his heart rate doubled almost jumping out of his chest. Bile rose in his throat as he thought of what Kellie must have gone through, and he wondered how much of the violence Harry had witnessed.

The sergeant came back into the kitchen. 'Dr Harvey, I'm Sergeant Stephen Campbell.' He held out his I.D. 'Are you okay mate?'

James nodded. 'Where have they taken my wife?'

'The Brisbane Women and Children's Hospital.'

'Good. Their obstetrics are amongst the best. She's in good hands.'

'Do you know who would do something like this?'

Suddenly like a bolt of lightning, James stood up and put Harry down. 'We need to check on my elderly neighbour right away.'

The cop got a surprise, but said, 'All right hop in my car.'

The officer pulled into Betty's driveway and James told Harry sternly to stay where he was.

They rushed in and found Betty groaning on the floor.

'Oh James,' she gasped. 'T-thank God you're here. Can you h-help me up?'

'No,' he said gently, 'stay where you are and we'll call an ambulance. Who did this Betty? It was Ross wasn't it?'

The old lady nodded as she wept. 'H-he wanted money.'

James shook his head, sickened by such brutality. 'Your left arm; let me have a look at it.'

'Ohhh, oh my God…'

'I think it's broken. We'll need to get this looked at and your nose needs attention. Your legs are twisted. How do they feel?'

Slowly, she moved them. 'Ahh!.. I think they're just bruised. I'll be all right.' She winced as she spoke. An angry welt stood out across her face and a blood-clot poked out from one swollen eyelid. 'Tell me James,' she slurred her words, 'what's with all the sirens, what's happened?'

'Kellie's been attacked.'

Betty sighed. 'Ross, do you think it was Ross?'

'Possibly.'

'Oh, James,' Betty sobbed, 'I'm so sorry. Is she badly hurt?'

He didn't want to add to the old lady's misery. She'd suffered enough. 'I don't know yet, they've taken her to Brisbane.' He looked at the police officer, busy taking notes. 'This lady needs to get to the Canungra hospital and have her injuries looked at ASAP. Can you organise that?'

'Sure, I'll call the ambulance now then drop you home.' He instantly returned his pen and pad to his shirt pocket then unclipped his radio and went outside.

James turned to the injured woman. 'Betty, I'll give the police Ross' details, do you know where he might have gone?'

She breathed deeply struggling to cope with the pain. 'All I know is that a mob of bikies have been here twice lately, looking for him. They said he owed them money.' She stopped for a minute. 'A bad lot they were; scared me half to death.'

The sergeant overheard what she said as he came back inside. 'I know Ross and his mates, we've crossed paths before.' He pursed his lips, then turned to Betty. 'You hang in there love, I'll take Dr Harvey and his son home now then I'll be straight back to stay with you until the ambulance arrives.'

After they left, Betty's troubled mind turned to Kellie. She prayed all would go well for her precious friend. Then she thought about Ross. Knowing her only child was capable of such violence shocked her beyond belief. He was now lost to her forever. Weighed down with grief and shame she wept and slid temporarily into another world.

***

On the way home, James updated the police officer with Ross Thompson's details. He took more notes then immediately radioed through to his supervisor.

Once back inside the house, Harry let the young policewoman wash his face and hands and change him into clean clothes. Then, while James chatted to the sergeant, she helped the young boy bring out a box of Lego and choose a building project from the instruction manual. This lad almost broke her heart. His eyes spilled the occasional tear.

Excusing himself, James went to his study and called the hospital. He didn't have much luck. They said Mrs. Harvey had only just arrived and her condition was still being assessed. He was told to call back later.

Next, he phoned Moira at the surgery.

'Hang on, James, I'll go and take this call in your consulting room.'

He waited until she got to his desk. 'Are you there? How is she? What's happened James?'

'Slow down now. Kellie has been badly injured. They've taken her by air-ambulance to the Brisbane Women and Children's Hospital. I called them, but they couldn't tell me anything as she had only just arrived.'

'Oh dear God, what happened?'

'We don't know yet. The police are still here, they want to speak to Ross, Betty's son. He went to her house demanding money. He must have been in an ugly mood as she's been knocked around quite badly. Then he obviously moved on to our place.'

'What about Harry, is he okay?'

'He seems fine at the moment, but I wondered if Don would come out and stay with him and Charlie while I go to the hospital.'

'Sure thing and I'll be coming along with him. Give us an hour, we'll grab a few things and drive out. It's not busy here and even if it was, they can still cope without me. Oh James,' she sighed, 'my heart breaks for that poor girl.'

'I know.' He went silent on the end of the phone. Moira felt dreadfully sorry for him, she knew he was becoming very fond of Kellie.

'Hang in there, mate and we'll see you soon.'

James put the phone down and shook his head. 'Why, why did this have to happen just when everything was starting to come right?' he asked himself, 'and what drives a man to attack a woman due to give birth?' He rubbed his tired eyes as he searched for some answers.

***

Moira immediately phoned Don and filled him in. 'Throw our pyjamas and toothbrushes in a bag. I'll be home in five minutes and we'll leave straight away.'

On the way out to Wonglepong, Don concentrated on his driving while Moira phoned Kellie's close friends. They were speechless and offered any help they could give.

The pain Sam felt for her friend could almost be heard over the phone. 'Oh dear God no,' she cried. 'Oh Moira as soon as I finish my shift I'm off to that bloody hospital. I need to be there for her.' She choked and howled out loud.

'I doubt they will let you in.'

'They won't be able to bloody stop me,' Sam wailed. 'I have to go, even if I just sit there.' The line went dead.

Moira and Don arrived at James' home to find two police cars still parked in the driveway.

He came out to meet them. 'Thanks for coming at such short notice.'

'How's Harry,' Don asked.

'He seems to be coping. He's with a young policewoman. They have the Lego out and she's helping him build something. The forensic people are here taking fingerprints and so on.'

Moira unpacked the car. 'I'll go and see if they'd like a cuppa and some of my fruitcake.'

'Thanks.' He turned to Don. 'Could I trouble you to go and check on Betty? She's been taken to the Canungra hospital with some nasty injuries. Will you let me know how she is?'

Don nodded and gently patted the doctor's shoulder. 'I certainly will. That poor lady's had such a rough spin. Don't worry mate, we'll make sure she's being well looked after.'

Moira grabbed James' arm. 'You'd better get off to the hospital, don't worry about anything here, Don and I can manage. I told them at the surgery to cancel or change all of this week's appointments, or they can see one of the other doctors.'

'Good,' said James. 'I'll ring later and let you know what's happening.' He had a quick word with the remaining police officers, said goodbye to Harry then left.

Chapter Thirty-Three

James arrived at the hospital and went straight to reception. He told them who he was, why he was there, and asked to speak to someone in charge. A no-nonsense middle-aged woman behind the desk made a phone call.

While he waited, his stomach churned. *How badly was Kellie hurt,* he wondered *and how much damage had been done to her unborn child?* He paced up and down then looked at his watch. *Twenty minutes I've been waiting, what the hell's going on?*

He marched back to reception. 'What's the hold-up here?' Angrily he banged his fist on the desk. 'Twenty minutes ago I asked to speak to somebody in charge!'

'Dr Harvey, please be patient... ah, here's someone to see you now.'

A tall, well-built man with bright red hair came towards him. 'Dr Harvey, I am Edward De Witt, head of A and E.' The two men shook hands. 'Please follow me.' He ushered James into a small sparsely furnished room off reception. 'Take a seat.'

'Your wife has some serious injuries. We suspect her uterus may have ruptured and she's in theatre at present.'

James dropped his head and covered his face with his hands.

'As you well know, Dr Harvey, time is critical when this happens and Mr. Lambert our chief obstetrician is performing a C-section. Your wife has lost a great deal of blood and after the delivery he will evaluate the extent of her injuries and proceed from there.'

The sick feeling in James stomach returned twofold. 'Did my wife understand the seriousness of her condition?'

'Yes. She was conscious when we explained the risk involved and she gave her consent to go ahead. She also has a deep gash above her right ear that will be cleaned and sutured in theatre.'

James took a deep breath, stood up and held out his hand. 'Thank you. I won't detain you any longer.'

Edward De Witt got to his feet and shook the proffered hand. 'Rest assured, Dr Harvey, your wife is in excellent hands.'

***

James desperately needed a strong coffee so he headed off in the direction of the canteen. He wasn't fussed on the cardboard mugs they served the drinks in, but there was no choice. While he sipped the hot liquid, it suddenly struck him. Harry had spoken! Yes, he had, on the telephone. He called him Dad. 'Oh, my Lord!' He couldn't bear to think what would have happened if his son had not made that call.

He needed fresh air to clear his head so he went outside and walked for half an hour. On his return, he made his way up to Theatre reception and spoke to the nurse on duty. She took his details and directed him to a small waiting area where several hard chairs were grouped around a television set. He looked at his watch, seven o'clock. He should phone Moira, but mobiles were not allowed to be used inside the hospital. 'Oh well,' he muttered to himself, 'I'll call her later.'

After three long hours, the door opened and a theatre-clad man came into the room with a mask dangling from his neck. 'Dr Harvey?'

James nodded and stood up.

'I'm Russell Lambert, chief of obstetrics.' Wearily he rubbed his eyes. 'Your wife should make a full recovery, but unfortunately she will never be able to have another child. I tried my best to repair the damage, but...' he shook his head, 'she hemorrhaged, then I had to do a hysterectomy. I'm sorry, I had no choice.'

'What about the child?'

'A baby girl. She's been taken down to the neonatal unit. When she left the theatre, she was barely alive. I don't have any details on her present condition, but you are welcome to go down and see her.'

'I'll go there now.' James shook his head, worn out with so much misery. 'Thank you for looking after Kellie. I'm extremely grateful for all you have done.'

Russell Lambert held out his hand. 'I just hope they catch the person responsible. Nothing can bring back what she's lost. All the best.' They shook hands and he left.

James took the lift down to the second floor, followed the directions to the neonatal intensive care unit, and saw the nurse at reception. He told her his name and asked to speak to someone about his baby daughter.

'Please take a seat, Dr Harvey. I'll see who is available.'

Once more, James waited with gripe-like pains attacking his empty stomach. On the wall were the rules of entry, what you could and could not do in this area. The list was huge. Thirty minutes later, the nurse came back followed by a white-clad person wearing a face-mask.

'Dr Harvey, I'm Sarah Duncan head paediatrician. Nurse will get you gowned and bring you through to the nursery where you can see your daughter. Her condition's not good I'm afraid, but we'll chat more in a few moments.'

James' muscles tensed after hearing further bad news.

Scrubbed and coated in sterilized gear from top to toe, he walked quietly behind the nurse. Even his watch and ring had to be removed. She said they might carry infection.

The unit was impressive. It featured all the latest hi-tech equipment and was well-staffed by doctors specialising in the care of seriously ill and newborn babies.

They entered a huge brightly lit room filled with machines and incubators. Sarah Duncan put her hand up and beckoned him over. She stood by a humidicrib with another doctor. He was taking blood from the tiny infant inside.

'This is your daughter, Dr Harvey. Do you have a name for her yet?'

James shook his head. He stood there lost for words, overwhelmed at the sight of the fragile scrap of humanity that was Kellie's child. Tubes were connected to her little body and machines stood by her bed beeping, and displaying graphs and other information. A miniature name band around her wrist had, 'Harvey' printed on it.

Dr Sarah Duncan chattered as she checked various monitors. 'It's too early to tell you much about her condition. It's critical at the moment. We are running tests and will know more in the morning. She'll be constantly monitored as she has a rapid heart rate and an irregular breathing pattern. At the moment, we don't know why this is. You can stroke her wee arm if you like.'

James put his fingers inside the incubator and gently picked up the baby's miniature hand. Something tightened inside his chest as he gently rubbed his thumb across her tiny fingers.

'Come back in the morning,' the doctor suggested, 'we'll call you if there's any change.'

Reluctantly he withdrew his hand and said a silent prayer for this little girl.

***

He desperately needed another coffee so he made his way back to the canteen, bought a hot drink, and carried it outside. A strong southerly wind howled cross the front of the building and it was cold on his face, but it felt good, it helped clear his fog-filled mind. He looked at his watch, it was nearly mid-night, but he thought he'd better give Moira a call. Knowing her, she would still be up watching some gruesome television programme.

'Hello, James here.'

She coughed and sputtered. 'Oh my God, James, I had a mouth full of coffee.' She cleared her throat. 'What's happening? I've nearly been out of my mind with worry.'

'Kellie sustained some serious injuries and her uterus was ruptured.'

'Oh no!' Being a trained nurse from way back, Moira knew the dangers of such an injury.

'She's had a baby girl.'

'I can tell by your voice something's wrong James, spit it out.'

'The baby's having breathing problems. They're doing tests as we speak, but won't know anything until the morning.'

'What about Kellie?'

'I haven't seen her yet, but I spoke to the surgeon who operated. He's hopeful she'll make a full recovery.'

'Are you okay, mate?'

'I'm outside in the cold wind trying to blow a few cobwebs out of my head.'

'Well don't worry about young Harry, he's fine. Don gave him horsey-rides around the house and it wore them both out.'

'What about Betty?'

'Her face looks a mess and her arm's in a plaster cast. Her legs are badly bruised but not broken, thank goodness. They rang and said she could go home so Don took Harry with him to pick her up from the hospital.'

'I can't believe they sent her home,' James growled.

'Don brought her back here so we can keep an eye on her. She's in Kellie's room, protesting that she wants to go back to her own house. She's a tough old rooster. She doesn't complain. Don went down and got started on her place. It's in a terrible mess thanks to that mongrel son of hers. We'll make sure its back up to scratch before we let her go home.'

'Thanks Moira and please thank Don as well. I'll let you get off to bed. I'm going up to see Kellie now. Hopefully she's out of recovery.'

'All right, call me in the morning. Goodnight, James.'

He walked for a while. He needed the fresh air. There was a great deal of activity around the hospital, ambulances left, more arrived: it went on and on.

Back inside he took the lift up to the level where the theatres were and asked if he could see his wife.

'Take a seat, Dr Harvey, while I'll call recovery,' said the night-sister working at a nurse's station on that level.

She made the call and waited. 'Her husband's here,' she pulled a face. 'All right I'll tell him.' She went pale and quietly put the phone down. 'I'm sorry. You can't see her at the moment. You're welcome to wait in the office, there's a comfy chair in there and I'll call you when they contact me.'

'Thank you.' He went in and sat down then leaned back and closed his eyes.

He woke to someone gently shaking his shoulder.

'Dr Harvey, you may see your wife when you're ready. She's been taken to our high dependency unit on level four.'

He stifled a yawn. 'Thank you, I'll need to freshen up first.'

'You'll find a visitors' bathroom as you enter the unit.'

He made his way to the fourth level. The lights were turned down low, as it was two-thirty in the morning. He freshened up in the bathroom then went to the reception desk, told them who he was and asked to see his wife.

'Room nine, Doctor. There is a nurse with Mrs Harvey. Would you ask her to report back to me? I can only allow you to stay a few minutes.'

'Thank you. What can you tell me about her condition?'

'She's very weak. There were complications during surgery and more problems in recovery. We'll keep her here for the next twenty-four hours to make sure she's stabilised then transfer her to our maternity unit.'

He found room nine, the door was open, and a nurse was adjusting a drip. She left and he stood quietly by the side of Kellie's bed. His eyes watered as he stared at the battered, bruised young woman. With a jolt, he realised just how much she meant to him.

He couldn't see much of her face for bandages, but the parts he could see were black with bruising and one eye was swollen shut. Life-saving blood flowed into a vein on one arm and a drip was connected to the other. Various drains came out from under the bedclothes.

Her good eye flickered open. 'James,' she whispered and a tear spilled out.

Gently, he laid a hand on her wet cheek. 'Don't cry. You're going to be all right.'

She seemed agitated. 'The baby,' she murmured. 'Tell m-me about the baby.'

'We have a little girl.' He waited for that to sink in.

'A little g-girl.' Kellie sighed. 'Is, is she all right?'

Oh, what could he say? 'She's had a rough time but she's getting the best of attention.'

'Have you s-seen her?' Kellie slowly whispered.

'Yes, she's very small. She weighs only two and a half kilos.'

Her mouth moved into a slight smile. 'Lucy, I'd l-like to call her, Lucy Marie.'

'Lucy, I like that. I'll let them know so they can put that on her chart.'

'Did Ross hurt B-betty?'

So it definitely was Ross that attacked these two defenseless women. 'She has a broken arm and a few bruises. She's staying at our place with Moira and Don. They came out to look after Harry.' He noticed her diamond wedding band was missing. 'Where's your new ring?'

Kellie slowly peered at her hand. 'I don't k-know.' Still sleepy from the anaesthetic she had trouble forming her words.

He made a mental note to check the whereabouts of that ring. 'I am only allowed to stay a few minutes,' he said as her good eye struggled to stay open, 'so I'll go now and see how Lucy is, but I'll be back later in the morning.' He leaned down and dropped a brief kiss on an undamaged part of her cheek then left. The nurse who had been waiting outside the door went back into the room to watch over her patient.

As he passed the reception desk on his way out, he asked about Kellie's wedding ring.

The nurse checked her paperwork. 'No, Mrs Harvey had no jewellery on her when she was admitted.'

'Thank you. I'll be back around lunchtime. You have my mobile number, please call me if her condition changes.'

He went back to the neonatal unit and spoke to the nurse at the desk. Once more, he garbed up and she escorted him to the unit where Lucy clung to life. A different doctor was adjusting a tube inside the baby's nose. 'Poor little mite,' James thought.

The guy stepped back, 'Caress her lightly, it will let her know you're here.'

James put his hand in the incubator and ever so gently picked up Lucy's fingers and willed her to hang on.

'Is there any change?'

'No, unfortunately, she's slipped back a bit.'

Before he left the hospital, he looked on the information board for directions to their Chapel.

Wearily, he went inside and sat down. There was a feeling of inner-peace as he gazed at the stained glass windows that filtered coloured light onto a wooden cross fixed to the plain front wall. A crystal vase filled with white carnations stood on a polished wooden table, adding a delicate fragrance to the quiet sacred room. James bowed his head in silence and prayed for the life of little Lucy and for Kellie's speedy recovery.

He left the hospital almost asleep on his feet and nearly banged into Sam.

'Oh James, thank God. How is she? I tried to see her, but they won't let me, told me I have to come back when it's visiting hours. Bloody cheek, she's my very best friend...' The distraught women went on and on.

'Come and sit down.' He guided her towards a bench seat a short distance away.

'I've been so worried, James,' Sam cried as she sat down.

He put his arm across her shoulders and gave her a gentle hug. She was a wonderful friend to Kellie and had been a great support to them all over the last few months.

'Sam, she's given birth to a baby girl, Lucy. Kellie's had a rough time but she will pull through.' He went on to explain her condition and that of the baby, trying not to upset her more than she already was. In the end, she agreed to go home and come back later.

The sun in all its brilliance peeped over the hinterland, ushering in a brand new day as James drove home. He quietly let himself inside, had a shower, then went straight to bed.

Chapter Thirty-Four

Later that morning, Kellie woozily opened her good eye. It took a while to work out where she was. A nurse stood next to her adjusting something.

'Good morning, Mrs Harvey, how is the pain?'

Who's she talking to, thought Kellie, *who's Mrs Harvey?*

'W-where am I?' she dopily asked the nurse.

'You're in hospital. You've had an operation and everything's gone well. Are you in much pain?'

'My head h-hurts.' She muttered and then fell back to sleep. The next time she woke, she remembered James had been there earlier and told her they had a baby girl. He'd left and she'd gone back to sleep. The nurses kept doing things, when all she wanted to do was shut her eyes, she was so tired. 'Why don't you leave me alone?' she muttered.

'Mrs Harvey, I need you to get out of bed and sit in the chair.'

Who's she kidding? Kellie thought. However, the nurse persisted and with her help, Kellie made it to the seat along with her drip stand.

'We have to get you mobile, even though it's a struggle.'

Back in her bed, she fell asleep. When she woke up, James was there, looking at the chart on the end of her bed. He had been home and had a short sleep then returned to the hospital.

He looked up. 'Oh, you're awake. How are you feeling?' He came over and sat by the side of her bed then gently picked up one of her hands.

'I'm so sore,' she whispered. 'I h-hurt all over.'

To take her mind off the pain, he quietly chatted about things at home. 'Moira and Don send their love along with all your girlfriends and I nearly banged into Sam early this morning. She desperately wanted to see you.'

'Oh, the poor girl, maybe I'll get to see her soon.' She spoke ever so slowly. 'When can I see the baby?'

'I'll go and ask.'

The door opened and Sam stood there, the look on her face said it all. 'Just as well you're here, James, or I wouldn't have recognised my very best mate.' She wiped her eyes. 'Oh Kellie,' she cried and tiptoed over to the bed then gently kissed her injured friend.

James walked towards the door. 'I'll go and see how Lucy's doing and be back in half an hour.'

They hardly noticed him leave as Kellie clung to Sam's hand and they wept together.

James made his way down to the neonatal unit, garbed up, and went in to see Lucy. A lady doctor stood by her incubator studying a chart.

She looked up. 'You must be Lucy's dad?'

He nodded.

'I'm Sally Hart, chief in charge today.'

'Is there any change in her condition?' He put a finger through the side of the crib onto her tiny hand.

'No, not yet. Lucy has us puzzled. At the moment we're waiting for Dr Davidson to check her over, he specialises in infant heart and lung problems.' She handed him a chart, 'here, you can see how rapid her respiratory rate is on these graphs and that accompanied by an accelerated heart beat is cause for major concern.

'My wife is asking to see her.'

'Come back later this afternoon. Hopefully we will know more by then.'

James went back to Kellie's ward and spoke to the sister in charge. 'When do you think my wife will be transferred to the maternity unit?'

She checked her paperwork. 'M-m, probably later in the day. Her condition has stabilised and her blood pressure is almost back to normal. All going well, about four-thirty we'll move her, before we get busy with dinners.'

'Thank you, she'd like to see her baby.'

'I'm sure she would. We can take her to the neonatal unit in a wheel chair after lunch if you like.'

'That would be great, thank you.' He returned to Kellie's room and told her what was happening.

'James, I really want to see Lucy.'

'You'll be able to this afternoon. The sister said they'll take you down in a wheel chair.'

'I hope I don't frighten the poor little girl.'

James smiled. 'Does that mean you've seen yourself in a mirror?'

'Sam held one up and I couldn't believe it was me.' She told him more about Ross Thompson. He was obviously playing on her mind.

After lunch, he phoned Moira, gave her an update, and asked if she would check Kellie's jewellery box to see if her new watch was in there. He waited while she had a look.

'No James, there's only a few coloured necklaces and other bits.'

'All right thanks. How's Betty?'

'She's away with the fairies quite a bit but otherwise she's doing well.'

'And Harry?'

'He's gone to the tip with Don. He spoke a couple of words. We were making your bed and he patted the pillow and said "Dad, dad sleep". Then when we made his bed, he patted that and said, "Bed, my bed". I told him how clever he was and his little face just beamed. James, I nearly cried.'

'I know. He saved Kellie's life by doing what he did. I'm so proud of him.'

He finished the conversation then called the sergeant at the Canungra Police Station and told him about Kellie's missing jewellery.

'I was about to call you Dr Harvey. I need to interview your wife – it will only take a few minutes.'

'It's not a good time.'

'I'm aware of that, but it's a must. I should be there in a couple of hours. Getting back to the jewellery, that's pretty important. Can you send us photos of the missing pieces and we'll circulate them to local jewellers, pawn shops and places where he might try to knock them off. He's after money this boy, so I pick he'll try and get shot of them fairly quickly.'

'I'll send that to you now. There are photos of them on my phone as I needed them for insurance purposes.'

'Good. By the way, how are your wife and baby doing?'

'My wife's had a rough time, but luckily she will recover, but its touch and go with the baby girl.'

'Send me those photos ASAP. I want this mongrel behind bars!'

James thanked him and ended the call, then found the photos and forwarded them to him.

He went shopping and bought Kellie magazines and ordered an arrangement of pink roses to be delivered to her room. He bought a coffee and went for a long walk to clear his head.

About four o'clock, he made his way back to the hospital where they were getting her ready to move. Her colour had improved, which was a good sign.

They moved Kellie in her bed, with a nurse wheeling the drip stand, down to a private room in the maternity unit. The room was opposite the nurse's station, which pleased James, as he knew they would keep his wife under constant observation.

There was a great deal of clatter and banging of dishes, people talked and laughed and babies cried; all normal noises. He knew she would be well looked after.

The nurse had just settled Kellie when the sergeant from the Canungra Police station arrived.

He nodded at James and introduced himself to Kellie. His face registered the shock he felt at seeing how extensive her injuries were. He had been first on the scene.

'I'm sorry to bother you, Mrs Harvey, but I need a few details.' He asked many questions and James stopped him when Kellie became distressed.

'I'm sorry to cause you more grief, Mrs Harvey, but we needed this information while it's still fresh in your mind. I'll go now, good luck to you and the baby.'

He left them and Kellie cried and cried. She had tried so hard to hold it all together.

'James I n-need to see Lucy,' she pleaded tearfully.

He struggled to compose himself after listening to what had happened. 'I'll g-go and see about it now.' He went over to the nurse's station and five minutes later returned with a nurse pushing a wheelchair.

'Come on, Mrs. Harvey, we're off to see your little girl.' She helped Kellie put a dressing gown on then gently assisted her into the chair.

***

The nurse wheeled the drip stand and James carefully pushed her along the corridor to the lifts. They passed several people on the way who openly stared at Kellie and one even put her hand to her mouth in horror.

James leaned over her shoulder and whispered, 'Take no notice of these people, look straight ahead, and focus on where we're going.'

In the lift, he explained more about Lucy's condition, and what she could expect to see. He watched the colour drain from her cheeks, but she didn't say a word. The nurse gently squeezed Kellie's hand. They reached the neonatal unit where she was helped into sterilised gear. James gently tied a sterile mask around her injured head. She was transferred into a special wheel chair.

Gowned up, James pushed her down the passageway into the intensive care nursery with its beeping machines and incubators. He stopped beside a doctor who was busy altering a monitor attached to the tiny child inside an incubator. Kellie gazed at a small pink heart above the baby's head and read, "Lucy Harvey", clearly printed in black letters.

Her stomach clenched and unchecked tears ran down her cheeks. Lucy was an unusual yellowy colour. She had a small tube up her nose, a hose type device taped into her mouth and another tube ran into her little tummy. Monitors were stuck on her chest with wires that led to machines that beeped continually. Kellie buried her face in her hands for a moment and tears squeezed out through her fingers.

James spoke to the doctor and asked if they could have a few moments alone with their child.

He smiled. 'Sure, I'll come back in five minutes.'

Kellie lifted up her arm, drip and all, and pushed her hand inside the incubator. With one finger, she softly caressed the baby's hand and in a gentle voice quietly whispered loving words.

'Oh James,' she whimpered, 'is she going to make it?'

He couldn't speak. He was so choked up. He put his arm across her shoulders and held her tight for a moment. 'They will do their very best to make sure she does.' Even to him his words had a false ring.

The doctor returned. He'd seen a great deal of heartache and suffering in this unit, but his eyes watered as he took in this tragic scene. The young mother had terrible injuries to her head and the paediatrician knew the chance of the child surviving was very slim. 'I'm sorry,' he interrupted, 'but I need to change her feeding tube.'

James gently squeezed Kellie's shoulder. 'We should leave now. I'll bring you back later.'

She couldn't speak. Her whole body shook with sobs as he wheeled her away.

The doctor grabbed a tissue and wiped his eyes.

***

James pushed Kellie back to her room and helped her into bed. Gut-wrenching sobs shook her body and tears ran unchecked onto her pillow. She didn't settle so he picked up her chart to see what medications they had her on then went in search of a nurse.

'My wife requires sedation, by the look of her chart there's none written up. Could you please attend to this straight away?'

The nursing staff were aware of Mrs Harvey's plight and immediately rang through to the duty doctor to get his approval for the medication James requested. Back in Kellie's room, he held her hand while the night-sister administered the sedation. James stroked her hair and held her hand until she fell into a drug induced sleep.

His stomach churned with hunger pains, he couldn't remember when he last had something to eat, so he left the hospital and went searching for a café. He came across a brasserie by the Brisbane River and ordered a coffee then sat staring out the window at the murky water.

He wondered why he felt such heartache for this woman. She had come to him as a housekeeper, hiding the fact she was pregnant. Then he married her to give Harry a mother and Kellie a roof over her head. The baby wasn't even his and yet he felt for Lucy. He felt a deep and tender love for the critically ill little girl.

He ordered a meal, but left most of it on his plate. He called Moira and told her what was happening.

'Oh James, how terrible. I don't know what to say...' She broke down.

Don grabbed the phone. 'Moira will be all right mate. She's been worried sick, we both have. Betty's doing well and young Harry's fine. He's fast asleep. I told him that pirate story he likes and he was out like a light.'

'Thanks, Don. I don't know what we'd do without you two.'

'We're pleased to be of some help. S-see you mate,' he spluttered as he put the telephone down.

***

Kellie woke up and looked at the clock on her bedside table. Ten pm, then she noticed something on the stand at the end of her bed.

She turned her overhead light on. Flowers! Then she reached down to pull the stand towards her and opened the card. There was just one word written there, "James". There must have been a dozen tiny pink roses surrounded by baby's breath with its miniature white flowers and dainty greenery.

He had been so kind and supportive and she vaguely remembered him touching her cheek, was it with his hand or his lips. Kellie couldn't remember, but it felt nice at the time. Then her thoughts turned to Lucy and she wondered if there was any update on her condition.

The door opened and James came in. 'You're awake. Can I get you anything?'

'No thank you, and thanks for the roses. They're beautiful. They give my room a lovely…'

The door burst open and a nurse hurried in. 'You are both wanted down at the neonatal unit. They said could you please hurry. I have a wheelchair outside the door ready to go.'

James jumped up and helped Kellie into her dressing gown. Nothing was said as the nurse pushed her chair and James wheeled her drip stand down to the specialised unit.

They quickly gowned up and got Kellie into a special wheelchair, then James pushed her down to the intensive-care nursery where two white-coated men stood talking next to Lucy's incubator.

One looked up, 'Lucy's parents, right?' He didn't wait for a reply. 'I'm Matthew Davidson.' James guessed he was the heart and lung expert they had been waiting on. The other doctor they had met earlier in the day.

The specialist took off his glasses and looked directly at Kellie and James. 'I'm very sorry, but Lucy's taken a turn for the worst. A blood vessel that usually closes over after birth has not done so and this has caused complications. She's been given medication that should have helped do that for her, but she's not responding. Normally I would operate and surgically fix this problem, but Lucy's too weak to survive the operation. Sadly she is slipping away from us.'

Kellie let out an anguished cry, like the sound of a wounded animal. James grabbed her hand and held it tight. He blinked back tears and swallowed the lump forming in his throat.

They stayed with Lucy for over an hour then James gently removed Kellie's hand from where it lay on the baby's tiny arm inside the incubator.

Matthew Davidson returned and checked Lucy's monitors.

'Well, she's no worse.' He pulled a slight smile. 'The medication could be kicking in, it's hard to tell. I think you should go back to your bed Mrs Harvey and I'll get a Nurse to call you in a couple of hours.'

They returned to Kellie's room and James helped her take off her dressing gown. She was like a zombie and couldn't even lift her arms to pull them out of the garment. Then she sat on the side of the bed and quietly sobbed. James kept one arm around her shoulders and with the other, he tenderly wiped her face every now and again as they waited.

It was three am when a nurse tiptoed in. 'You're wanted down in neonatal unit. I have a wheelchair ready outside the door.'

Mr. Davidson, the specialist, stood by Lucy's incubator. He looked up and nodded as they came in.

'I think she might be over the worst, her vital signs are slowly picking up. We'll do another ultra-sound shortly to see if we've been successful in closing off that blood vessel.'

He looked at Kellie. He knew of her condition and how it came about. 'I wanted to give you some hope. She's not out of the woods yet, but I feel she's gaining ground.'

Kellie's head dropped onto her chest, she was unable to stop the rush of tears that streamed down her cheeks underneath the sterile mask. James grabbed some tissues and wiped her face then she carefully put her hand inside the incubator and stroked Lucy's arm. She tried to pass her love through to this tiny child. 'There's hope,' she cried, 'at last there's some h-hope.'

Chapter Thirty-Five

Kellie picked up after being given such wonderful news and as the days passed, Lucy's condition slowly improved. The young mother tried to express milk, but she had to give that idea away. It was hopeless. There was nothing there to express. The doctor said not to worry as babies thrived on formula and had done so for many years.

Then came the day when Kellie was allowed to hold her for the very first time. She beamed as a nurse lifted the tiny girl out from the incubator and carefully handed the baby to her.

James stood and watched. There were times when he thought this would never happen. The child's condition had been so grave.

'Oh James, just look at her, she has so much lovely hair.' They couldn't see that before as Lucy always wore a miniature beanie to hold in her body heat. 'I don't know where her red hair comes from. My family were fair-headed, and it looks as though she's going to have curls, isn't that lovely?'

He watched on and couldn't hold back a grin. He couldn't get a word in as Kellie slowly looked over her small daughter.

'Oh James, she's opened her eyes – they're blue, how about that?' She felt her heart might burst with love and pride. How lucky were they to have this beautiful baby girl.

***

Kellie spent another week in hospital. Friends came bearing gifts and flowers. There were days when she felt totally worn out because she'd had so many visitors.

Moira came with James and they brought Harry with them. He was shy at first but soon came right after eating some of the chocolates Kellie had been given. Then they all went down to see the baby, viewing her through a window in the special nursery.

'What a little pet,' Moira said with a break in her voice. 'Look at her hair, my goodness; she's going to be really beautiful.'

James lifted Harry up so he could see his new sister. 'There's Lucy, she'll be coming home soon.' Harry pulled a funny face and wriggled to get down.

Back in the ward, he soon became bored and knocked over a stand then grizzled when he couldn't have more chocolate.

'Someone's tired, I think,' Moira muttered as she sat him on her knee so he couldn't touch anything else.

As they all left, Moira kissed Kellie goodbye and Harry gave her a big hug then took off.

James called out from the door. 'I'll see you tomorrow afternoon. Give me a ring if there's anything you need.'

That was it. She shook her head. He had been very attentive while she was ill, but now it seemed everything was back to normal. She sighed. 'I think he forgets I exist once he leaves here,' she told herself in a moment of self-pity.

Sam came the next afternoon with another gift for the baby.

'You bring her something new each time you visit!' Kellie exclaimed.

'I know, but that's what Aunties do.'

Kellie looked in the gift-bag and undid the tissue paper to find a tiny summer top and pants in daffodil yellow with a matching sunhat, it was gorgeous.

'I can just see her in this,' laughed Kellie.

'Especially with that bright red hair,' commented Aunty Sam.

***

Kellie had just finished her dinner that evening when James arrived.

'Hello there. You're looking much better and there's some colour in your cheeks.'

'It's probably all that healthy blood they pumped into me,' joked Kellie.

He reached inside his jacket and brought out a small parcel. 'There are two gifts here. One is for you and one for Lucy.'

Kellie didn't know what to say as she undid the ribbon and sticky tape. There were two jewellery boxes. She opened one, inside was a beautiful gold chain bracelet with a heart clasp and safety chain. It took her breath away. 'This is so lovely,' she uttered and put it on her wrist. 'I've always admired these in jeweller's shop windows, never thinking I'd own one. Thank you James.'

He passed her the other box and inside was a tiny replica of the bracelet he'd given her. 'That one's for Lucy – a mother and daughter gift.' He looked somewhat embarrassed. 'It can be adjusted as she grows.'

Kellie's eyes watered and she swallowed a lump in her throat.

'Now, now,' James murmured, 'we've had enough tears.'

'I k-know,' blubbered Kellie. 'It's just that you are so kind and these g-gifts are so beautiful.' She stared at the small bracelet, imagining it on Lucy's tiny wrist. 'What a lovely thing to do, James.'

'That reminds me, I have her registration papers here.' The moment was lost as the papers were produced.

Shortly after that, he left with a brief, 'I'll see you tomorrow night.'

Kellie opened the boxes once again and lay back against the pillows admiring the contents. 'I wouldn't want to guess how much these bracelets cost him,' she whispered, shaking her head.

***

James drove home deep in thought. He was so confused. He hadn't stayed long with Kellie because he felt he might do something foolish. He'd wanted to hug her and say the gift was for her because he missed her so much and he'd wanted to tell her how proud he felt to be Lucy's dad. 'Hell, I'm getting myself all mixed up,' he grumbled and sighed for what might have been but knew he could never have.

***

The next day, the nurse removed the stitches from the side of Kellie's head. 'You may have to bring your hair forward for a while to cover this scar, but in time it won't be so noticeable.' The bruises on her face were now multi-coloured: blues and greens with patches of yellow.

'I can cope with the scar. From what I gather, I'm lucky not to have brain damage.'

'That's true and each day that passes, those bruises are fading a bit more. I'd say you'll be going home soon.'

'What about Lucy?'

'They'll keep her here a few more weeks, just to be on the safe side.'

Kellie bit her bottom lip to stop herself from bawling out loud. *How am I going walk out of here and just leave her behind? I thought they might do this, but it's going to be so hard.* She grabbed a fistful of tissues as a few tears escaped. However, commonsense soon kicked in and she pulled herself together. Deep down, she knew that only specialised medical staff could give Lucy the extra care she needed.

The nurse adjusted her bed. 'Now lay down Mrs Harvey and I'll remove the staples from the incision on your tummy.' It took the nurse a few minutes. 'That's healed nicely,' she commented. 'You'll have to be careful for the next few months not to exert yourself as you have many internal stitches and they will take much longer to heal.'

When the nurse left the room, Kellie studied the ugly scar on her tummy and wondered what exactly they had done in there.

When James visited after dinner, she asked him if he knew.

His face changed and he went over to the window and stood quietly staring at the bright lights of Brisbane, then he turned around. 'When you arrived here you had a ruptured uterus, which is a very serious condition. The hospital called in a surgeon who specialises in obstetrics. He carried out an emergency caesarean section and later told me he did his best to repair the damage to your uterus, but you haemorrhaged. To save your life, it had to be removed.'

'So, if I have no uterus that means I'll have no more babies doesn't it?'

'I'm afraid it does, but you have Lucy and you have Harry as well.'

Slowly she got off the bed and shuffled over to the window, gazing at nothing in particular. 'He did a real number on me didn't he, that mongrel Ross Thompson.'

'He certainly has a great deal to answer for.'

The room went quiet and James could hear the nurses out in the corridor giggling over something.

'How's Betty?' Kellie asked.

He shook his head. 'Don took her home yesterday. She'd been nagging to get back there, but she needs to be assessed. Physically she's much better, but I don't think she'll be able to live by herself for much longer. They'll keep an eye on her.'

'Oh, that's awful, the poor darling. We'll have to see how we can help.'

James took her down to see Lucy, then left shortly afterwards. Kellie went back to her room and sat in the dark, staring out the window, trying to absorb all that James had told her. She put her hands on her tummy, an empty tummy, one that would never produce another child. Then she got up and removed a vase full of pink chrysanthemums someone had given her. Their strong perfume was too much and they irritated her nose, so she put them outside in the corridor.

'Oh well,' she muttered, 'there was no likelihood of me getting pregnant at any rate. James and I don't even share the same room and there's certainly no hope of us sharing the same bed.'

She felt quite miserable about it all and then she got angry.

'Ross Thompson will pay for all of this, one way or the other,' she whispered to herself. 'No one gets off scot free in this world. I wonder if he's heard of karma!'

Kellie slept badly that night as her mind worked overtime. She fell into a deep sleep just as a nurse came in with her morning cup of tea and pulled back the curtains to reveal a wet cloudy day.

'Wakey, wakey, Mrs Harvey. I have it on good authority that you can go home today.'

A bleary-eyed Kellie answered. 'Really, what time can I leave?' Thinking, *I need time to organize James. He'll be off to work soon.*

'Later this afternoon. The doctor's going to check your wounds and then you'll be free to go. Make a note of any questions you have, especially regarding Lucy.'

'I will thanks.' She got out her phone. 'I'll just let my husband know.'

***

Back at Wonglepong, James' mobile went off as he stepped out of the shower. He looked at the caller – 'Kellie' – then pressed the answer button.

'Good morning, is everything all right?'

'Morning James, the nurse just told me that I can go home later today, but Lucy needs to stay here a while longer.'

He quickly grabbed a towel and sat on his bed. 'Crickey, I didn't expect you home just yet. But that's good. You'll get more rest here.'

'That's true. I've had a terrible night. There's so much noise.'

In his mind, James quickly reorganised his day. 'I'll leave work early and, hopefully, I can be there around four.'

'The doctor has to check me over before I leave; but surely he'll be here before then.'

'If not we can visit Lucy and wait. It's no bother. I'll see you this afternoon.'

James ended the call, finished dressing, and went in search of Moira. He found her having a coffee on the back verandah.

'Kellie's just called to say she can come home later today.'

Moira spluttered, 'What?'

'Lucy has to stay, which is understandable. I'll finish work early this afternoon then go straight to the hospital.'

His phone buzzed. He looked at the caller's name. 'It's Kellie again.'

'James, would you ask Moira to find me some clothes to wear home. Something loose. My tummy can't stand anything tight. I have to go, see you later.'

'That was short and sweet,' James commented. He looked at Moira and repeated Kellie's request.

'Sure, I'll get them ready now before we go into work. Can you drop me back here before you go to the hospital?'

He nodded. 'Of course.' Then he grinned. 'How excited will Harry be when he finds out she's coming home?'

'I know, the little pet. He dearly loves Kellie.' She started pulling the rollers out of her hair. 'Give me twenty minutes James and I'll be ready.'

Chapter Thirty-Six

Moira being James' head-receptionist, went to work with him each weekday and Don stayed with Harry. He drove him to and from kindergarten and helped the child learn a few more words. Once a week either Don or Moira returned to check their home in Broadbeach and collect their mail from a kindly neighbour.

Don loved pottering around out at James and Kellie's home and, with Harry's occasional help, had the back garden looking a real picture. Spring bulbs flowered in large clumps and the fruit trees were in full flower. Freesias had popped up along the side fence and they filled the air with their sweet tangy perfume. While Don gardened, Harry played in his tree-house. Every now and again, he called out, 'Hey mate', and Don would look up from whatever he was doing and wave. Harry grew in confidence, his little face filled out and his cheeks glowed with healthy colour from the lifestyle he now had amongst those who loved him dearly.

***

Mid-afternoon, James dropped Moira back at Wonglepong and made his way to the hospital. He found Kellie down in the special nursery. Lucy lay in her incubator sleeping, with her tiny hand wrapped around one of her mother's fingers. James, clad in a sterile surgical gown and mask walked over and put his hand on her shoulder.

'She's starting to fill out,' he commented, 'the nurse told me that next week they will remove her feeding tube and start her on a bottle.'

'I know, her grip has become a little stronger and her colour is improving.'

'They are small things, but very important. They said they expect her to be here another four to six weeks. By then, she will have all this behind her.'

'I want to visit her every day, James. I need to see for myself that all is well.'

'Don't worry; we'll make sure you do. Has your doctor been?'

'Yes, and he explained the details of the hysterectomy to me. He said they had no option but to do what they did. Then he went on to say the usual things, plenty of rest etc, and he'll see me in two weeks.'

'Good, when you're ready, we'll get on the road.'

'Okay, just give me a few more minutes with Lucy. I need to somehow let her know we'll be back. I feel terrible leaving her here all by herself, but that's how it has to be.'

James nodded then picked up Lucy's chart, studied it, then walked over to where a neonatologist, worked at a computer screen. They discussed Lucy's progress and ongoing treatment.

Satisfied with the programme outlined by the neonatal team, James returned to Lucy's incubator and passed on the details of his conversation to Kellie. He gave her a few more minutes to say farewell to Lucy then insisted it was time to leave.

Back up in her room Kellie struggled to compose herself. She sniffed and wiped her eyes then unpacked the clothes James had brought in for her to wear home.

'Moira chose the biggest trousers she could find so they wouldn't hurt your stomach.'

'Yes, these are b-big ones,' she sniffed again as she held up the pants. 'They're pretty daggy, but they'll do.'

James gathered up her flowers. 'I'll take these down to the car while you get changed.'

'Okay, I won't be long.' She put the trousers on and they only just fitted with the zip left undone. 'Blimey, I didn't think I was still so big,' she muttered looking in her bathroom mirror. The loose blouse only just buttoned up, but at least the length of it hid the top of her pants.

James came back with a nurse pushing a wheelchair.

She grinned at Kellie. 'Hop in, Mrs Harvey. I think you'll be home in time for dinner. Got everything, have you?'

Kellie looked around. 'Yes, everything except my baby,' she answered and her eyes watered.

James reached for her hand and held it tight. 'We'll be back tomorrow, keep that in mind.' He gave her a reassuring smile. 'It's all right nurse, we're ready to leave.'

They arrived home just as the setting sun slipped over the horizon. What a welcome she had. Charlie barked madly and ran around in circles, while Harry clapped his little hands and jumped up and down yahooing like mad.

Don gently helped her out of the car and gave her a loving hug. 'Welcome home, Kellie, it's so good to see you.' He sniffed. 'Oh no, now you've got me all emotional.'

He kindly held her arm as they walked inside. The awesome smell of roast beef filled the room and the dining room table was set with roses and a lighted candle. Betty was there as well, but she appeared vague and not completely in touch with reality.

'Lovely to have you home, Kellie. I bet you're pleased to be out of there.'

Kellie hugged her. 'Yes, Betty; and its lovely to see you. How's your arm?'

'Nearly mended. I fell over you know.'

'I know darling, you'll have to take better care of yourself.'

Betty sat down at the table with her handbag on her lap and smiled at everyone, so happy to be part of this homecoming.

Kellie went out to the kitchen. 'Oh Moira, the dinner smells good. Hospital food leaves a bit to be desired.'

The older lady put her arms around Kellie. 'Welcome home, Love. I'm sorry you had to leave Lucy behind, but it won't be for long, chin up now.' They held on tight to each other.

The fuss they made of the young mother helped lift her out of the depression she had been slowly sliding into. Harry sat next to her and kept touching her leg, as though to say, "You really are home". Kellie rubbed his little hand each time and gradually he realised, she was home to stay.

After dinner, James drove Betty home and Moira ran Kellie a warm bath. She helped her into the steaming water then left her to lay back and relax in the perfumed bubbles.

A short while later, Moira returned with a large warm towel. She helped Kellie out of the bath, then gently wrapped the towel around her still bruised body.

'Oh Moira, this is lovely. My own mum isn't here and you're looking after me just like she would have done. I feel so loved, thank you, dear friend.'

Moira patted the young woman's arm. 'Believe me love, the pleasure's all mine. We only have one lovely daughter and we've always looked on James as our son, but now we also have a fantastic daughter-in-law and two extra grandkids. How lucky are we?'

She helped Kellie get ready for bed then tucked her in and turned out the light. She slept nine hours straight. When she woke the next morning, it took a few minutes to work out where she was.

James knocked and came in with a cup of tea. 'Morning, Kellie.'

'Goodness, you're already dressed for work.'

'You needed your sleep, so we didn't disturb you. Moira's staying here with you today, but I'll be home around two to take you to the hospital. Don takes Harry to kindy then collects him later on. I'll see you about two o'clock.'

'I'll be ready.'

***

That formed the pattern for the next few weeks. Lucy came out of her incubator and off the feeding tube. They had a few problems getting her to take the bottle, but that was overcome with perseverance. Kellie stayed through two feeds each afternoon. Gradually, the child put on weight. She clung to her mother's finger each day when Kellie fed her. It was as though her mother's strength was being absorbed through this loving contact.

Each day they were given a report on the child's condition and three times a week they had an appointment with her pediatrician. She explained where she was at and what progress they could expect. When James couldn't get home to take her to the hospital, Don drove her there, and later in the day, James would come to take her home.

Kellie went to her appointment with the obstetrician. He did a thorough examination and was pleased with her progress.

'Don't resume sexual relations just yet. I'd like you to wait a couple more months, but you should have no problems in that area.'

'Thank you, doctor,' mumbled Kellie feeling very embarrassed. *If only he knew*, she thought.

***

They were driving home from the hospital late one afternoon when Kellie became fidgety.

James wondered what was bothering her. 'Are you feeling unwell?' he asked. She shook her head and said nothing, but he persisted. 'Tell me Kellie, what's up?'

She bit her lip, 'I'm worried about Ross. Do you think he'll come back?'

James frowned. 'He'd better not, but I'll call into the Canungra police station tomorrow on my way home and speak to Steve and find out what's happening.'

The next afternoon, he walked into the local police station, went up to the glass window, gave his name, and asked to see Sgt. Campbell.

After a few minutes, the police sergeant came out. 'James, I was about to call you, come on through.'

They went into a cluttered office and the sergeant waved his hand. 'Have a seat.'

'Thank you.'

'Ross Thompson has been picked up at a Cash-Converters outlet down in Sydney. The dumb bastard tried to sell several items of jewellery. He told the shop assistant they were his elderly mother's trinkets and she had no need of them anymore. He can't be very bright to come up with an old yarn like that. Amongst those trinkets were a watch and ring similar to the ones in the photos you sent me. The salesman became suspicious and made an excuse to leave the room. Then, unbeknown to Ross, he called us.'

'Smartarse Ross got wind that something was up and did a runner, but one of our cars was patrolling close by. They gave chase and brought him down. He's being extradited to Queensland next week, along with all the jewellery. Boy, are we pleased to get a slimeball like him off the streets.'

James nodded. 'My wife will be pleased as well. She's terrified he's going to return.'

The sergeant leaned over and looked James right in the eye. 'Mate, he's going nowhere. He'll get years for what he's done, and inside they'll give him heaps. Even crims have standards you know. To savagely beat a heavily pregnant woman like he did, and his own old mother as well, goes against their code of ethics. He'll cop it in there mate, believe me.'

When James arrived home, Kellie was sitting on the back verandah enjoying the late afternoon sun. He dropped down to sit next to her. 'Ross Thompson has been caught.'

'What?' Kellie's head jerked around to face him.

'I said he's been caught.' He repeated what the sergeant had told him.

'Thank goodness.' She breathed a huge sigh of relief. 'Oh dear God, at last he'll pay for what he did.'

James nodded. He understood how she felt. 'There'll be a court-case, which you will probably have to attend.'

Kellie took a deep breath. 'I'll do it, not just for me but for what he's done to his mother. He hurt her badly, time and time again, the rotten mongrel.'

'Don't work yourself up over it. He won't be back here, that's all you need to think about. He'll be on an attempted murder charge for what he did to you and Lucy. That alone will get him many years behind bars. Imagine what the jury will make of what he did to his own mother.' He gently patted her arm. 'I told Steve I'd go and let Betty know.'

To Kellie, the relief of knowing Ross was behind bars was huge. Night after night, she suffered bad dreams and had trouble sleeping. She worried about staying home by herself with the two small children. Now it had all changed and changed for the better.

Chapter Thirty-Seven

James made his way down the road to Betty's house and knocked on the front door. 'It's James, can I come in?'

The old lady wandered out. She looked a mess. Her clothes were filthy, food was caked around her mouth, and the house was a pigsty. 'James come on in, I haven't had breakfast yet. What day is it – is it Tuesday yet?' Her eyes were twitching and she seemed agitated.

'No, it's Friday.' He then made a snap decision. 'How about we find you a nice safe place to live, one where you'll be well cared for. Somewhere you can have a small garden and you'll have other people to chat to. You'll be taken on outings and we can visit you.'

'That place sounds nice, James?' She had a faraway look in her eyes that told him she didn't really register what he had suggested. He sat and chatted with her a while longer and hugged her tight when it was time to leave. He felt he could easily throttle Ross Thompson for what he'd done to his mother. Not just the injuries he inflicted, they were bad enough, but he'd caused her to shut off from the normal world and live in one where nothing mattered.

James remembered the strong self-sufficient woman he'd known since he moved next door and it broke his heart to see the mindless soul she had now become.

Two years ago, she'd given James her 'enduring power of attorney' as she hadn't seen her son Ross for several years. James found out later he'd been in jail. It was for the best that Betty never knew.

'I know you will always make good choices on my behalf,' she had said, 'It pleases me to know you'll be there for me in case I can't make my own decisions.'

Now he would make a decision for her and move her in a good well-run nursing home owned by some friends of his. Her house would have to be sold to pay for her care.

Kellie's eyes watered when James told her. 'I know she needs this sort of help, but when I think of how she'd pop down here with her baking and always be ready to help, it's very upsetting.' She grabbed a handful of tissues. 'It's criminal the damage her mongrel son has done to us all, especially his own mother.'

'I know, don't distress yourself. We'll visit her and make sure she has everything she needs. I'll get on to it straight away.' He rubbed his eyes, distraught by what he had to do. 'Once she's out of her home, I'll get commercial cleaners in and get the place tidied up ready to go on the market.'

***

James got Betty into care fairly smartly and made sure everything was how she would have liked it. By then she didn't really know where she was, but kept a smile on her face. He frequently dropped by after work to check on her. She didn't know him anymore, but smiled and looked content. Her health was good. Her room had doors opening onto a patio where he'd put flowering pot-plants for her, so she could do a bit of gardening. Some days she remembered to water them and sometimes James rescued them. He always replaced the ones that didn't survive.

***

One afternoon, a few weeks later, Lucy's paediatrician came over to her cot just as they were leaving. 'You can take her home tomorrow,' she announced with a big smile. 'We're particularly pleased with her progress and have kept her here a few days longer than she needed as we wanted to make sure all was well. She's now seven weeks old and has just passed her birth weight.'

Kellie almost burst with happiness, but one thing still worried her. 'Is she likely to have any ongoing complications from the problems she had at birth?'

'No. Definitely not. Lucy is now able to lead a normal happy life, just like any other child.'

James shook the doctor's hand. 'Thank you. We're extremely grateful for the care and attention Lucy has received from you and your staff.'

'She certainly had us worried for a while. Now, I would like to see her in two weeks' time just to be on the safe side. She'll be discharged in the morning. I'm very pleased to see you looking so much better, Mrs Harvey.'

With that, she left them and Kellie sank down in the nearest chair. 'Oh

James, tomorrow we can take her home. Isn't that wonderful?'

***

The first few days at home were hectic. Lucy had to be fed every three hours. Moira took turns during the night to let Kellie get a decent sleep.

The next weekend Moira and Don went home. They had been out there helping for nearly two months.

'We'll never be able to repay you both for all you've done,' Kellie tearfully told them.

'You're like family to us love and we enjoyed helping out,' Moira told her as she hugged them all goodbye.

Don piped up, 'Yer love, when you get old like us it's nice to be wanted, and feel needed.'

Harry really played up when they left and nearly pushed Lucy's bassinette over.

James grabbed the baby's bed just as it rocked over on two legs. 'Harry!' he shouted, 'stop that. You'll tip the baby onto the floor, you naughty boy.'

The child screamed. He didn't like his dad yelling at him and he didn't much like that baby either. She cried all the time and Kellie cuddled her and not him. His bellowing upset Lucy and she cried as well. It was bedlam. Then the phone rang.

It was Sam. Kellie burst into tears and couldn't speak.

'Well,' said Sam, 'I'm ringing to say I was coming out to visit. Hang in there love, I'll be there shortly.'

Peace reigned by the time she arrived. James and Harry took Charlie for a long walk and Kellie fed the baby and grabbed a quick shower.

Sam organised someone to feed her cats and stayed the night. She was a great help and her hard-case stories about her current Italian lover had Kellie in stiches.

James went cycling the next day and Harry settled down. He still wasn't fussed on Lucy and did naughty things. So far, he had put Charlie's disgusting old bone in the bassinette as well as a dead frog. Still, it was early days, and Kellie hoped he would soon settle down and accept the baby.

The boy missed Don. He'd had the man's undivided attention for the last few weeks and now he'd left, and Harry had to learn to share Kellie with the new baby.

***

Monday came and so did Joy Brennan, Harry's case worker. When she arrived, Kellie was trying to bring up Lucy's wind, without much success. Harry yelled and carried on as he wanted his box of Lego out of the top cupboard. It had been put away as punishment for refusing to pick it up the night before. That was when the front doorbell rang.

Kellie hushed Harry and carried the crying baby to open the door.

'Got your hands full have you, Mrs Harvey?' Joy commented.

The old bitch had a grin on her ugly dial. 'Nothing I can't handle. Do come in.' Joy followed Kellie into the lounge-room where Harry bawled at the top of his voice. He stopped when he saw who the visitor was and pulled a rude face.

'You get on with what you were doing, Mrs Harvey, I'll spend a few minutes with the child.'

'All right, I'll be in the kitchen if you need me.' Kellie turned and spoke quietly to the sulky young boy. 'If you be good while Joy's here, we'll go for a walk and check out the young plover you spotted.' The child immediately lost his cranky look and grinned. He liked birds and quickly sat down and folded his arms, looking like a little treasure.

A few minutes later, Joy came into the kitchen. Lucy had burped and lay in her bassinet without her nappy on, enjoying a few little kicks.

'I see a big improvement in the young boy. Kindergarten is obviously doing him good. The inter-action with other children has helped with his speech.'

'He's surprising us every day,' Kellie added.

Joy turned to leave. 'Who was the woman housekeeping here last time I called, I found her extremely rude.'

'That woman, as you call her, is a good family friend, and was here to help out while I was in hospital. Moira did a wonderful job of running the house and looking after Harry.'

'She may be your friend, but I found her uncooperative and insulting. I didn't stay long, as I don't have to put up with people being rude to me.'

Kellie stifled a grin. She could just imagine Moira's reaction to this old cow.

'I didn't report the incident as she was temporarily in charge.' Joy Brennan made it sound as though it was a big deal. 'I'll be back in one month's time.' She picked up her folder. 'I'll see myself out.'

'Thank God and good riddance,' Kellie muttered after the front door had closed.

'Come on, Harry, let's go.' They set off up the road. Lucy's pram had large wheels making it easy to push and Harry's job was to hold Charlie's leash and lead the way.

***

The following Saturday the thirtieth of October was the young boy's birthday. He knew all about birthdays – with his mates at kindergarten it was a popular topic. She mentioned it to James when he came home.

'Hmm, maybe we could take him and a few of his mates to Macca's – what do you think?'

Kellie grinned. 'That's a great idea and he'd think that was pretty cool. He's been there before to a birthday party and loved it.'

'Do you feel up to organising his party and getting some invites?'

'I'd enjoy that. What about his birthday gift?'

'Can I leave that to you? I'm up to my ears in paperwork at the moment. I haven't caught up since Lucy was born.'

'I thought of getting him a budgie – you know how much he loves birds. It would do him good to learn how to look after a small pet.'

'Sounds good to me. Do you know where to pick one up?'

'I've a few places in mind. Now that I'm able to drive again, I can check out what's available.'

'Good, now I must get on with my work. Give me a call when dinner's ready.'

Their relationship had gone back to how they were before Lucy was born. James the boss and Kellie still the hired help. But he was a good man with a strong sense of right and wrong and there had been times at the hospital when he looked at her as though he somehow cared.

Maybe at the time I read him all wrong, she thought, *Oh well, I entered into this marriage knowing it was to be in name only, so I'll just have to stick to my side of the bargain.*

***

Kellie invited their friends to Harry's birthday party. Most of them couldn't make it, but Moira and Don replied that 'they wouldn't miss it for quids'. Harry excitedly gave out invites to seven of his little mates at kindy and their mums agreed to deliver the boys to Macca's at Canungra. Kellie assured all the parents that their children would be safely taken home.

The budgie was a real hit. Harry immediately loved the little bird. It was a pretty blue colour and in a pale blue cage.

'What do you want to call her, Harry? She's a girl bird.'

He looked thoughtful for a moment then said, 'Lucky.'

'That's a strange name for a bird.'

'No, it's not. I'm calling her, Lucky.' His speech had improved a great deal and Kellie told James he was turning into a bit of a chatter-box.

***

His mates all turned up to the party and the noise was unbelievable. Luckily, Moira and Don decided to stay back with Lucy. For them to cope with such a racket would have been too much.

Kellie had a word to the mums as they dropped their children off at the party venue. Two of the voices she recognised from the day she'd been in the toilet at Isaac's birthday party a few months ago. At the time, they had made unkind comments about her and James. Kellie had been so upset she'd grabbed Harry and left the party. What a turnaround. Now they carried on as though they were her best friends.

Harry enjoyed partying with his mates, they ate like little pigs, and the mess they left was disgraceful. James apologised to the staff when he paid the bill.

The bright eyed assistant was very pleasant about it all. 'Don't you worry about the mess, Dr Harvey. The kids had a great time and that's what it's all about. We're geared up for these occasions and this lot will be cleared away in a few minutes. Hopefully, we'll see you again.'

'You can be sure of that,' James replied and left them a healthy tip.

They transported all the kids safely back to their parents. Some looked decidedly green, as though they were about to throw up. Kellie couldn't get them home fast enough.

After the last young guest was dropped off, they made their way home. Moira and Don were staying the night and had everything under control. The dinner was simmering away in the oven. It smelt delicious.

'Yum, what's cooking,' Kellie asked, 'Whatever it is smells divine.'

'Roast chicken with apricot stuffing and baby vegetables,' Moira replied.

'Wow that sounds real yummy. How's Lucy?'

'She's in the lounge-room. Uncle Don just fed her and she's nearly ready to go back to bed. Go and see them. He's having a great time.'

When she went in, Don was holding Lucy up and poo was running down her leg onto his trousers.

Kellie grinned. 'Hang on Don, I'll fetch a cloth and clean you up.' She laughed as she left the room to grab a bucket and some cleaning gear.

After dinner, when the children were both in bed, the adults relaxed in the lounge-room with a few red wines. For Kellie it was the first drink she'd had in months and it went straight to her head. James downed a few glasses and got up quite a sparkle.

About eleven o'clock the two visitors went to bed and left Kellie to feed Lucy. James sat next to her on the sofa gazing at the baby. The night had turned cool and the cardigan Kellie had over her shoulders suddenly slipped off.

'Oops,' said James and leaned over to put it back. He adjusted it then left his arm loosely around Kellie's neck. Lucy finished her bottle and Kellie sat her up to burp. The hand across her back moved and was now running up and down her arm. Tingling sensations ran through her body and she turned her head to meet his smiling eyes.

'Kellie,' he murmured, 'I...' he leaned over and gently kissed her on the lips. 'Kellie I want...' he hesitated as they heard Harry call out and start to choke.

'What the...' James jumped up and took off. Kellie put Lucy down in her bassinet then followed. Harry had vomited in his bed. He coughed and cried then vomited some more.

She quickly sobered up and once more fetched the bucket and cleaning gear. *The poor little guy*, she thought, *what an awful end to his birthday*.

When he was all cleaned up and fresh sheets were put on his bed, James lay down next to him and Charlie took up his normal position on the child's other side. Later, when Kellie was ready for bed, she peeped around the door. The three of them were fast asleep, snoring loudly, and they sounded like a collection of old steam trains.

'Oh well,' she muttered, 'I'll leave you all to it.'

She fell asleep straight away. It had been a long day. About one thirty, she woke up and remembered what had taken place on the sofa with James.

'Oh my God,' she muttered to herself. 'Why did I let him do that? I wonder what it was he wanted.' All sorts of things ran through her mind. She couldn't believe he'd kissed her and she couldn't believe she'd let him.

'I must be dreaming. How much wine did I have?' She racked her brains trying to work out how many glasses she'd had. 'How on earth am

I going to face him in the morning,' she whispered and her mind kept going back over the incident, again and again. She was still awake at five o'clock when Lucy woke up demanding to be fed.

A while later, Moira cooked them all breakfast. Kellie pushed hers around on her plate and then James appeared in the kitchen with a grumpy, 'Morning', and made himself a coffee then took it outside.

'Well,' commented Moira. 'We can see who woke up with a bad head today, can't we?'

Don looked at Kellie and winked. 'I think we'll get packed up shortly and hit the road. James doesn't look too good. It must have been a potent drop he was drinking.' They all laughed.

***

Later in the day, a clean-shaven James came out to the kitchen where Kellie was busy preparing Lucy's bottles.

He looked hesitant, which was most unlike him. 'Um, Kellie, I'm sorry if I over-stepped the mark last night. Please forgive me, it won't happen again.'

Kellie couldn't meet his eyes. 'You have nothing to be sorry about. I had far too much to drink and most of the evening's a blur, apart from poor Harry being so ill.'

'Oh, um, that's all right then. Harry seems to have shaken off whatever was upsetting him.' James studied his shoes for a few moments. 'I have paperwork to catch up on so I'd better get started.' He turned and walked out of the room leaving Kellie totally gob smacked.

Chapter Thirty-Eight

No more was said about the incident. On Tuesday, he took the day off to take them back to the hospital for Lucy's appointment with the pediatrician. They kept Harry home from kindy so he could come with them. Kellie thought that was a good idea, as she didn't look forward to the trip there and back trying to make conversation with James.

Dr Sarah Duncan was extremely pleased with Lucy's progress. 'She's doesn't seem to have suffered any set-backs from her traumatic start to life, which is great. I think she can go onto four-hourly feeds now and if she doesn't wake during the night don't worry about it. She'll let you know when she's hungry.'

Kellie agreed. 'She certainly does.'

The doctor looked at her calendar. 'I'd like to see her again when she's six months old, just to check that she's progressing as she should be.' She gave Harry a jelly baby and then saw them out.

The next day James came home in a shiny maroon four-wheel-drive Land Rover.

'Wow,' said Kellie admiring the vehicle, 'Is this yours?'

'This brand spanking new vehicle is for you.'

'What?' squealed Kellie.

'You heard me. You need the extra room now we have two children and apart from that, this is one of the safest vehicles on the road.'

She could hardly speak and covered her mouth with both hands. 'Oh James, goodness me, I hope I'll be able to handle such a big wagon.'

'You'll be fine. It's automatic and very easy to drive. I'll change over the children's car seats and then you can take it for a test-run.'

***

Two weeks later, James' mother phoned from Bribie Island and invited them to stay the weekend. It was getting near Christmas and she knew how busy they would be in the coming weeks. James asked Kellie what she thought.

'I think it would be nice for them to meet Lucy, and Harry would love a weekend at the beach. When shall we go?'

'She said this weekend suits them.'

'Okay, that sounds good to me.'

***

They left Charlie with a neighbour and set off early Saturday morning. Harry was terribly excited to be going on a 'trip' in Kellie's new wagon. He wanted to bring his bird, but James said no as they had enough to take, but maybe some other time.

As they crossed the long road-bridge onto the Island, Kellie admired the magnificent scenery.

'This is the Pumicestone Passage,' James said as she gazed at the sparkling blue stretch of water with its white sandy beaches and numerous boats and people swimming.

'What a lovely place,' Kellie uttered dreamily. 'It's almost like a small slice of heaven.'

'What's heaven?' Harry asked.

Kellie looked at James. 'It's a very beautiful place just like this.'

Then the child noticed some brilliantly-coloured birds. 'What are they?'

'King parrots, Harry. There are lots of them around this area,' his dad replied.

***

James' parents, Wally and Vi Harvey, were terribly excited to see them and made Kellie very welcome. They had a lovely old home in a quiet leafy street close to the beach. The garden was well kept and their house was beautifully furnished with a beach influenced style of elegance.

They fussed over the children and thought Lucy was gorgeous. Harry beamed, he knew when he was on to a good thing and kept them well entertained.

When they had finished their morning tea, Vi turned to her son. 'Would you like to bring your luggage in from the car and I'll show Kellie where you're all sleeping.'

Kellie followed the older lady along the hallway to their guest room, tastefully decorated in white and turquoise with glass sliding doors opening onto a small balcony.

Then Kellie noticed the double bed!

Vi smiled. 'I thought you and James could sleep in here with Lucy and Dad put a camp bed up in our room for Harry.'

Kellie was momentarily stunned. *Oh no,* she thought, *I have to share this bed with James. What on earth am I going to do?*

'Is that all right with you dear?' Vi asked, 'It's just that you look a bit shocked.'

The younger woman quickly pulled herself together. 'Sorry, I was thinking about Lucy and how she might disturb you both when she wakes during the night,' Kellie lied.

Vi patted her hand. 'Don't you worry about that, she won't bother us. I'll leave you to get settled in and please call me if there's anything I can help you with.' She stood back and smiled.

Kellie liked this friendly woman and gave her a hug. 'My own mum died along with my dad several years ago and it's nice to find that I now have a caring mother-in-law.'

A few minutes later, James came in with the bags and pulled up short. 'Is this where we're both sleeping?' His mum had just gone back to the kitchen.

'Yes,' replied Kellie. 'Lucy's sleeping in here as well and Harry's bunking down on a camp bed in your mum and dad's room.'

James quickly closed the door. 'Oh Kellie, I'm sorry. There is another small bedroom and I thought one of us could sleep in there with Harry.' He opened the door and walked down the hall. The 'other bedroom' had a large walking machine and other bits of gym gear squeezed in. There wasn't even room for a chair.

'I could have slept in a chair,' muttered James. 'Oh, dear Lord, what a mess.'

He went back and gave Kellie the bad news about the 'other bedroom'.

Wearily she sank down on the side of the bed. 'Oh well, we'll just have to share this one.'

'No, I'll sleep on the floor.' said James.

'You don't need to do that. We'll each stay on our own side of the bed.'

James gazed out through the sliding doors. *She doesn't exactly sound thrilled to be sleeping with me,* he thought sadly.

Kellie was in a state of shock. How was she going to spend the whole night next to him and not do something stupid? She had feelings for this man. His thoughtfulness and attention during her hospital stay showed her the 'real James' and in his stand-offish way she'd felt he somehow cared about her. Since she'd been home, she hadn't seen that side of him again. Although, there was the night he'd had too much wine and he put his arm across her shoulders and kissed her – if you could call it a kiss.

***

Harry played up to his grandparents and ran around like a headless chook. Being silly, he managed to knock over a small table in the lounge-room, sending the potted maidenhair fern that sat on it crashing to the ground. As it fell, it spilled dirt all over their unmarked carpet.

'Harry,' roared James, 'Look what you've done!'

The boy started to cry and Kellie called him over. 'I told you not to run inside. You did and look what's happened, now poor Grandma's plant is all broken.'

'We'll get you another maidenhair fern, Mum,' James went on, 'he's not usually this naughty.'

'He's terribly upset. I think he's learned his lesson, so please don't worry. I can get a plant anytime.'

James was red-faced and after the mess was cleaned up, he grabbed the boy's hand. 'Come on Harry, we'll go down to the beach. Are you coming Dad?' Off they went and Vi went to have a quiet read on her bed.

***

Kellie desperately wanted to call Sam and talk to her about what was happening, the double bed etc. When the men left, she walked down to a children's playground and pulled out her mobile phone.

'Kellie, it's nice to hear from you. How's it going with the in-laws?'

'Not good, not good at all, Sam. I have to sleep with James in a double bed!'

'What, you and the doc are sharing a cot! Wow things are hotting up!'

'It's not a joke, Sam, we have a double bed, and Harry has a camp-bed in their room.'

'Has the doc brought his condoms?' She roared with laughter at her own joke.

'It's not funny, this is deadly serious. What on earth am I going to do?'

There were more giggles on the other end of the phone. 'Well like they say darling, "just lay back and think of England".'

'Some friend you are, here I am stressed to the max, and you think it's one big joke.'

'Look, just go along with it. He won't try anything, he's probably shit scared like you are. I have to go Darl, but let me know how it goes, rate him out of ten.'

Kellie pressed 'end call' and put her phone back in her pocket. 'That was a total waste of time,' she muttered.

James' mum cooked a wonderful roast-beef dinner, roast potatoes, pumpkin and fresh peas out of Wally's garden. The desert was apricot pie with whipped cream and ice cream.

'Wow,' said Kellie when they finished, 'As apricot pies go, that was the best I've ever tasted Vi.'

'I don't make it very often as we have to watch our diet, but it used to be James' favourite.'

'It still is, Mum. That was a great meal; even if Harry didn't eat his vegies.'

'I only like meat,' piped up a small voice.

'Time you were in bed, young man, come with me and I'll run your bath.' James left the table and Kellie helped Vi clean up, then it was time to feed Lucy.

'She's a lovely little thing, Kellie; I can see some of James in her.'

Kellie almost choked and turned it into a cough. 'Lucy's a good baby. What was he like as a youngster?'

'Colicky, he nearly drove us mad. At about six months, he settled down, but he was never a good sleeper. Not like your little girl, she drops off to sleep with no bother. She must get that from your side of the family.'

They had supper at nine-thirty and Kellie gave Lucy her last feed then tucked her in.

Returning to the lounge room, she announced, 'I'm off to bed now, so I'll say goodnight.'

Vi and Wally both called out, 'Goodnight Kellie, see you in the morning.'

She went to the guest room grabbed her pyjamas and toilet gear then headed for the bathroom. This was spacious with white tiles, glass shelves, and turquoise shutters. Thick matching towels were piled neatly on a stand beside the bath. Before she stepped into the shower, Kellie looked at her figure in the floor to ceiling mirror. Luckily, she had very few stretch-marks. The scar on her tummy still stood out but she knew that would fade in time. Then she pulled a face as she studied her boobs, they had sagged!

That's a shame, she thought, *they used to be quite perky. Oh well, it's not as though anyone's going to see them.*

Feeling fresh and clean, she hopped into bed the same side as Lucy's bassinette. She left James' bedside lamp on so he could see where he was going when he came in. About ten minutes later, the door slowly opened and he crept in, she pretended to be asleep with the sheet pulled right up over her ears.

James quietly gathered up his toilet gear and pyjamas then tip-toed to the bathroom. He kept seeing the sheet almost covering Kellie's head.

'What does she think I'm going to do to her, for heaven's sake,' he muttered to himself as he showered.

He went back to their room, closed the door behind him, then crept over to his side of the bed. He carefully pulled back the bedclothes so he could get in without disturbing Kellie. He lay down and faced the wall, extremely conscious of her soft body lying next to him. It awoke all sorts of feelings that he had no right to have. He wished he could tell her how he felt, but that wasn't part of their bargain.

This is going to be a long night, he told himself, *and this bloody mattress should have been thrown out years ago.*

Kellie lay facing the other wall and Lucy's bed, very much aware of James lying so close to her. In her heart of hearts, she desperately wanted to turn over and put her arms around him, but she had to keep such feelings to herself. She 'had' him, but in name only.

Sleep eluded her; the mattress was lumpy and funny things ran through her mind. *What if I pop off*, she thought, *how embarrassing would that be?* Her tummy always played up when she felt anxious. *Oh good heavens, I hope that doesn't happen.* In the end, she dozed and woke up when Lucy whimpered in her sleep. Then realization hit her and she remembered where she was and who was with her. She turned over; James lay on his back snoring. It wasn't overly loud, but it made her smile and she fell back to sleep.

Morning came, and Kellie woke up to find her head resting on James' shoulder. He was still asleep so she gently moved away and got out of bed. Lucy was awake making soft cooing noises and studying her fists. Kellie pulled on her dressing gown then picked up the baby and quietly left the room. In the kitchen, she changed the little girl's nappy and warmed up her bottle.

James had woken earlier, content to let Kellie's head nestle into his shoulder. He hadn't wanted to move, just savour the moment. Then she'd woken and taken Lucy out to be fed. Disappointment overcame him and he wondered how he would get through another night of being next to her, but not able to hold her, and tell her his true feelings.

Not letting himself dwell on the situation, he showered and dressed then went to find Harry. His dad was up having a coffee and the boy had dressed himself. They decided to go for a walk along the beach.

What a great morning it was – the sky was streaked with golden orange against a vibrant blue background and seabirds squabbled over tit bits left on the sand from yesterday's picnickers. Joggers made light work of sprinting along the foreshore and kayakers paddled through the almost still waters of the Pumicestone Passage. James enjoyed spending these quiet times with his dad. Wally had prostate cancer and they discussed his latest test results after several weeks of chemo and radiation therapy. They weren't a close family but James intended to change that in the future.

***

By the time breakfast was ready, Kellie had showered, done her hair and made their bed. 'Morning Vi, something smells good,' she called as she walked into the kitchen.

'Morning, Kellie. I've made pancakes, and there's some nice maple syrup that my friend Donna brought me back from Canada when she went to see her family. I keep it for special occasions like this.'

James and his dad returned with Harry. The young boy had much to report from down at the beach. 'Granma, I sort some dolphins – didn't I Dad?' He looked at his father and wrung his small hands together, 'and I sort some pelicans, one had a fish hanging out its mouth – didn't it Dad?'

'Yes, Harry, now go and wash your hands then sit up to the table, Grandma's made pancakes.'

'Yummy,' he called as he ran to the bathroom.

Kellie was on her second coffee when she noticed Vi looking at her left hand. 'Don't you wear a wedding ring, Kellie?' The younger woman turned red.

James quickly piped up. 'Yes, she has a nice gold and diamond wedding ring, but her fingers slimmed down after Lucy was born and it's at the jewellers being resized.'

Vi smiled, 'Yes, I forgot about that for a moment. When you're pregnant, your fingers do tend to swell. The ring sounds nice; I'll look forwards to seeing it next time you visit.'

Kellie's mobile went off indicating a txt had come through. She dragged the phone out of her pocket.

It was from Sam. "Are you still a virgin bride?"

Kellie could have killed her. James looked at her as though to say, 'What does she want?'

'It's just Sam, a girlfriend of mine asking after us,' she lied.

She helped with the dishes then went to the loo and got out her phone to reply to her cheeky friend. "Do pigs fly?" she txted Sam.

An answer came straight back. "Better luck tonight." Kellie shook her head in disgust.

***

They filled the day with walks to the playground and the beach. Harry loved it. He couldn't get enough of being able to splash around in the gentle waves that suddenly crept up on him. He shrieked and yelled, and his trousers had to be changed several times.

'Lucky, we brought plenty of pants for him,' Kellie said looking up at her husband.

'I really enjoy watching him have fun after the traumatic life he lived with his mother,' James replied and his mind went through emotions that Kellie could only guess.

All too soon, it was her bedtime and Kellie wished James' parents goodnight then went to their room. As she showered, she remembered some of the looks she'd caught James giving her during the day when he thought she wasn't watching. At times, she had seen a sort of anguish in his face and couldn't work out why. 'Oh well...' her phone went off with another txt. She dried herself and looked at the message.

It was from Sam. "Darling be prepared in case the doc wants his conjugal rights."

Kellie laughed. 'Just wait until I see you Sam Stewart,' she muttered, 'You're in deep shit!'

She sent a return txt. "Some friend you are, get lost."

One came back. "Yep I just might do that, I have this great new sunshine yellow Mr Buzzy."

Kellie replied. "You are quite disgusting, good night."

Feeling like a bag of nerves, she hopped into bed. 'This mattress is shocking, hard, and lumpy,' she moaned and pulled up the sheet. She pretended to be sleep when James tiptoed in and gently slid into his side of the bed.

Then Lucy started to grizzle. Kellie got up and tried to pacify her. That didn't work, so she grabbed her dressing gown, picked up the crying baby and went out to the lounge room, where she and walked her up and down.

No luck. Lucy cried and cried. Kellie rubbed her back, changed her nappy, but nothing worked.

An hour later, James came out in his pyjamas. 'Here, give her to me and you hop back into bed. She sounds colicky.' Kellie passed the upset infant over to him and went back to their room.

Out in the lounge, James gave Lucy a quick once-over and decided that she was full of wind. He massaged her tummy then sat her on his knee and whispered encouraging words to her. He loved this little girl and felt blessed that he was her dad. She stopped crying and gave him a wobbly smile, then burped. He kissed the top of her head then carried her back to her bassinet. She gurgled happily as he tucked her in then he crept back into his side of the bed.

Kellie had been asleep, but woke when the bed moved as James got in beside her. She tried to stay still, but her heart thumped so loud she was sure he must hear it beating. Then a mosquito buzzed around her ear. She hated the damn things. It must have landed on James' face as she heard him swipe at it.

James struggled with the knowledge that he loved this woman beside him, but wondered how to go about telling her. A bloody mossie landed on his cheek – whack – he hoped he'd killed it. He rolled over to face Kellie and heard her make little snoring noises in her sleep. Her back was towards him so he moved himself closer, but she slept on. Next, he put his arm around her waist and waited for it... no response, she slept on. He left it there and didn't let it stray up towards her breasts as he wanted to. At the moment, he felt content with this small amount of progress. Warm and fuzzy feelings relaxed his body and he fell into a deep sleep.

Kellie woke as daylight filtered through the wooden shutters. She felt cosy. Then she really woke up. She was cuddled in James' arms! She stayed still and enjoyed the moment. How safe this felt and how tender were his arms. She loved this stiff and starchy man, but she would never tell him. 'I'll just enjoy this wonderful moment in time and notch it up in my memory,' she sighed, 'He probably doesn't even know what he's doing.'

Lucy stirred so Kellie reluctantly moved James' arms from around her middle and crept out of bed. She tried not to disturb him, as she picked Lucy up and took her out to the kitchen to organise a bottle.

James woke soon after she left, and for a few moments, he remembered how lovely it had been to hold Kellie while she slept.

Feeling quite miserable, he got out of bed, showered and dressed then dressed Harry. His dad was waiting for them to go down to the beach.

As he smelt the fresh salty air and gazed over the tranquil blue water, he thought about Kellie and knew he would have to toughen up if he was going to carry on with this platonic relationship.

Meanwhile, Kellie pulled on a light track-suit and tucked Lucy in her pram then headed down the street. She felt the need to get out. The walls seemed to be closing in on her, surrounded by James and his family as she was. They were really nice people, but Kellie felt she was there under false pretences and keeping up the pretence had become hard work. James was attentive, but in a distant sort of way, even his mother remarked on it.

'He is so much like his dad, Kellie, neither of them show their emotions, but deep down they're loyal and loving.'

Kellie nodded when Vi said this, she didn't know how to answer. Luckily, at that moment, Harry came running inside bawling at the top of his voice.

He'd tripped over. 'There's lots of blood,' he tearfully told them. His knee was grazed and some ointment and a 'Disney' plaster soon fixed the problem.

They left after lunch. Vi and Wally hugged them all and told Kellie how lovely it was to meet her. Their eyes watered as they watched their son and his family drive away.

Kellie felt quite tense on the drive home. The little ones had fallen asleep and an uncomfortable silence filled the car. She sat back and shut her eyes, but with James being so close, her over-stretched nerves prevented her from falling asleep.

***

They quickly settled back down to everyday life. James was polite but cool. He helped when he could with Lucy and sometimes gave her a late night feed so Kellie could get to bed early, but things were strained between them.

Chapter Thirty-Nine

The following Thursday the case worker was due for another visit. Harry was up in his tree-house when Joy Brennan arrived.

'Morning, Mrs Harvey,' she almost choked over those words, 'Where's the boy?'

'Harry's playing outside. I'll call him in.'

'Rude, smelly cow,' muttered Kellie under her breath. When he came in and saw who their visitor was, he started to grizzle – she had that sort of effect on him. Joy liked to see the boy alone, but Kellie stayed until he quietened down, then went into the kitchen to feed Lucy.

Ten minutes later, Harry rushed outside at great speed. Joy came behind him, pulled out a chair, and sat down. 'His speech has improved, but his behaviour leaves a lot to be desired.'

Kellie was not going to listen to such rubbish. 'We don't have problems with Harry; he has the odd nightmare, a legacy from his traumatic past as you well know. Apart from that, he behaves much the same as any other four year old – ask the ladies at his kindergarten. In fact, they tell me the opposite; they say he's well-adjusted and mixes well with other kids. They are amazed at the progress he's made in the few short months he's been with them. So don't you come out here moaning to me about his behaviour.'

Joy picked up her clipboard. 'I'll send in my report, and check with his kindergarten myself. Thank you, Mrs Harvey, and I don't need to be spoken to like that.'

'I will also send in a report. One you won't like.'

The front door banged as the rude cranky woman strode out, leaving the smell of stale-smoke in her wake.

Kellie related the incident to James when he came home.

He grinned and shook his head. 'They are probably typing up their letter of complaint as we speak.'

Kellie banged a pot on the stove. 'And probably, they'll hear from me too,' she spouted, still angry about Joy's visit.

***

The next weekend James was away at a seminar for two days and Sam came out to stay. She arrived early Saturday morning before he left.
'How's it going, James?'
'Good, thank you, Sam, and yourself?'
'Not too dusty, but the traffic coming out here was shocking.'
'I know it's getting worse. Come on in, Kellie's around somewhere.'
They both went inside and suddenly there was a great commotion. Harry shrieked loudly when he saw Sam then ran to her for a cuddle and Charlie jumped up on them barking with excitement. It took a moment for the poor woman to detached herself and hug Kellie.
'Wow,' laughed Sam. 'What a welcome.'
James called out, 'I'll be off now. You girls have a good time.'
'We will,' stated Sam with a big grin.
James ruffled Harry's hair and nodded at Kellie then left.
'Did you see the look on his face, Kel?'
'What look?'
'He's got feelings for you, girlfriend.'
'What?' Kellie retorted.
'Don't tell me you didn't see the look on his face as he left you.'
'No, I didn't, and you're making all this up.'
'No, I'm not. Oh good grief, this is starting to sound like a soap opera.' She glanced at Kellie. 'You've turned bright red my girl; you've fallen for him as well haven't you?'
Kellie turned and looked out the window, hiding her embarrassment. 'You're such a dreamer, Sam Stewart. Now to change the subject – have you had breakfast?'
'Don't change the subject. This is me you're talking to, your old mate Sam. Come on girl, spill your guts.' She walked over to her friend and looked her straight in the eye.
'All right, I do have feelings for him, but we have an arrangement and I will stick to my side of the deal.'
'Fair go, Kel; I should bang your two heads together.'
'Leave it Sam, come and sit down. I've made us a yummy omelette.'
They finished their breakfast, but Sam was like a dog with a bone.
'You know, I've noticed James softening somewhat. He used to be a real stuffed shirt but no, even though he's still up himself, he's quite...'
'Oh Sam, what an awful thing to say.'
'No, I'm being serious. Since you had Lucy, I've seen a change in the

man. I'm seeing a softer side of him and I quite like what I see.'

Kellie's face turned pink. 'I know. He was so good to me when I was in hospital,' she looked sad and wistful as she spoke. 'He made me feel quite special, now he's stand-offish again. Oh well, that's how it is.' She shrugged her shoulders.

'Honestly Kel, I don't know what I'm going to do about you two, you're a worry, you really are.'

***

James arrived home Sunday afternoon just as Sam was about to leave. He pulled her to one side when Kellie went to the loo.

'Sam, I heard on the four o'clock news that Ross Thompson has escaped!'

'Oh God, no!'

He nodded. 'They didn't give any details, but I'll call Steve, the local sergeant and find out more.'

'She doesn't need this.'

Kellie returned to the kitchen. 'What are you two whispering about?'

Sam pretended nothing was wrong. 'Were just saying how close it is to Christmas. Harry'll love it this year, that's for sure.'

'Yes.' Kellie laughed. 'He tells me what he wants, but changes his mind each time he comes home from kindy.'

'Kids ah, well I'll be off. I've had a great weekend,' she hugged Kellie. 'We'll do it again soon.' Sam gave James and Harry a hug then drove off.

***

The next afternoon James called into the Canungra Police station and spoke to Steve.

'Ah James, I wondered how to go about letting you know the mongrel got away.'

'How, how could they let that happen?'

'He was being transported to another facility. It's a long story mate, but because of a cock-up, he's loose. We're on the look-out as they thought he'd somehow make his way up here to his mother's place.'

'It's sold. New people moved in last week. A couple with four children and about as many dogs and cats brought it. Nice guy, he's a teacher at the local school. Security wise, Kellie was extremely pleased to see them move in.'

'That low-life will get a shock to find them there. Well, they've sent us three extra unmarked patrol cars and half a dozen guys plus a dog squad. Mate, we want Thompson back behind bars and quickly.'

James frowned and shook his head. 'There are two families at risk here.'

'I know James, and we'll keep a close eye on them. Our boys will patrol past your homes and watch your houses from a distance. We don't want to alarm the womenfolk.'

James left, not at all happy with the situation. He felt like moving his family out until Ross Thompson was caught. Meanwhile, he'd have to tell Kellie. It was up to the police to let the neighbour in Betty's old place know.

Chapter Forty

The next day it started to rain and as it often does in tropical places like Queensland, the rain continued almost non-stop for a week. Fortunately, Kellie had just bought a whole carton of disposable nappies for Lucy and she had a tumble clothes drier.

Getting Harry to kindergarten and back was a nuisance, but she coped. The roads were a mess as the nearby river had risen and spilled over low lying areas. The sides of the road were under water, but Kellie in her four-wheel drive managed well on the wet roads.

James became frustrated and Kellie didn't worry too much about it. She thought it was because he couldn't get out to ride his new push-bike after work. He had started a keep fit regime.

The real reason for his anxiety was Ross Thompson. James still hadn't told Kellie that the offender was on the loose. With all the rain and bad weather, she hadn't noticed the extra police cars patrolling the area as she mainly stayed inside. Also, to be living with Kellie and yet not able to tell her how he felt was driving him crazy.

She enjoyed James' company, but had trouble coping with the tension between them and was scared she'd do something stupid and make a fool of herself. Then he'd find out how she felt about him.

***

Harry had become a right little chatter-box. Kellie didn't mind as it was great to watch his on-going progress, but he also picked up on different things and made embarrassing comments.

The previous night at the dinner table James had sat silently picking at his meal.

Harry watched him. 'Dad what's wrong with you that you're not talking?'

His dad replied. 'I'm tired Harry and I have a lot of things on my mind.'

'What sort of things Dad, do you mean like flies and moths – those sort of things.'

Kellie and James grinned. 'No son, I meant problems. Do you know what they are?'

Harry screwed up his face. 'Well, mmm, are they like your headaches?'

'Sort of. Now tell me which book you'd like me to read to you tonight?'

'The pirate one, caus I like the ho, ho, hos!'

***

Lucy was nearly twelve weeks old. She smiled and slept right through the night, which Kellie thought was wonderful. James often picked her up and sat her on his knee as he watched the news. She would chuckle and gurgle with delight. There were times when colic upset her and she wouldn't settle. He would come out of his study to give Kellie a break so she could go and take a shower or soak in a nice hot bubble-bath.

But when he smelt 'number twos' as Harry called it, he handed the baby straight back to her mother announcing, 'She's all yours.'

***

After days of being stuck inside because of the rain, Harry couldn't wait to get back to kindy on Monday. He now went five days a week. The sky was overcast as she dropped him off in the morning. Heading home, she heard the weather-forecast on the car radio.

They guy from the Met office warned of flash flooding in the hinterland and Kellie thought, *We'll be okay, our house is elevated and we're well away from the swollen river,* and kept driving. She had to cross the bridge over that swollen river and noticed the level of turbulent water underneath was high, but she didn't think it looked dangerously high.

At quarter to two, she woke Lucy. It was time to leave to pick up Harry. She tucked her warmly in her baby-capsule, carried her out, and clicked it on to its base on the back seat of her car. As she drove over the bridge, the river level was higher, but still had a long way to go before the bridge was unsafe to cross. The filthy fast-moving water was pushing logs and other rubbish downstream at an incredible pace. Her heartbeat quickened as she headed into town.

While she waited outside the kindergarten, she had a quick look in her handbag for her mobile phone. *I'll get James to pick up a cooked chicken on his way home*, she thought feeling a bit lazy. In her bag there were old shopping dockets and tissues, but no phone. 'Blast!' she muttered as she realized she'd forgotten to put it in. *Of all the times to forget it, oh well, we'll be home before long.* She chatted to other mums who also felt anxious about the rising river level and like herself couldn't wait to get safely home. Harry came out and waved goodbye to his little mates then Kellie helped him into his car-seat, making sure he was clicked in safely. The sky had darkened, so she turned the headlights on high-beam as they set off for home. Lucy grizzled, she had a touch of the snuffles, and Kellie thought she would get James to look at her when he came home.

Abruptly, the sky opened and the rain pelted down as she approached the river bridge. She slowed right down and noticed that the water level had risen, but was still well under the old wooden structure.

'I'll be so pleased when we're all safely home,' she told Harry who wasn't worried at all. 'We should be all right, the waters not across the bridge,' she muttered and proceeded cautiously.

Suddenly, there was a powerful thump then a loud roar. They were dropping. She screamed as the Land Rover was swept along with the now dislodged bridge. The noise was horrendous as logs and rubbish bashed into the side of them and wild water spun the wagon around time and time again. 'Oh dear God,' yelled Kellie, 'Please help us.'

She couldn't see through the windows, filthy brown water crashed against the glass as they banged and bounced along with the raging river. Her head kept banging against the side window and the children screamed. Luckily they were strapped into their capsules or they would have been thrown around the car.

'Oh no,' Kellie whimpered after the wagon was struck again, 'We aren't going to make it.'

Suddenly, the Land Rover spun around violently then jolted to a stop, it seemed to be teetering on something.

'Oh God,' she shrieked, 'what's happening?' She took a few deep breaths; panic was getting the better of her. 'Harry darling, just be quiet for a moment.' There was a lull as he stopped screaming. Even Lucy went quiet. The car tilted over to one side at a funny angle, shuddered, and then stayed put.

There was an almighty crash as a solid object smashed into the back of the Land Rover breaking the rear-back window. The vehicle spun sideways, rocked, and then steadied itself again.

Kellie felt cold air on her neck; she turned and saw a hole in the glass! Cracks fanned out across the window, but luckily, it stayed in one piece.

The raging river thundered past them on both sides with sticks and other debris continually crashing against the side of the car. The water level outside was half-way up the doors, and looking down, she noticed water seeping in somewhere down by the accelerator pedal.

'James!' Kellie cried, 'Please, please help us!'

She wiped her eyes with her sleeve then turned to check on the children in the back seat. They were terrified, but unhurt. Lucy was due for a feed and grizzled as she slobbered over her little fists. By now, they were all shivering with cold and she needed to hold the little ones close, so she decided to climb over to the back seat.

Frightened that she might cause the car to sink or move somehow, she undid her seatbelt and cautiously worked her body across the console over to the back seat where the children were strapped in. There was a loud smack! Another branch crashed against the side window, the car shuddered and rocked. Kellie held her breath then waited for it to steady itself. 'Oh my God,' she muttered.

Then she remembered there was an old rug they kept in the back of the wagon for when the dog travelled with them. Carefully, she leaned over to reach the blanket; but it was covered in bits of broken glass so she decided to leave it there as she didn't want the children injured.

Peering through the windows, she could see the water level had fallen.

'Oh, that's something,' she murmured and tucked an arm around each child as they shivered in their car seats.

***

Back at his Miami surgery, James was in between patients when Moira caught up with him. 'James, do you think Kellie and the kids would be home from kindergarten by now?'

He looked at his watch. 'Hm, five-past-three. Yes, they should be, why?'

'I heard there's been a flash-flood up that way...'

He straight away picked up the phone and rang home. 'They should be back by now,' he said as the answer machine came on. 'Surely Kellie wouldn't go shopping in this weather.' He tried her mobile and let it ring until the message bank came on. Moira felt the bile rising in her throat as she went back to reception.

Next, he phoned the Canungra police station and asked the receptionist for some details of the flood.

'Well, a wall of water came down the river and swept away the old Canungra Creek Bridge,' she told him.

'My wife and two children would have been on that road in the last half hour and I can't contact them.'

'Oh,' he heard an indrawn breath on the end of the phone. 'A motorist reported seeing a vehicle crossing the bridge when this happened.'

James felt a rising panic. 'Can I speak to one of the guys?'

'No, all the men are out searching that area.'

James dropped the phone.

Moira came in. 'What? What's happened James?' He didn't speak. 'For hell's sake man, tell me what's wrong?' He told her.

'Oh dear God no, it wouldn't be them, surely not. Have you tried ringing home? They might be there.'

'I did, there's no answer.' He felt sick inside. 'I'm out of here Moira; get Richard to see my patients there's only two to go.' With that, he raced off.

'There's one love-sick man. I just wish he'd realise it. Dear God,' she prayed, 'Please keep his family safe. If they all come out of this okay, I'll give up alcohol altogether like my doctor wants me to. Please, please keep his family safe.'

***

With the bridge washed away, James had to take the long way home. The rain continued. His chest pounded and his mind went into overdrive to the swish of the wipers. *Where were they, what was happening to them, were they still alive?* He shook his head in frustration. Roads were blocked, detours were in place, and the whole trip to Wonglepong was an absolute nightmare.

Eventually he reached home, left his car in the driveway, and ran inside. 'Kellie! Kellie!' he shouted. 'Is there anyone here?' Charlie barked madly and jumped up on him.

'Get down boy, get down.'

He ran through the house calling her name. He stopped when he saw her mobile phone on the kitchen table. 'Oh no,' he muttered, 'No wonder she's not answering.'

The dog barked incessantly so James decided to feed him to shut him up. When he opened the fridge to get the dog-food out, he saw Lucy's bottles – three of them standing there. At this time of the afternoon, there should only be two left. The baby usually had a bottle at three o'clock and it was now after four. He grabbed one and packed it in a cold-bag then tried ringing the Canungra police station. He couldn't get through so he jumped back in his car and took off. With the bridge gone between Canungra and Wonglepong he had to take a back road almost up to Tambourine then turn off and head back down to Canungra that way. Eventually, he arrived at the police station and went looking for the local sergeant.

The receptionist recognised James as he ran in.

'Where's Steve?' he shouted; panic caused him to lose his cool.

'He's gone to the bridge wash-out.'

'Get him on your radio. Tell him it's James Harvey.'

She called up the sergeant, Steve answered.

James yelled at her. 'Tell him Kellie and the two children are missing, they would have driven over the washed out bridge on their way home from pre-school this afternoon.'

Steve heard. 'I'm on my way back to the station now. Tell James I'll be there in ten.'

James marched up and down a couple of times then rang Moira to let her know his family was still unaccounted for.

The police car pulled up and Steve jumped out. 'James, mate, I can't believe what's happened here. The motorist who alerted us thought the vehicle he saw washed away was a dark reddish... what was Kellie driving?'

'A maroon coloured Land Rover.'

'That fits the description. Okay, we'll take it from there. Someone else thought they saw a motorcyclist washed away as well. I've called up the rescue chopper and it will follow the flow of water. We need to find them before the light goes, as it is, visibilities poor.'

A call came though and the sergeant walked away to take the message. He came back to James. 'The chopper's on its way. They'll use the sports oval at the school to land when they bring them in so we will head there now. The paramedics are due to arrive shortly.

James heard the helicopter fly over. He shuddered and goose pimples broke out on his body. He prayed like he'd never prayed before.

'Climb in the front seat, James, and we'll head out to the school.' The sergeant kept up the chat as he could see the doctor struggling with his emotions. 'Tell me about your little fella, James. I hear he's come a long way with his speech, my sister takes her girl to the same kindergarten as young Harry, and she said he's a right little chatterbox.'

'He's that all right, but it's a great sound after months of nothing at all.'

'It certainly is.' They soon pulled up outside the Canungra School and an ambulance pulled in the same time. James shivered as he watched it drive in through the school grounds.

'Oh dear God, please help us.' he breathed.

Steve noticed the doctor go very quiet. 'Many people will be praying for you mate, look over there.'

James looked across the schoolyard and saw people arriving dressed in warm jackets and carrying food.

'I know it looks like they're nosey parkers, but they too will be praying. Those people are here to offer support if we need it. This is a great community.'

James nodded and grabbed the cold-bag with Lucy's bottle inside then they walked over to where the ambulance was backed up. The sergeant introduced him to the paramedics and James handed over the bottle explaining how Lucy was due to be fed over two hours ago.

'Leave it with us mate and when we're notified the choppers on its way in we'll warm it up.' He could see James was almost beside himself. *As you would be,* thought the paramedic, *when your family was in such grave danger.*

James walked away and stared at the darkening sky searching for a miracle.

***

Meanwhile, Kellie faced the thought of dying, along with the two small children. Constant tears streamed down her cheeks. She couldn't stop crying. Harry had wet his pants and wanted a hot drink and Lucy, well overdue for her feed, had cried herself to sleep. She whimpered each time branches and pieces of wood jolted the wagon.

Harry wanted to go home – he went on and on.

Kellie tried to pacify him. 'Maybe we could sing some of the songs you learn at kindy.'

'No,' he cried, 'I want to go home. I don't like being here and I want my dad.'

'I want him too. I bet he's already sent someone to rescue us so we just have to wait until they come. It shouldn't be much longer.' She tried to believe what she told the child and started to sing in a broken voice. 'The wheels on the bus go round and round...' she poked Harry gently in the ribs. 'Come on mate, help me sing!'

He looked at her and grinned through his tears then started to sing. 'Wound and wound, wound and wound, the wheels on the…oh look Kellie, there's a snake!'

She nearly died. A long brown snake slithered across the muddy windscreen onto the bonnet of the Land Rover and off again. 'It's all right Harry, he can't get in here.' She hoped she was right. 'He's just looking for dry ground, a bit like us really. As long as we don't open the windows, we're all right.'

Fear gripped her. She was so scared. More objects hit the car with a loud crash. One after another. 'Oh James,' she sobbed, 'please get us out of here.'

She wiped her eyes then undid Harry's seatbelt and pulled him close trying to think of something to distract him. 'Just think of this as an adventure Harry, you'll have so much to tell your dad and friends at kindy. Think of 'show and tell' what a story you'll have for them.'

'Yer,' he giggled, 'Miss Hayley will think we're berry brave, won't she?'

'She certainly will... Oh listen! I can hear something...'

'What, what tis it?'

'I'm not sure but it's getting louder. Ssh-listen…' she looked at Harry. 'It's a deep thumping noise, can you hear it?' Suddenly she knew their prayers had been answered.

Harry jumped up and down on the seat, 'I can, yer, I can hear it. Oh Kellie, it's Dad. He's come to get us. Yayyyy,' he yelled. Poor little Lucy woke up with a fright because they were making so much noise.

Kellie tried to hush the excited boy. Then crash! Another tree or something hit the car causing it to shudder … then another. 'Oh God, this is terrible.'

She released the safety belt on Lucy's capsule and held her close; the poor little girl was beside herself. It was heart-breaking to listen to her hungry cry and not to be able to do anything about it.

'Shhhh, soon, darling, soon,' Kellie whispered and rocked her in her arms.

Harry patted her hand. 'Look, Kellie, look!'

She looked up. 'Oh my God.' A man in dark clothing with a light on his helmet was outside the window next to Harry. 'Oh dear God, we are going to be saved. Oh, praise the Lord.'

The man yelled something, but she couldn't make out what he said. He spoke into a handset as he peered through the filthy window.

Chapter Forty-One

Back at the school sports oval, the police sergeant received the call he'd been waiting for. He spoke into his radio then walked over to James. The smile on his face said it all.

'The choppers located the wagon. It's a fair way downstream wedged on a shingle bed. One of our guys is outside the vehicle as we speak. They're all safe, upset but safe. The baby's making plenty of noise and that's good. Let us know she's ok.'

For a moment James couldn't speak, he just nodded and shook the policeman's hand with both of his. The watching group of people lip-read his every word and let out a loud, 'Yipee!'

Another call came through for the sergeant; he excused himself and walked away. 'Okay mate, we'll get someone out there first light tomorrow.'

James wondered what that was all about, but then his thoughts quickly returned to the expected arrival of his family.

***

Meanwhile at their Broadbeach home, Moira and Don had just turned on the five-thirty local news – the hinterland flash flood was the first item.

The news reader looked grim as he read out the details. 'A young mother and her two small children are missing, washed off a bridge by the huge wall of water that swept down the Canungra Creek this afternoon. The already swollen waterway became a raging torrent when a flash flood hit the hinterland around two-thirty this afternoon. A four-year-old boy and his twelve-week-old baby sister were returning home with their mother after she collected her son from kindergarten. Grave concerns are held for their safety.'

Tears ran down their faces and not a word was said.

***

Back at the rescue sight, night was fast approaching and it was freezing cold. The wagon was suddenly lit up from above and a guy banged hard on the right hand passenger window indicating he wanted the window down. The windows needed the ignition turned on to work. Kellie strained forward over the console, reached the ignition key, and turned it. Nothing happened. She tried again, still nothing. She looked towards the guy and shook her head. Then Crash!

She nearly had a heart-attack and the little ones screamed. He'd busted the window – it shattered and almost dissolved.

His helmeted head came straight in through the gap and he quickly assessed the scene inside. 'Kellie, is it?' She nodded, unable to speak.

'Okay, this is what we're going to do. We have to be quick, so hand me the baby. I'll put a harness around her then take her up. Quickly, pass her over here now!'

Kellie hesitated, kissed Lucy, and with her heart in her mouth handed the cold screaming baby to the rescuer. He secured the child, gave the okay signal, and disappeared upwards. A few minutes later, he appeared again.

He put his arms in for Harry. 'Come on mate, put this harness on.'

'Is my dad there? Ohhhh.' His teeth chattered with cold. 'I want my dad!'

'Your dad's waiting at the school. Come on now, quickly!' The guy manoeuvred Harry through the window and into a harness. It was tricky as the boy cried and carried on. Then crash! The vehicle suddenly shuddered and tipped sideways.

'Kellie, are you okay?' the guy shouted.

She called out, 'Y-yes.'

'Good, now while I take this nipper up, I want you to wriggle through this window then grab the roof-rack. Make sure you hold on tight! I need you out here to put your harness on. Won't be long.' They vanished upwards to the waiting chopper.

Without letting herself think of the danger, she quickly twisted her way out of the vehicle and grasped hold of the roof-rack. The water wasn't too deep where the Land Rover was wedged. It appeared to be stuck on some sort of bank. On either side of the car, the river looked deeper and rushed past, choked with branches, rubbish, and what looked like old fence posts.

Then crash! 'Oh!' The car shook violently and slipped sideways. 'Help!' She screamed and hung on tight to the roof rack, then turned to see what had hit the unstable vehicle. She thought she could see handlebars and in the strong light from the aircraft above, she saw what looked like a motorbike! Then, to her horror, a leather-clad body caught up in branches ploughed into her car. 'Oh what the...?' A muddy bike helmet was perched at a funny angle over the person's head and she could see writing tattooed across the rider's neck – venge. *It must be revenge*, she thought feeling squeamish and horrified! *Oh no! No, it can't be. It can't be him. He's locked up!* Then the body rolled over. It was. It was Ross Thompson!

Her mind went into turmoil and she had to really concentrate to hang on. Vomit rose up and spilled out over the car again and again. Then suddenly... a loud voice broke through her horror-filled subconscious.

'Kellie, Kellie, hurry-up! Give me your hand.' She did. 'Now grasp the rope. Try and keep your feet on the vehicle so I can clip this harness around you.' Like a robot, she followed his instructions. Then he signalled up to the chopper and looked straight at Kellie. 'Now put your arms around me firmly and keep them there, off we go!'

She clung to him and kept her eyes shut. It was terrifying; she was so scared of heights!

Once they reached the aircraft, another pair of hands pulled her inside. She heard Lucy crying and looked over to see her wrapped warmly and firmly belted into a seat with Harry strapped next to her. They put a jacket and headset on Kellie and secured her to a small seat along the side of the helicopter. Instantly she covered her mouth with both hands as vomit threatened to erupt once again. She shivered. She was cold, so cold. A crew member hurriedly put earmuffs on the children, then the door closed and the chopper turned sharply and headed towards the school oval.

The wind had got up and the trip was bumpy. Kellie retched again and again. One of the rescue guys handed her a plastic bag and gently patted her back until they were safely on the ground.

He undid his seatbelt and removed their headpieces then filled a cardboard cup with water and gave it to Harry.

'Pass that across to your mum, please, young fella.'

'She's not my real mum ya know,' Kellie's pale face turned red as Harry continued. 'My real muver's in heaven and Dad and me married Kellie, and then we got Lucy.'

The guys grinned and Kellie shook her head. The relief of being safe after hours of incredible fear sent her floodgates into overdrive. The men waited until she had herself under control and then opened the outside door.

***

Down on the school oval, James held his breath as he watched the aircraft get buffed around in the strong wind as it come into land.

'Everyone stay back,' the police sergeant called, 'Stay back please.'

In the dark, they saw the chopper door open and a man flip down a set of steps. The crowd hushed as the first person out was one of the rescuers holding the baby wrapped in his jacket. A roar of delight went up from the people. James closed his eyes to stop the tears spilling over. A waiting paramedic carried the infant over to the ambulance. Her cries were loud – she was cold wet, and desperately hungry.

Next out was Harry. Carefully he was helped down the steps then he took off. 'Dad, Dad!' he yelled and another roar of delight went up from the waiting crowd. His little legs raced over to where James stood and he jumped up into his father's open arms and clung on tight.

'Dad,' he said excitedly, 'we had this aventure, you know.' The people around him laughed as Harry held tightly to his dad and gabbled the whole time.

Then the crowd hushed once more as the pilot slowly helped Kellie down the steps. James felt his heart was about to burst.

The sergeant tapped him on the arm. 'I'll look after your nipper mate – you go to your wife.' That was it. James hurried over to meet Kellie with tears streaming down his face. She looked up and saw him coming then let go of the pilot's arm.

James held his arms out. 'Kellie, oh Kellie,' he whispered for her ears only. 'My darling girl.' He held her close. 'I thought I'd lost you forever.' They clung to each other oblivious of all the people watching on.

'James,' she wept, 'I thought we were going to die.'

'Ssssh,' he whispered. 'You're safe now, my love. Come on we'll check on Lucy, although I know she's in good hands.' With his arms supporting her, he slowly led her over to the waiting ambulance. Inside the vehicle, Lucy, wrapped in an insulated blanket, was being fed by a paramedic.

Steve, the police sergeant came over to them. 'Excuse me, Mrs Harvey but we need to have you all checked out at the local hospital. James, you come with me and pick up your car from where you left it at the station.' Then one of the paramedics reached for Harry and lifted the young boy up into the ambulance.

James drew Kellie to him, held her tight, and whispered. 'You will never know what I went through when I thought I'd lost you.' His voice cracked and it took a moment for him to pull himself together. He gulped. 'I'll see you at the hospital.'

Her heart swelled with love for this humble man as she pulled away and stepped into the ambulance.

***

Steve and James hopped in the police car. 'James, it's not confirmed yet, but we're fairly sure Ross Thompsons dead.'

James, whose head was in a different place, suddenly took note of what the police officer was saying. 'Dead – how?'

'It looks like he was also caught in the flash-flood. One of the guys from the chopper crew thinks he saw his remains caught in debris as he went down to get Kellie.'

'Did she see him?'

'From what I gathered, she did, we're not sure if she recognised him or not. I personally, think he was following her.'

'What!'

'That's what I think has happened. He's watched to see what time Kellie went out each day, when she goes to collect your young fella from kindy, then followed her. With such poor visibility, he didn't see the bridge had gone and couldn't pull up in time to save himself.'

'Dear God,' James shook his head in disbelief.

'However, don't lose any sleep about it. Here's your car.' They'd arrived at the police station.

'Thanks for the lift.'

'My pleasure. I'll call you late tomorrow when I have an ID on that body.

***

Back at Broadbeach, Moira and Don didn't bother with dinner, neither of them felt like eating. The channel nine news finished and they were about to switch to the ABC for their seven o'clock news bulletin when they heard. 'We have breaking news! The mother and her two children thought lost in this afternoon's flash flood at Canungra are safe and well. All three were rescued by the police helicopter and at the present time are being checked over at the local hospital.'

Moira looked at Don. She covered her face with both hands and howled in relief. 'That's it,' she stated when she could get the words out,

'I'm giving up the grog.'

'What,' wailed her bewildered husband?

'Well, this afternoon I told the good Lord that if James' family were saved I'd give away the couple of wines I have every night, as my doctor advised. They're safe now and I'm so grateful that I'll cheerfully give up the grog!'

'Good grief,' uttered Don completely stunned.

Both their hearts overflowed with gratitude for the brave police officers who safely rescued Kellie and the children.

***

James picked up his car, drove to the hospital, then went in search of his family. He could hear Harry as he walked into the accident and emergency department.

Kellie was sitting on a bed as a young doctor listened to her chest. He looked up as James came in.

'Ah, you must be Dr Harvey,' the young medic smiled, 'You are just in time to take these two home.'

'What about the baby?'

'We'll keep her overnight just to be on the safe side. Her body temperatures a bit low. Come back in the morning and we'll see how she's doing then.'

'Thanks, doctor. Are these two all right?' James gazed lovingly at his wife and son.

'I'm sure this young man will grow up to be a politician, he's never short of a word. We've bathed and dressed a few cuts; there are several bruises, but nothing serious. I think some warm food, a warm bath and a warm bed is what they require, they are both quite shivery.' He held out his hand. 'Nice to meet you, Dr Harvey, we'll see you all tomorrow morning.'

They checked on Lucy, who was fast asleep in a heated crib, then Kellie and Harry waited on a seat by the hospital entrance while James brought his car around.

Once more, James had to drive almost to Tambourine before turning off to get back to Wonglepong. Harry chattered the whole way home, but Kellie was content to just lay back, feel safe, and be close to the man she loved. James went inside first and switched on the heating. Charlie was overjoyed to see them all and ran around in circles barking with excitement.

James put an arm around Kellie and dropped a kiss on her cheek. 'You go and have a warm bath, my love, and hop into bed. I'll see to Harry and tuck him in. We'll talk tomorrow, when you're not so tired.'

She thawed out in the bath, but didn't stay there long as she was scared she might fall asleep.

Later, as she lay in her warm bed with her warm flannelette pyjamas on, she smiled thinking of James and how wonderful it had felt to be held in his arms.

'Knock, knock.' He came in carrying a tray. Kellie sat up and he put it down on her lap. Her tummy rumbled just looking at it, a steaming mug of hot chocolate and melted cheese on toast.

'Thanks, this looks great.' She smiled up at him, her tired eyes filled with love.

He tried to keep a grip on his emotions as he sat on the side of her bed. 'I nearly lost you today and all I could think of was that I have never told you how much I love you.' He picked up her hand and held it against his cheek. 'I've tried to a few times, but we made a bargain and loving you wasn't part of the deal. I was so scared of losing you.' His eyes watered as he spoke.

'Oh James, I love you too, but have never been brave enough to tell you. Today, when I was so frightened, I kept calling your name, over and over. I knew you wouldn't stop searching until we were found.'

'Oh, my darling girl, have your drink while it's hot. I'll take Charlie outside then have a shower and come back to you.' He leaned over and gave her a brief kiss then left.

***

Kellie could hardly believe all that had happened. He loved her. Dr James Harvey, who was so stiff and starchy, loved her. She closed her eyes and could still see the look of pure joy on his face when he told her of his love, then with a contented smile she drifted off to sleep.

Later, he returned and stood watching her while she slept. There were a couple of cuts on one cheek and a bruise colouring up on her chin. She was so brave and plucky and she loved him, he felt as though he was the luckiest man alive.

He turned out the light and carefully pulled back the bedclothes then crawled in beside her. She never stirred as he put an arm around her waist and tenderly kissed her goodnight.

Author profile

Fay and her husband Graham live out in the Brisbane Valley where they are caretakers for a 100 acre life-style property. Originally from New Zealand, they have called Australia home for the last twenty-four years.

They foster old, unwanted cavaliers, and have a budgie, two parrots, and five red hens. Fay always wanted to write a book, but with raising five children and work commitments, there wasn't the time. This is her first book, and her second manuscript, called 'Be Afraid' is under way.

www.ingramcontent.com/pod-product-compliance
Lightning Source LLC
Chambersburg PA
CBHW070555300426
44113CB00010B/1260